For Steve Poskanzer
and Carleton College,

With deep appreciation for support
with this project and for giving me
a true intellectual home!

[illegible]

January 17, 2013

The *Kipper und Wipper* Inflation,
1619–23

Yale Series in Economic and Financial History

Sponsored by the International Center for Finance, Yale School of Management

The *Kipper und Wipper* Inflation, 1619–23

An Economic History with Contemporary German Broadsheets

Martha White Paas

WITH BROADSHEET DESCRIPTIONS BY

John Roger Paas

TRANSLATIONS BY

George C. Schoolfield

Yale UNIVERSITY PRESS

New Haven and London

Yale University Press books may be purchased in quantity for educational, business, or promotional use. For information, please e-mail sales.press@yale.edu (U.S. office) or sales@yaleup.co.uk (U.K. office).

Designed by Lindsey Voskowsky.
Set in Bembo type by Tseng Information Systems, Inc.
Printed in the United States of America.

Library of Congress Cataloging-in-Publication Data
Paas, Martha White.
The Kipper und Wipper inflation, 1619–23 : an economic history with contemporary German broadsheets / Martha White Paas ; with broadsheet descriptions by John Roger Paas and translations by George C. Schoolfield.
p. cm. — (Yale series in economic and financial history)
Includes bibliographical references.
ISBN 978-0-300-14676-9 (cloth : alk. paper)
1. Inflation (Finance)—Germany—History—17th century.
2. Broadsides—Germany—History—17th century. I. Paas, John Roger. II. Title.
HG997.P33 2012
332.4′1094309032—dc23
2011047238

A catalogue record for this book is available from the British Library.

This paper meets the requirements of ANSI/NISO Z39.48–1992 (Permanence of Paper).

10 9 8 7 6 5 4 3 2 1

For Bronwen, Hugo, and Montagu

Contents

Preface

The study of inflation since World War II has had its theoretical base either in the real demand and supply of goods and services under the influence of Keynesian economics or, on the monetary side, in the emphasis on the quantity of money available. Most economists agree that it is in the interaction of both of these, together with expectations of change, that inflations are instigated, supported, perpetuated, or extinguished. The recognition of this mechanism implies the appreciation of developments in institutional and structural parameters over time. While these parameters may be held constant in short-run analysis, the peculiarities of their origins and characteristics should not be ignored in a more comprehensive understanding of the phenomenon of inflation in general.

The economic history of inflation provides insights into these structural parameters and allows a clearer and more focused study of inflation within simpler structures than those in the current global environment. Such historical studies can help to facilitate a more complete understanding of the physiology of inflation. While history does not necessarily repeat itself, it does provide precedents that can benefit economists and historians concerned with the vital topic of inflation.[1]

The inflation of 1619–23, the so-called *Kipper und Wipper* inflation, was the most serious inflation in Germany prior to the hyperinflation following World War I. It has been studied primarily as an acute monetary phenomenon in Germany alone, broadly akin to later wartime inflations. Although it does bear some important resemblances to these later inflations, it also

1. For a comparison of the *Kipper und Wipper* inflation with later episodes, see Charles Kindleberger, "The Economic Crisis of 1619 to 1623," *Journal of Economic History* 51 (1991): 149–175.

occurred in the context of broader and longer-running structural dislocations, which were international and had their roots in sectors other than the monetary. This structural context in addition to the short-run events is essential for understanding the origins of the inflation.

Moreover, this inflation has left behind a clear record—in the form of broadsheets—of its effects on the social fabric. These contemporary polemics provide us with a rare window into a seventeenth-century society in turmoil.[2] It is in such times that underlying beliefs, prejudices, and anxieties reveal themselves most clearly. Published here in their entirety and in English translation, the extant broadsheets give a voice to the people who were actually devastated by the inflation. Thus, it is possible to go beyond the statistics and to give a humanity to the economic analysis, which allows a more complete study of an early inflation than has hitherto been possible.

2. All extant broadsheets, including the various variant printings, are reproduced in John Roger Paas, *The German Political Broadsheets 1600–1700*, vols. 3 and 4 (Wiesbaden: Harrassowitz Verlag, 1991 and 1994). Selected sheets with commentaries can be found in Michael Goer, "'Gelt ist also ein kostlich Werth.' Monetäre Thematik, Kommunikative Funktion und Gestaltungsmittel illustrierter Flugblätter im 30jährigen Krieg" (Diss. Tübingen, 1981); Gabriele Hooffacker, *Avaritia radix omnium malorum. Barocke Bildlichkeit um Geld und Eigennutz in Flugschriften, Flugblättern und benachbarter Literatur der Kipper- und Wipperzeit (1620–1625)*, Mikrokosmus, 19 (Frankfurt am Main: Verlag Peter Lang, 1988); *Deutsche illustrierte Flugblätter des 16. und 17. Jahrhunderts*, ed. Wolfgang Harms, vol. 1 (Tübingen: Max Niemeyer Verlag, 1985).

The German Inflation of 1619–23

In order to understand the *Kipper und Wipper* inflation, we must begin with the inflationary pressures that started a century earlier and contributed to the precarious economic situation of the early seventeenth century. The debate about the nature and course of the price revolution of the sixteenth century and its subsequent effect on wages and profits has intrigued scholars for over a hundred years.[1] Economic historians now generally agree that the influx of bullion and the growth of demand promoted a modest but sustained rise in prices over most of the sixteenth and into the seventeenth century. Real wages fell and profits may have increased, though the extent is unclear. Agricultural prices appear to have risen fastest of all. These trends accelerated the movement from a barter to a money economy with the accompanying growth of credit.[2]

Despite great regional variations, inflation as a Europe-wide phenomenon was recognized and was a matter of concern. By the beginning of the seventeenth century the price rise became less marked on the Continent, and in some places, such as Paris, prices appear actually to have declined. England, meanwhile, had experienced a growth in exports in the second half of the sixteenth century due to a reform of the currency under Elizabeth I and the relatively lower prices of English goods compared to those

1. The first modern, systematic study of the price revolution was written by Georg Wiebe: *Zur Geschichte der Preisrevolution des XVI. und XVII. Jahrhunderts* (Leipzig: Duncker & Humblot, 1895). It was, however, Earl J. Hamilton's classic article, "American Treasure and the Rise of Capitalism," *Economica* (1929), which sparked the major debate and led to further research.

2. For an estimate of the differential rates of inflation for various products, see Bernd Sprenger, *Das Geld der Deutschen: Geldgeschichte Deutschlands von den Anfängen bis zur Gegenwart* (Paderborn: Schöningh, 1991), 117–120.

on the Continent. This led to an upsurge in prices in England during the first decade of the seventeenth century, which gave the Dutch an advantage in the important textile trade. Such developments were significant, for prices played a fundamental role in the development of mercantile policy and practice. The common way to lessen risk and to protect profits from the vagaries of a free market was to erect barriers, and nowhere were these barriers more in evidence than in the German territories.

Despite the agreement among scholars about this broad outline of events, the complexity of the inflation made it difficult to specify the contributory factors. Although these differed in importance because of timing and location, the most important factors appear to have been: (1) changes in the patterns of domestic production and importation of gold, silver, copper, and lead; (2) an increase in demand; and (3) a growth of credit accompanied by a change in the velocity of money. In the German case, two additional factors were important: (1) the passive trade balance, and (2) the structural flaw in the Imperial Coinage Regulations of 1559. We will examine each of these before looking at the specific events that triggered the *Kipper und Wipper* inflation of 1619–23.

Traditionally, gold and silver imports from the New World have been seen as the most important factor initiating the price revolution. Gold imports from America to Spain rose throughout the first half of the sixteenth century, culminating in 1551–60, but thereafter they declined, with the exception of 1591–1600. However, it is also the case that gold was produced in Europe and was imported from Africa and Asia as well, and research has shed light on the importance of these sources in enhancing the growth in supply of these precious metals. Although most of the main sources of gold in Europe had been worked out by the end of the Middle Ages, it continued to be produced in many areas in significant amounts throughout the early modern period, especially in Silesia, Slovakia, and later in Salzburg and the Carpathian Mountains.[3]

African gold was also important, especially from the thirteenth century onward as Genoese trade expanded toward the western Mediterranean. By the time of the influx of American gold to Spain, gold from Africa was coming into Lisbon in amounts equal to 30–60 percent of the American tonnage. When we add to these crown imports gold from other markets, the Portuguese imports of African gold in the first two decades of the sixteenth century must have been at least 75 percent of that coming into Spain from America.

3. For details, see Hermann Kellenbenz, "Final Remarks: Production and Trade of Gold, Silver, Copper and Lead from 1450–1750," in *Precious Metals in the Age of Expansion: Papers of the XIVth International Congress of the Historical Sciences,* ed. Hermann Kellenbenz and Jürgen Schneider, Beiträge zur Wirtschaftsgeschichte, 2 (Stuttgart: Klett-Cotta, 1981), 307–361.

In the second half of the sixteenth century the Portuguese had to contend with rivals in West Africa: other Europeans, Moroccans, and the owners of caravans who organized trade through the Sahara. Nevertheless, they managed to monopolize the gold in areas of East Africa. Since most of it, however, went to India for minting, it is unclear how much came into the European market via Lisbon. Another competitor of the Portuguese were the Dutch, who made inroads into the East African trade after 1593 and consequently brought gold into the Republic. Substantial amounts of gold were also produced in the Far East, but because most was consumed in India and Persia, there are no accurate estimates of how much may have entered Europe.

The estimates of American silver exports to Europe are complicated, because the official statistics of imports through Seville tell only part of the story. How much was taken by pirates, how much was smuggled to avoid taxes, and how much went via the Pacific and eventually to Europe are questions to which we have only partial answers. Nevertheless, these are important questions which must be answered before definitive estimates of the impact of American treasure on the European money supply can be made.

In addition to the impact of American silver, the production of silver in Europe itself was significant in the monetary history of the period. The revival in the early modern period of the prosperity of mining and metallurgy in Europe originated in the mid-fifteenth century with the development of the Saiger process, a method that used lead to help separate silver from the rich argentiferous copper ores. In the sixties, seventies, and eighties new technology was developed to recover flooded or buried mines, at the same time that new seams of ore were being discovered. According to John Nef, there was probably not a single mining center yielding 10,000 marks of silver a year in 1450, whereas around 1530 there were eight or more centers producing from 10,000 to upward of 50,000 marks.[4] By the middle of the sixteenth century, beginning about 1540 in most places, production began to decline and did so steadily into the next century. The exceptions were the Saxon town of Freiberg in the Ore Mountains (Erzgebirge), where production continued to grow, and Rammelsberg in the Harz Mountains and Kuttenberg in Bohemia, where production remained steady in the latter half of the sixteenth century. Scholars largely agree that the central European mining industry experienced a general collapse in the half century before the Thirty Years' War, and as the war began the mines were probably little more productive than they had been at the onset of the silver expansion around 1450.

4. John Nef, "Silver Production in Central Europe," *Journal of Political Economy* 49 (1941): 586.

Central Europe in 1620

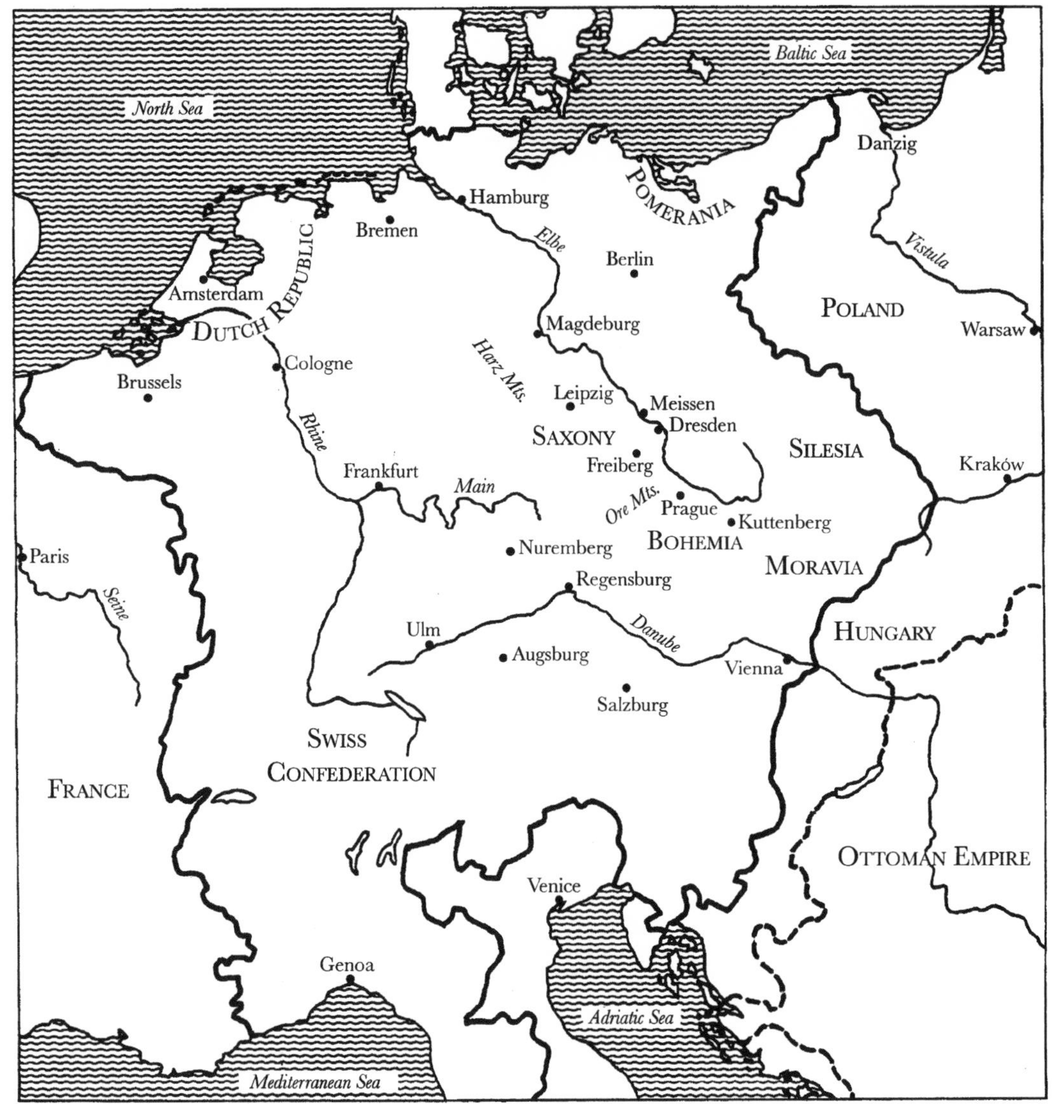

The copper trade was also important in the history of the European money supply. Europe is rich in copper, and there are records of significant copper production in England, Norway, Sweden, and Central Europe from the Harz Mountains to the Carpathian Mountains and the Tyrolean Alps. The trading houses of Nuremberg and Augsburg, particularly that of the Fuggers, dominated this trade and made fortunes in the process. In the second decade of the seventeenth century, Sweden's emergence as a European power of the first order was based largely on its capitalizing on the large copper reserves at the Stora Kopperberg, which were mined and exported in large amounts throughout Europe. Spain had seriously debased its currency from 1599 to 1606 by coining 22,000,000 ducats in vellon, a copper alloy, a move which led to bankruptcy in 1607 and the concomitant failure of the Fuggers and several Genoese bankers. Spain promised to cease coining copper and did so for a decade, yet under the pressure of inflation and the need for coins it resumed the practice again in 1617. Thus, while the supply of precious metals for coinage was growing, prices were also rising.

Economic theory helps us to specify the relationship between these events. The quantity theory of money in modern economics, for example, holds that initial price changes are a function of the money supply and that all prices and incomes should rise proportionally, assuming there is no change in the rate at which money is spent (i.e., its "velocity"). In this formulation, an increase in the money supply acts to raise the price level and is therefore an exogenous variable. Keynesian and Post-Keynesian economists, on the other hand, regard changes in the real economy (i.e., the demand and supply of goods and services) as being the source of most inflation. They argue that the money supply changes in response to changes in demand through changes in debt and is therefore an endogenous variable. This debate is not merely academic, for a thorough understanding of how inflation is initiated is critical to our understanding of how it can be combated.

Until the 1950s, a less restrictive version of the quantity theory of money, "the price-specie-flow" formulation, which sees a positive but not necessarily proportional rise in prices resulting from the growth of the money supply, was the dominant theory used to explain the sixteenth-century price revolution. Jean Bodin (1530–96), a French philosopher, was the first to make explicit the link between the quantity of money and inflation,[5] and mercantilist writers seem to have generally accepted Bodin's view. Gold and silver from Mexico and Peru were believed to have flowed through Spain to pay for the war in the Spanish Netherlands (1584–85) and in turn to have initiated the price revolution and the rapid development of markets.

By the 1950s, scholars investigating this process discovered a problem in the timing of this explanation. Prices appeared to have actually risen throughout Europe *before* the Spanish treasure reached them.[6] If this is true,

5. Jean Bodin and François Garrault, *Discours de Iean Bodin sur le rehaussement et diminution des monnoyes, tant d'or que d'argent, & le moyen d'y remedier* (Paris: Iacques de Puys, 1578).

6. For regional evidence, see J. Blum, "Prices in Russia in the Sixteenth Century," *Journal of Economic History* 16 (1956): 182–199; I. Hammarstrøm, "The Price Revolution of the Sixteenth Century: Some Swedish Evidence," *Scandinavian Economic Review* 17 (1964): 249–266; Y. S. Brenner, "The Inflation of Prices in Early Sixteenth Century England," *Economic History Review* 14 (1961): 225–239; Y. S. Brenner, "The Inflation of Prices in England, 1551–1650," *Economic History Review* 15 (1962): 266–284; Peter H. Ramsey, ed., *The Price Revolution in Sixteenth-Century England,* Debates in Economic History

the quantity theory of money in its price-specie-flow formulation would appear to be inapplicable to the price revolution, and other explanations must be sought. Moreover, agricultural prices rose faster than other prices, which would suggest that something other than the flow of bullion was at work to cause the differential in rates of inflation.

The main alternative to the quantity theory as a theoretical explanation for the price revolution has been the "population hypothesis," which emphasizes the growth of the real economy in a Keynesian theoretical framework. This hypothesis holds that European population rose perhaps as much as two- or threefold from 1500 to 1618. Along with this rise was a growth of urbanization and a gradual monetization of economic life as trade expanded and specialization increased. It is argued that this explanation satisfactorily accounts for the relatively faster growth of agricultural prices and is consistent with the timing of the inflation. Population grew most rapidly in the first half of the sixteenth century and more slowly thereafter. In the seventeenth century, population and prices both stagnated.

This argument also links the population growth and the price level to monetary theory. It holds that population growth would itself have generated growth in the supply of money by releasing money previously hoarded or by stimulating the minting of precious metals and the growth of credit. Urbanization and specialization accompanying the population growth would also have caused large increases in velocity.[7]

More recently, economists favoring a monetary explanation have utilized a more sophisticated approach to the quantity theory, the "monetary approach to the balance of payments," to argue that it was indeed the growth of precious metals which is the key to the price revolution. This approach argues that the actual physical money is irrelevant in a time when prices are largely determined internationally. Therefore, the actual physical presence of specie or lack thereof is not inconsistent with a monetary explanation of the inflation. These economists argue that a growth of demand using a Keynesian model is inappropriate for long-term analysis, and they challenge the suggestion that investment may have expanded in response to population growth when, by the second half of the sixteenth century, real wages were falling.[8]

(London: Methuen, 1971); R. A. Doughty, "Industrial Prices and Inflation in Southern England, 1401–1640," *Explorations in Economic History* 12 (1975): 177–192.

7. For evidence that these shifts in velocity did occur, see Peter Lindert, "English Population, Wages and Prices, 1541–1913," *Journal of Interdisciplinary History* 4 (1985): 609–634. An interesting theoretical formulation of the possible magnitude of such shifts using network theory is given by Jack A. Goldstone, "Urbanization and Inflation: Lessons from the English Price Revolution of the Sixteenth and Seventeenth Centuries," *American Journal of Sociology* 89 (1984): 1122–1160.

8. See Dennis O. Flynn, "'The Population Thesis' View of Inflation Versus Economics and History," in

A more detailed consideration of the theoretical debate is beyond the scope of this work.[9] Nevertheless, both theory and the current state of historical research allow us to tentatively conclude that the growth of the money supply—in minted coinage from domestic and imported gold and silver, and in credit—facilitated the growth of output and trade as population grew in the sixteenth century. Seen from a macroeconomic perspective and with hindsight, the long-term movement toward market capitalism is undeniable from the sixteenth century onwards, with interruptions due to war, disease, and famine. How the other historical forces at work—the advent of Protestantism, new technologies, urbanization, the growth of nation-states, expansion of long-distance trade and business practice—figure in the calculus of causation likewise defies quantification, yet these forces are undeniably involved.

It is against this background of structural change in Europe that the *Kipper und Wipper* inflation must be viewed. There are in addition three important factors relating to the inflation which were peculiar to the German case. The first was a deterioration in the agricultural sector after 1600, a development which exacerbated the crisis of 1619–23. Agriculture, especially the cultivation of grain, expanded in the sixteenth century in response to price rises and demographic expansion, and while there were some advances in agricultural method, the technical innovations that were to produce huge surpluses in the eighteenth century were not yet on the horizon.[10] The main way to increase agricultural output was to put more land under cultivation. This was increasingly expensive in Germany, as forests had to be cleared and marginal lands brought under the plow. Such difficulties accentuated the rise in grain prices. Farmers, counting on the price of grain remaining high, acquired more land and consequently more debt. By the last decade of the sixteenth century the slowing of population growth caused agricultural prices to decline, although good harvests in 1598, 1599, and 1600 buffered the effect of the price decline for farmers.

Münzprägung, Geldumlauf und Wechselkurse, ed. Eddy van Cauwenberghe and Franz Irsigler, Trierer Historischer Forschungen, 7 (Trier: Verlag Trierer Historischer Forschungen, 1984), 361–382.

9. Readers interested in a monetarist view of the debate may wish to consult Dennis O. Flynn, "Use and Misuse of the Quantity Theory of Money in Early Modern Historiography," in *Münzprägung,* 383–417; Douglas Fisher, "The Price Revolution: A Monetary Interpretation," *Journal of Economic History* 49 (1989): 883–902; Jack Goldstone, "Monetary Versus Velocity Interpretations of the 'Price Revolution': A Comment," *Journal of Economic History* 51 (1991):176–181; David Hackett Fischer, *The Great Wave: Price Revolutions and the Rhythm of History* (New York: Oxford University Press, 1996); Peter Kugler and Peter Bernholz, "The Price Revolution in the 16th Century: Empirical Results from a Structural Vectorautoregression Model," Wirtschaftswissenschaftliches Zentrum der Universität Basel, Working Paper 12/07, August 2007.

10. For an account of the sixteenth-century innovations in agriculture in England, see Eric Kerridge, *The Agricultural Revolution in the Sixteenth Century* (London: Allen and Unwin, 1967).

When, however, harvests stagnated after the end of the century, the possibility of saving and spending in the dominant agricultural sector was further reduced. In such a market farmers had difficulty paying their debts, and many lost their farms.[11] In addition, the harvest failures in 1618–22 and the outbreak of the Thirty Years' War caused agricultural prices to rise dramatically, and this cyclical crisis coincided with the monetary crisis and served to intensify it.[12]

The second German problem was the stagnation of industry as a result of territories adopting a defensive stance in response to increased competition from other parts of Europe. The shifting of trade routes to the Atlantic with the opening of trade with the New World and the development of the lucrative entrepôt trade in the Atlantic ports had put German industry at a geographical disadvantage. German merchants continued, nevertheless, to produce expensive, high-quality handicrafts and textiles for export even as the market was moving toward lower-quality bulk goods.[13] In the course of the sixteenth century, however, the German trade balances turned negative with Italy, England, and the independent Netherlands. In addition, trade in raw materials and cattle with Poland and Hungary also resulted in a negative balance. (Only to the Spanish Netherlands, Switzerland, and Lorraine did German lands export more than they imported.) This unfavorable trade balance put pressure on the increasingly scarce money supply as silver flowed out to settle accounts.

The third peculiar problem was a structural flaw in the Imperial Coinage Regulations of 1559.[14] Medieval monetary theory held that there was a difference between *valor impositus* and *unitas intrinseca*.[15] That is, the value of a coin was determined by the value given to it by the highest authority in the land instead of by the market value of the metal it contained. This is understandable for the medieval period, when markets were not so well developed and the number of coins in circulation was relatively limited. But it obviously made currency reform difficult in the early modern period, when the supply of gold and silver increased dramatically and a

11. Wilhelm Abel, *Agrarkrisen und Agrarkonjunktur* (Hamburg: Parey, 1978), ch. 12.

12. Ruggiero Romano, "Between the Sixteenth and Seventeenth Centuries: The Economic Crisis of 1619–22," in *The General Crisis of the Seventeenth Century,* ed. Geoffrey Parker and Lesley M. Smith (London: Routledge and Kegan Paul), 213.

13. Excellent examples of these goods, including hundreds of different kinds of metal products as well as precision instruments for navigation, surveying, etc., may be seen at the Germanic National Museum in Nuremberg.

14. An excellent introduction to this problem is Fritz Redlich's *Die deutsche Inflation des frühen siebzehnten Jahrhunderts in der zeitgenössischen Literatur: Die Kipper- und Wipper,* Forschungen zur internationalen Sozial- und Wirtschaftsgeschichte, 6 (Cologne: Böhlau, 1972).

15. This difference is noted by Arnold Luschin von Ebengreuth in *Allgemeine Münzkunde und Geldgeschichte des Mittelalters und der neueren Zeit* (Munich: Oldenbourg, 1904).

separate market existed for the precious metals. Add to this the problem peculiar to the Holy Roman Empire, namely, that it was made up of many cities and principalities with the right of coinage, so that no central mint was responsible for striking money. Under these adverse conditions, the morass in which the monetary sector found itself is not surprising.

The sixteenth century had witnessed a gradual monetization of life with demographic growth, expansion of trade, urbanization, and specialization. Yet, the Imperial Diets seemed consistently to misunderstand the indispensible function of small-denomination coins for transactions as well as the coins' relationship to larger denominations. They relied solely on *valor impositus* for maintaining the value of the coins in circulation. When the Imperial Diet met in Augsburg in 1559 to discuss the need for reform of the coinage regulations, the amount of silver content prescribed for the small coins was less than that for the larger coins, but not proportionately less. The result of this miscalculation was that smaller coins were uneconomical to produce. Mints could produce a larger total value of output of coins with the identical amount of silver and labor by producing the larger denominations rather than the smaller ones. As the price of silver began to rise in the second half of the sixteenth century, with the decline of silver production and imports and the growth of demand for money with expanded trade, this differential became greater, and the price of silver rose above the price stipulated in the Imperial regulations.

An interesting example from the writings of the Saxon master of the mint Heinrich von Rehnen in 1606 illustrates the problem.[16] For 100 Marks of fine silver the profit for the larger coins (that is, Thalers and Guldens)—calculated solely by the value of the coins produced—was 14 Florins, 17 Groschens, and 10 1/2 Pfennigs; for Groschens there was a loss of 18 Florins, 2 Groschens, and 11 Pfennigs; for Pfennigs, a loss of 28 Florins, 14 Groschens, and 11 Pfennigs; for Hellers, a loss of 37 Florins, 18 Groschens, and 3 Pfennigs.[17] In addition, the mint had to figure the interest on the 50,000 Guldens which it had to invest each year in silver, copper, and lead. When this is added, it is clear that the minting of coins under the Imperial regulations

16. The monetary history of Germany is extremely confusing and intricate. The emperor had no power to enforce Imperial edicts on coinage, so they were largely disregarded by the separate circles of the empire as well as by the princes or union of princes. However, a relationship between the coins serves to illustrate the problem of minting small coins. The Third Imperial Ordinance of 1582 fixed the relationship between large and small coins as follows: 1 Gulden (Florin) = 60 Kreuzers = 15 Batzens (also: Batzners) = 20 Groschens = 240 Pfennigs = 480 Hellers; 1 Reichsthaler = 68 Kreuzers; 1 Goldgulden = 2–3 Guldens; and 1 ducat = 4 Guldens. Although in German the singular and plural forms of the coins are identical, in the present volume the plural forms have been anglicized with an added *s*.

17. Robert Wuttke, "Zur Kipper- und Wipperzeit in Kursachsen," *Neues Archiv für Sächsische Geschichte und Altertumskunde* 15 (1894): 126–127.

was not nearly as profitable as contemporaries seemed to believe and that there was a strong disincentive to mint the smaller coins.[18]

Mints, therefore, began to concentrate on making larger silver coins and produced "pagament" instead of the smaller silver coins.[19] The potential for profit was great enough, as the price of silver rose, to tempt mints to engage in various kinds of illegal activity, including the melting of larger coins and the debasing of smaller coins, both of which the regulations of 1559 explicitly forbade and for which the Imperial Diets of 1570, 1571, 1576, and 1594 set out penalties. The fact that increasingly severe penalties were imposed reveals that the regulations were being ignored.

The result was that small silver coins were melted down to make more small, debased coins, with the silver mixed with copper or lead or silver of lesser quality (see Plates III, IV, V, VI, VII, and VIII). The chronicler of Sangerhausen records, "Boilers, kettles, pipes, gutters, and whatever was made of copper was removed, taken to the mints and turned into money. . . . If a church had an ancient font . . . it was sold by those who had been baptized in it."[20] This "new-lamps-for-old" mentality led the public to rush to sell larger, pure coins for smaller ones and even to sell silver plates and other items for their silver content. They believed themselves to be profiting, because the nominal value of the smaller coins they received was greater than the nominal value of the silver they sold. Treasure and savings alike flowed into this illegal activity at the same time that clipping of coins became commonplace (see Plate XXI), and all of this caused the inflation to worsen.

Debasing a coinage to provide the treasury with money was particularly effective when the debased coinage could be exchanged in neighboring territories for good coins, as was the case in the dozens of small territories and principalities in the German lands. The good coins could then be brought back to strike still further debased money, and the neighboring territory, which was then inundated with bad coins, would try to attract good coins by raising the price of silver in the coins. This, along with rising labor costs, made it increasingly unprofitable to mint subsidiary coins, so people either debased them further or stopped striking them altogether.

18. For a useful discussion of the complicated nature of the German coinage problem and the history of coinage in other European countries, see William Arthur Shaw, *The History of Currency 1252 to 1894: Being an Account of the Gold and Silver Moneys and Monetary Standards of Europe and America, together with an Examination of the Effects of Currency and Exchange Phenomena on Commercial and National Progress and Well-being,* 2nd ed. (1896; rpt. New York: Augustus M. Kelley, 1967).

19. The exact meaning of *pagament* is unclear, although it is a term frequently found in the seventeenth century. Basically, it meant coins made of scrap silver, melted foreign coins, and the like, while larger coins were made from silver of uniform quality.

20. Gustav Freytag, *Bilder aus der deutschen Vergangenheit,* vol. 3 of *Aus dem Jahrhundert des großen Krieges (1600–1700)* (Leipzig: Bogeng, 1927), 266–267.

Good coins disappeared and bad coins circulated (see Plate VIII), and Gresham's Law operated in the German lands increasingly with a vengeance.[21]

Records of mint trials held in Nuremberg reveal several examples of this debasement. In 1606 the city of Frankfurt am Main minted Six-Kreuzer (Sechs-Kreuzer) pieces lacking nearly 37 percent of the Imperial standard. The Duke of Tesch minted Three-Kreuzer (Drei-Kreuzer) pieces lacking almost 27 percent, and the Count Palatine of the Rhine minted Three-Kreuzer pieces lacking 30 percent. The Count of Solms minted Three-Kreuzer pieces lacking 31 percent, 34 percent, and more. In 1609 the list of debasers had grown to more than twenty, including among others the counts of Waldeck, the Count of Stolberg, the dukes of Holstein, and Count Simon of Lippe.[22]

The situation became so critical that the Nuremberg town council took steps on its own to try to stabilize the currency.[23] At the Diet in 1613 in Regensburg the delegates once again urgently discussed the problem, and shortly thereafter the Imperial authorities circulated a draft of a reform act among the cities and territories. This attempt, however, was ineffective, as was the one by the leading trading cities to cooperate with one another to find a solution. There were a number of reports issued by the officials of various mints about the causes of the crisis, and various suggestions for reform were made, but these too came to naught.[24] Although the economic understanding—as shown in these texts—is remarkable for the times, the political unity necessary for reform was lacking, and debasement continued unchecked.

This then was the situation in the German lands shortly before 1618: structural weakness in agriculture, chaos in the monetary sector, a worsening of trade balances, a tradition of inflation, and no central authority capable of reform. The last weakness was crucial for monetary reform, because individual cities and territories stood to lose unless every one of them cooperated fully. When the lingering conflicts of the Counter-Reformation came to a head with the Defenestration of Prague in May of

21. Gresham's Law, named for Sir Thomas Gresham (c. 1519/21–1576), a minister under Elizabeth I, states that debased money will drive good money out of circulation, as people hoard the full-valued coins. The principle is actually wrongly attributed to Gresham, for it may already have been understood by Aristotle and was clearly articulated by Nicole Oresme, Bishop of Lisieux, in his *De Moneta* in the mid-fourteenth century. Gresham had, however, made the case for reforming the currency debased under Henry VIII, which is undoubtedly the reason for the attribution.

22. J. C. Hirsch, *Des Deutschen Reichs Münz-Archiv,* vol. 3 (Nuremberg: Felßecker, 1757), 397.

23. The copy of the *Nürnberger Münzdekrete* cited by Redlich in this regard as being held in the Harvard Law Library is not, in fact, held there under the call number he cites, nor can the library locate it. However, a wealth of records concerning attempts within the empire to take action, including the coinage decrees from Nuremberg from 1609, 1611, and 1612, mentioned by Redlich as being available on microfilm, are printed in Hirsch, *Münz-Archiv.*

24. See Hirsch, *Münz-Archiv,* for these texts.

1618, and the Thirty Years' War broke out, the political crisis in the empire was compounded by these structural weaknesses, and the *Kipper und Wipper* inflation was the economic result.

In order to raise the armies necessary for the war, governments needed to raise large sums of money to pay mercenaries, yet since capital markets did not function efficiently, it was hard for the governments to borrow the sums needed. Taxation was difficult without broad-based cooperation, for if taxes were not unified across territories, suppliers and customers would gravitate to the area of the lowest tax rate. A unified tax code was impossible in the "crazy quilt" of territories which formed the empire, each with its own partisan interests. The easiest solution for those in power was to strike more debased coins. The effect of debasing within one's own borders could be further enhanced by going outside the territory, exchanging the debased coins for good coins, and then returning these for further debasement, as previously discussed. Those dealing in this theft were people from all walks of life, although the rampant anti-Semitism of the age often led people to point their fingers solely at the Jews. Pastors, millers, and peasants were particular targets of theft, for pastors and millers turned over coins frequently but did not travel enough to know firsthand what was happening, while peasants, who might have small sums set aside, were simply naïve (see Plate XIX).

The period of inflation which broke out in the German lands in 1619 is known in German as the *Kipper- und Wipperinflation*. The origins of *Kipper* and *Wipper* is uncertain, though both words originated in Lower Saxony. They may refer to the Low German *kippen,* which means "to tilt," or *abkippen,* "to cut off," and to *wippen,* which means to "to wag," recalling the action of the scales on which silver was weighed. (A *Wippe* was also a means of torture.) It is also possible that they are a more recent version of the early German alliterative rhyme, of which *Kind und Kegel* and *Mann und Maus* are examples still in use. Together their musical sound made them come into the language as a unit. *Kippen und wippen* may also be onomatopoetic, suggesting the back and forth action of the scales during weighing, which was not always done honestly, so the perpetrators became known as the *Kipper und Wipper.*[25]

Whatever their origin, the words came to mean the chaos in the monetary sphere resulting in an acute inflation in the early years of the Thirty Years' War. Instead of poverty being the direct consequence of profligacy or sloth, which the people understood (as shown in Plates I and II from before the war), this inflation was something new altogether (see Plates IX,

25. The inflation resulted, in fact, in the creation of an entirely new family of words. See Redlich, *Die deutsche Inflation,* 20.

EXCHANGE VALUES OF LARGE SILVER AND GOLD COINS IN KREUZERS, 1566–1623

	Reichsthaler	Reichsgulden (Guldenthaler)	Goldgulden	Dukat
1566	68	60	75	104
1590	70	62	79	110
1600	72	64	80	116
1610	84	75	100	135
1616/17	90	80	112	150
End of 1619	124	105	140	192
End of 1620	140	120	150	210
End of 1621	390	330	480	720
1622/23	600+	500+	700+	900+
after 1623	90	80	110	150

Note: The figures are only averages, for large regional differences existed.

X, and XI). While not a hyperinflation in the modern sense such as Germany experienced after World War I, it was nonetheless unprecedented for contemporaries. The extent of the depreciation of the coinage in circulation has been illustrated by Bernd Sprenger (see table above).[26]

In July 1622 the city of Nuremberg imposed the death penalty for trading in debased coinage, though records of actual action are scarce. This is understandable given the chaos and the lack of a good communications network. Because we lack sufficient records for the smaller coins, all that we can confidently say is that mints sprang up "like mushrooms after a warm rain"[27] and that debased coins "poured from them in avalanche proportion."[28] Herbert Langer cites the particularly telling example of Brunswick, with its seventeen mints in 1620 and forty by 1623, including the monastery at Amelungsborn, which had converted within a few months into a mint employing three to four hundred workers.[29]

Most of the records we have are limited to a single *Kreis,* or circle, into which the empire had been divided in 1512 for purposes of administering the Imperial Coinage Regulations. This makes research into the course of the spread of the *Kipper und Wipper* inflation extremely difficult. For example, scholars have suggested that it spread from the German lands to

26. Sprenger, *Das Geld der Deutschen,* 114.

27. Herbert Langer, *Hortus Bellicus: Der Dreissigjährige Krieg, eine Kulturgeschichte* (Leipzig: Edition Leipzig, 1978), 30.

28. Gustav Schöttle, "Münz- und Geldgeschichte in ihren Zusammenhang mit derjenigen Schwabens," *Württembergische Vierteljahrshefte für Landesgeschichte,* n.s. 31 (1922–24): 84.

29. Langer, *Hortus Bellicus,* 80.

Poland through the port of Danzig (Gdańsk), which the Dutch dominated and whose prices and exchange rates they controlled. Another possibility is that it may have moved to Poland along the coast from Pomerania, where debasement was rampant, or that it entered Poland through Kraków, which was the center for the export of Polish coins to the Czech lands and Silesia. Yet another suggestion is that Leipzig was the origin, since it was a central city for coins and paid the highest prices for silver in all of Germany. In addition, Leipzig's fair was the entry for much of eastern trade, including Poland's. These commercial dealings all provided a possible conduit for the spread of debased coinage and, thus, inflation, but we cannot so far pinpoint the exact historical course.

As in all inflations, there were winners and losers. One famous group of profiteers was a consortium which included Prince Carl von Liechtenstein, governor of Bohemia, and Albrecht von Wallenstein, general in the Imperial army. Under the terms of a lease from Emperor Ferdinand II made in January 1622, the consortium was to control all the mints in Bohemia, Moravia, and Lower Austria and to deliver to the emperor specified amounts of coinage to support the army. Profit accrued to the members of the consortium through their selling of silver to the mint at exorbitant prices or in such large volumes that they made vast sums. All circulating coins were to be turned in to the nearest mint for a set price and then melted and reminted with a copper alloy. In order to enhance profits, the consortium devalued the money even more than allowed for in the contract. With profits thus made, Wallenstein enhanced a fortune he inherited on the death of his wife, who had been a wealthy widow, and this great wealth allowed him to acquire some sixty estates in Bohemia. When the Protestants were defeated at the Battle of the White Mountain in November 1620, their confiscated estates were quickly acquired at imposed prices with debased coinage by people like Wallenstein. After Emperor Ferdinand II became bankrupt and unable to outfit and supply the Imperial army, Wallenstein used his own vast fortune to do so.

As the effects of the inflation spread, people initially suffered from money illusion and increased their spending, for based on the higher nominal value of the debased coinage they mistakenly considered themselves wealthier than before. A temporary economic boom resulted, and profits may also have risen as raw material and labor costs lagged behind prices. Since foreign imports—such as English cloth—had to be paid for in silver and, thus, became increasingly expensive, local industry had a windfall of demand (e.g., Meissen textiles). By the same token, exports also boomed, as traders in linen, wool, wax, leather, yarn, and horses bought locally in debased coins and sold abroad for full-bodied coins.

Although the nobility involved in debasement profited along with long-distance traders, others, especially those paid in cash in the cities, suffered disastrously. These would have included servants, day laborers, building craftsmen, teachers, miners, parish priests, carters, boatmen, and municipal officials. Without the ability to grow their own food, they faced increases of food prices of 500–800 percent over the course of the inflation. Elsas's figures for foodstuffs and wages for journeymen in Augsburg in this period suggest that real wages fell by more than half from 1619 to 1621 and perhaps to a third in 1622.[30] To make matters worse, those who supplied foodstuffs from the surrounding land began to demand payment in the larger silver coins or payment of exorbitant prices in an attempt to hedge against the inflation. In Ravensburg it was written in 1623, "The farmers are treating the starving population so horribly that even a stone would be moved to pity."[31] As money broke down as a medium of exchange and as laborers' wages no longer supported them, people were forced to sell their household possessions for food, and hunger was widespread (see Plates IX, X, and XI).

Violence broke out as the frustrated population directed their aggression toward the people they considered responsible for their plight.[32] In 1621 in Halberstadt, for example, citizens plundered the house and property of the mintmaster and then turned upon the wealthy manufacturers. In 1622 in Magdeburg a mob destroyed the houses of the coin minters, even though the city government had intervened earlier and confiscated their equipment. Sixteen people were killed and two hundred injured. There was unrest in Dessau, Erfurt, Halle, Eisleben, Mansfeld, and Leipzig, and in Freiberg the citizens stormed the houses of the minters.[33] Jews were often singled out as the target of blame, for they had traditionally been involved in coinage, money lending, and long-distance trade (see Plates IV, VI, VII, VIII, XII, XIII, XIV, XV, XVI, XX, and XXV).

Direct evidence for the effect of the inflation on merchants is lacking, yet it is clear from the coinage reports contained in Hirsch's *Münz-Archiv* that there was continual pressure on the emperor from cities like Nuremberg and Augsburg, whose merchants depended on a stable currency, to take action to end the inflation and to develop deposit banking. Following the example of Amsterdam, which founded the Amsterdam Exchange Bank in

30. M. Elsas, *Umriß einer Geschichte der Preise und Löhne in Deutschland vom ausgehenden Mittelalter bis zum Beginn des 19. Jahrhunderts,* vol. 1 (Leiden: Sythoff, 1936), 595, 602, and 623.

31. Gustav Schöttle, "Die große deutsche Geldkrise von 1620–23 und ihr Verlauf in Oberschwaben," *Württembergische Vierteljahrshefte für Landesgeschichte,* n.s. 30 (1921): 41.

32. Martha White Paas, "Wie können wir wissen, was sie wussten? Deutsche Flugblätter und die Kipper- und Wipperinflation (1620–26)," in *Arbeitskreis Bild Druck Papier, Tagungsband Ravenna 2006,* ed. Wolfgang Brückner et al., Arbeitskreis Bild Druck Papier, vol. 11 (Münster: Waxmann, 2007), 37–52.

33. Freytag, *Bilder,* 318.

1609, Hamburg established a deposit bank in 1619 to help stabilize the exchange rates in the western Hanseatic trade by reducing trade in coinage and by making transfers from one account to another possible.[34] By accepting only full-bodied Reichsthalers, the bank effectively excluded the debased coinage from its transactions and preserved the value of the money in trade within the bank.

The situation elsewhere became intolerable when debased money was no longer accepted by merchants and farmers in payment for goods. The nobility, which had played a major role in the inflation, began to be paid rents in debased coinage, and when debtors began to repay loans in worthless money, "what goes around" came around. At this point it became in the interest of everyone to end the inflation.

Some faltering first steps were attempted—in Lower Saxony in 1619, in Württemberg in 1620, with the Treaty of Ulm in 1620, etc.—but these all failed. The first successful step came when a mint treaty concluded in 1618 by the Hanseatic cities of Hamburg and Lübeck was joined in 1620 by the Duke of Mecklenburg, the Lower Saxon Circle, and by the Hanseatic city of Bremen in agreement with Wismar. A commission established by the local diet in Lüneburg in April 1621 set up a committee on the minting question. Its report in 1623 was adopted and was the crucial step in bringing the inflation to a halt in the Lower Saxon Circle, where it had been so rampant.[35]

The Upper Saxon Circle took decisive action in 1623 by immediately returning to the imperial ordinance of 1559, establishing a *valor impositus* that matched the *unitas intrinseca.* It ordered all coins to be reminted on that basis and reinstated the mint trials, which had not been held since 1618, to enforce the regulations. The Swabian, Franconian, and Bavarian Circles undertook a more measured reform considered by Schöttle to have caused the "necessarily painful transition period to be unnecessarily severe and prolonged."[36] Finally, on 8 February 1624, Emperor Ferdinand II issued a mandate reaffirming the Imperial coin laws.

As with any inflation, the debts incurred during the period were a major problem in the aftermath. A regulation from 1572 stated that debts should be repaid in the currency in which they had been contracted, and there was much support for basing a resolution on this principle. In the end, however, different circles worked out different solutions over a period of years, depending on who stood to lose and who to gain from the various options

34. Amsterdam's bank was itself modeled on the Venetian Banco della Piazza di Rialto, founded in 1587.

35. Richard Gaettens, *Geschichte der Inflationen,* 2nd ed. (Munich: Battenberg, 1982), 91.

36. Schöttle, "Die große deutsche Geldkrise," 53.

and on how much influence they had in the courts.[37] The resolutions of the court cases took years, and the courts were still bogged down with cases at the time of the Treaty of Westphalia in 1648. Those left holding debased coins received only the value of the metal they contained, which was a fraction of their previous market value. Langer estimates that people lost on average about 90 percent of the value when new coinage was introduced.[38] So widespread was the fallout from the inflation that in many cities and towns, a majority of the population was economically ruined. Freytag's assessment of the damage is fully supported by contemporary accounts: "The evil of this sudden devaluation of money fomented passion and discontent in families, hatred and indignation between creditors and debtors, hunger, poverty, begging and homelessness. It made upstanding citizens into gamblers, drunkards and brawlers, drove priests and teachers from their posts, brought well-to-do families to the point of begging, threw authority into hopeless disarray, and threatened city-dwellers in heavily populated areas with starvation"[39] (see Plate XIX).

The present account of the events of the inflation is based on official written records, including prices, wages, and government documents, and the analysis of its pathology is based on current economic theory. But whatever insights this episode may have for economists, it is certainly at least as interesting to political scientists and historians, for its foundation lay in the weakness of the government structure and in the lack of checks on the government's officials, who were allowed to exercise their greed. Clearly, there was far more to resolve in seventeenth-century German society than was accomplished on the battlefields of the Thirty Years' War. In order to enhance our understanding of these broader issues, it is important to consider another contemporary source, the German political broadsheet. These broadsides provide a type of eyewitness account of the inflation and its impact and give insights which are otherwise lost over time.

Martha White Paas

37. See Redlich, *Die deutsche Inflation,* for details of some of these resolutions.

38. Langer, *Hortus Bellicus,* 31.

39. Freytag, *Bilder,* 152.

Note on Broadsheets

By the early seventeenth century broadsheets had become a major component of the burgeoning news network in early modern Europe. Appearing as single sheets printed on one side only and issued irregularly to meet public demand, broadsheets were for centuries the most popular literary medium in German-speaking areas of the Holy Roman Empire. As they dealt with virtually any subject of topical interest, whether it was political, religious, social, or economic, broadsheets enjoyed a wide circulation, especially in times of political unrest or social turmoil. They appealed to a broad audience and reflected general contemporary public interests like no other printed or visual medium could.

During the turbulent years of the Reformation Martin Luther's criticism of the Church soon went beyond strictly theological issues, and Europe was confronted for the first time by the extensive powers of the political press. In a concerted effort to gain or to maintain the support of the common people, Luther, the formidable theologian and gifted translator, never shied away from also putting his pen to paper as an aggressive publicist. As a result of his and others' zealous efforts in print to proselytize on the one hand and to condemn on the other, there was in the years from 1518 to 1524 at least a sixfold increase in the output of the German presses. The publication of polemical German and Latin works continued in the decades that followed, as advocates on both sides sought widespread support for their causes. The types of works that were issued by both lawful and clandestine presses ranged from erudite treatises to argumentative pamphlets to scurrilous lampoons.

The production of broadsheets in the empire in the sixteenth century was exceeded by that in the following century, when unresolved religious tensions led to the carnage of the Thirty Years' War. In the atmosphere of intense hatred, fear, and instability that marked the early decades of the seventeenth century, broadsheets were in such demand that by the end of the century hundreds of thousands of impressions of several thousand different broadsheets had been published. Their engaging content and illustrations were intended to catch the interest of a wide range of readers (and listeners), but their popularity is perhaps best explained by the seminal role they played in filling a significant gap in the informational network in German-speaking areas. Since German newspapers did not begin to appear on a regular basis in many of the larger and some of the smaller cities until the second half of the century, and since those which did were subject to censorship, broadsheets (along with pamphlets) often appeared clandestinely and supplied people with the information and interpretations denied them in the newspapers.

Broadsheets about current events served two primary functions, which remain integral to modern newspapers. With bold headlines and reports of major events or topics of general interest to the public, some sheets transmitted news as we find it on the front page of today's newspapers. The role of other sheets was closer to that of the modern editorial page with its political cartoon and opinions on current issues. Into this second group falls the corpus of broadsheets focusing on the devastating *Kipper und Wipper* inflation in the 1620s. Since there were no events per se to be reported, the journalists focused their attention on the causes and disastrous consequences of the inflation, and they were not averse to drawing on prejudices, such as anti-Semitism, to convey their message.

The manner of reporting or interpreting to be found in broadsheet texts varied from seemingly impartial factual accounts to extremely caustic, often obscene lampoons. The bite of a well-constructed print could be much more successful in delivering a message than could a polished written text. Although authorities throughout the empire tried to establish effective censorship over all types of printed works, the repeated issuance of decrees bears witness to the failure of both civilian and ecclesiastical attempts to stem the activities of the popular press. Materials were seized and arrests made, yet as long as there was a market for broadsheets, there were enterprising printers and publishers willing to take the necessary risks for profit.

The printing and publication of broadsheets in the early modern period was a highly risky undertaking that required special business acumen if one was to flourish, let alone survive. Competition was stiff, and to make ends meet printers often found it necessary to find sources of income outside of the printing trade. In the early modern period free imperial cities such as Frankfurt am Main and Strasbourg (Straßburg) were centers of production, but two cities—Augsburg and Nuremberg— far surpassed other German cities in the production of popular literature. Located on the major long-distance trade routes from north to south and east to west, these two cities were natural collecting points for news from throughout the empire. In Augsburg many of the enterprising publishers of broadsheets took care to establish their shops in close proximity to the city gates, through which all news passed as people entered and left the city.

The free imperial cities were also cultural centers in their own right. Among the citizens residing there, publishers had little trouble finding educated men—primarily students, lawyers, and churchmen—to compose the texts for broadsheets in either prose or verse. The names of these authors were rarely stated, for theirs was to be an anonymous voice of the people, and what they wrote was in no way considered important creative work. Most of these cities had long been centers of art and printing, and, thus, they also had a ready supply of printmakers to produce the illustrations. Whereas woodcuts had been the predominant form of illustration in the sixteenth century, taste changed rapidly after the invention of engraving and etching, and by the early seventeenth century the vast majority of illustrations were etched on copperplates. Frequently a printmaker also acted as a publisher, as, for example, the Augsburg artist Daniel Mannasser, the publisher of Plates VI, XI, XV, and XVI as well as of different printings of some of the other sheets.

Once a publisher had decided to have a broadsheet printed, his goal was to have it on the street as fast as possible. Under normal circumstances it would take no more than a few days to have copies ready for sale, and the often sloppy presswork—smeared text, crooked illustrations, and overlapping text and illustration—are a clear indication that speed of production was the overriding concern. As soon as a broadsheet was ready, if its content was in no way threatening to the local authorities, it could be openly offered for sale in town; additional copies were routinely sold to peddlers and hawkers, who carried them to other towns and villages.

Because of the rampant piracy of popular works such as broadsheets throughout the early modern period, publishers had to take great care in gauging the number of copies of a sheet they might reasonably expect to sell before that sheet could be reprinted by a competitor. The copperplates for the illustrations could have been used to produce upwards of two thousand copies of varying quality—and many more if the plates were retouched—but in actuality it was the cost of paper that was the decisive factor in determining the size of an edition. Paper accounted for a larger percentage of production costs than did labor, and, thus, a publisher would routinely choose to publish editions of five hundred or fewer sheets and then have a second edition printed, if necessary, rather than run the risk of having one larger edition remain unsold. There exist two or more different printings of Plates VI, VII, XI, and XXVII. There are also pirated editions of several sheets: Plates I, III, IV, VI, VIII, X, and XI. Almost all of the reprints and pirated copies come from the first year of the inflation, which possibly indicates a declining public interest in broadsheet comments about the inflation.

When having broadsheets printed publishers endeavored to make each sheet as topical and saleable as possible. Most broadsheets have a clear tripartite construction—title, illustration, and text—and the first two of these were particularly important in piquing the interest of the potential buyer, who would then later read the text. Frequently titles would emphasize the novelty of the sheet (for example, Plates VI, VII, VIII, and XVII), and at other times they would stress the sensational content of the report (for example, Plates VIII, XIV, and XVII). The illustrations often went even further in engaging the buyer through the use of eye-catching, sometimes frightening visual images, as on Plates V, IX, X, XI, XIII, XIV, XVI, XVII, XIX, XXV, and XXVI. As the artist worked on his illustration he could conceive of it as a close visual representation of the printed text, but a common technique used to underscore the message of the text was to depict a clear dichotomy between good and evil. For example, on Plate XI the impoverished mother and two children in the foreground are contrasted with the people engaged in hedonistic activities in the background; on Plate V the mintmaster is flanked by money debasers to his left and honest poor people to his right; on Plate XIII the usurer again stands in the middle and is flanked by Moses and the Ten Commandments to his right and the gaping maw of hell to his left.

The message conveyed by the broadsheets from the *Kipper und Wipper* inflation is one that varies little: the activities of those engaged as moneychangers are unchristian and sinful, and anyone who accumulates ill-gotten wealth on earth will find eternal damnation. Such a tendentious message makes no pretence of objectivity, and, thus, scholars were for a long time wary of basing research upon them in historical studies. Broadsheets have become, however, important primary sources for the early modern period, for they can help us understand what people at the time knew, thought, and believed. They help to bring to light the everyday concerns of people and by so doing help to give depth to our understanding of the historical past.

John Roger Paas

Note on the Translations

The form used by the anonymous authors of the broadsheet texts is *Knittelvers* (or *Knüttelvers*), rhymed pairs of more or less regular iambic tetrameter lines. The pattern, deriving from the classical Middle High German epic, was demotic, easy to master and easy for readers, or listeners, to follow, and throughout the later fifteenth and entire sixteenth centuries, it was the verse form of choice among poets. Sebastian Brant and Johann Fischart in Strasbourg, Hans Sachs in Nuremberg, Paul Rebhun in Saxony, and Sixt Birck in Augsburg—to mention just a few—all used *Knittelvers* in their literary writings. It was enormously popular in the lands of the German tongue, and although the somewhat pejorative sobriquet it acquired comes from *Knüttel,* a rough cudgel or club with a knotty surface, it was still the favored verse form at the time of the *Kipper und Wipper* inflation.

The literary provenance of the *Kipper und Wipper* versifiers (who occasionally deserve ranking as poets) can readily be made out; but we have little idea of who they were. The printmakers themselves? The printer-publishers (for example, Plate XXII)? Impecunious students eager to pick up some extra income? Or underpaid pastors? Whoever these versifiers were, their texts show a good amount of run-of-the-mill classical learning; for example, the appearance of the goddess Discordia on Plate IV, the account of the bad Roman emperors on Plate XX, the confrontation of Democritus and Heraclitus before Apollo on Plate XXIII, Pallas and Apollo on Plate XXVI. The author of Plate XIV is especially erudite: witness the references to Cicero's *De Officiis* and Seneca's *Epistolae Morales;* his whole text may have its prime source in the first of Horace's *Satirae.* The legal terms on Plate XXIII may also point to legal studies, popular then as now, and the same text displays a very modest knowledge of modish Spanish words. However, the Latin on Plate XIX might betray someone not wholly firm in the language, and the allusion to what Aristotle said about false coiners "in a poem" might be a symptom of shaky learnedness. The clever parody of highfalutin epistolary style in Lucifer's letter to his subjects (Plate XXV) indicates, perhaps, the hand of a copyist or secretary.

A trait common to the "poets" is a thorough grounding in Holy Scripture, a familiarity they would have expected their audience to share. The writers were virtually all Protestants; the towns indicated at the conclusion of Plates I, IV, VI, XI, XV, XVI, XIX, and XXII (Augsburg), Plate XXVII (Strasbourg), and Plate II (Frankfurt) had embraced the Reformation by the 1530s and along with Nuremberg remained centers of Protestantism, that is, Lutheranism, throughout the seventeenth century. Across the Roman Catholic lands, lay Bible-reading was discouraged or forbidden, and references to the Old Testament in particular would have caused difficulties of comprehension. To be sure, that exceptional author of Plate XIV makes scriptural references to the Vulgate but appears to number Saint Jerome among "profane and worldly authors." Lutheran clergymen still kept their knowledge of the Latin Bible, but how conversant was the audience of Plate XIV with his marginal references? Although this one sheet seems to be aimed at a particularly well-lettered target, the general level of sophistication varies from text to text.

The authors had grown up with the moralizing-satirizing conventions of *Knittelvers* and its paradoxical union of commonplaceness and vividness, and they employed the tradition to the full: witness the money-transport on Plate III; the coiners' shop on Plates IV, V, and XXI; the leprous money on Plate XV; the mirror of greed and usury on Plate XIII; the landscape of devastation on Plate XIX; the laments of the purse and its owner on Plates I and II; and the anti-Semitism on Plates IV, XIII, XV, XX, and XXV, which fits neatly into the age's carefully nurtured expectations of Jewish trickiness and skullduggery. The reader is engaged (or teased) in the guessing game on Plates VI and VII, and made to look into himself by the debate between the master coiner and his conscience on Plate V; further, the reader must (or should) sympathize with the supplicants on Plate XII, and test himself against the temptations listed on Plate XVIII. The atrocities of the Thirty Years' War were just beginning, but the speeches of the ravaged poor man and the boastful lansquenet on Plate X could remind the reader that, even though he had been spared as yet from plundering, rapine, and worse, an insidious—if less bloody peril—was at the door. At times, the broadsheets come close, in their search for ways to depict and persuade, to the time-honored serial technique of German drama in the late Middle

Ages and the early decades of the Reformation in which the representative of one calling after another steps forward and speaks his piece—a technique already intimated in the several self-descriptions in the coin catalogue on Plate VIII. Nor is the residual force of the polemic dialogue-literature of the Reformation to be forgotten, so strikingly represented a century before in the Latin dialogues and then the vernacular *Gesprächbüchlein* (Conversation Booklets) of the knight-humanist Ulrich von Hutten, a tradition that had certainly not died out: see, for example, Plate X (poor man and lansquenet), Plate III (rider and wagoner), Plate IV (Jew and Christian), and Plate V (master coiner and Miss Conscience).

The broadsheet texts can be regarded as lay sermons, delivered to a non-captive audience whose attention must be aroused and held; sometimes the verses attain an impressive solemnity—in the finale of Plate III, in the accusation against "worldlings" on Plate XII, in the charges against the devil near the end of Plate XVIII, and in the frightening conclusion of Plate XXII with its mention of Judgment Day and its plea for redemptive Christian charity. The versifiers demonstrated considerable powers of rhetoric as they sat in their parsonages or swiftly improvised on the spot in the publisher's house.

The translations do not attempt to reproduce the rhyme pairs of the originals, except at the end of each text. But it is hoped that the metrical energy of the originals will shine through, to an extent, in the English-language renderings, which have bravely been given a pseudo-archaic character, while trying to be as accurate as possible. It would be foolish to pretend that the texts do not contain murky patches confronting the translator with vague referents, jumbled syntax, unhelpful punctuation, and idioms long since dead as a doornail. The translations therefore represent a best effort to do justice to the meaning and spirit of the *Kipper und Wipper* broadsheets, even across four centuries.

George C. Schoolfield

PLATES

Trawrige Klag/
Vber meinen Seckhel.

Traurige Klag vber meinen Seckel.

SV tragen Samet vnd Seiden/
Mein Seckel nit wol kan erleiden/
Vil Gelts vnd Guts zuverschencken/
Mein Seckel hefftig thun bekrencken/
Ein Pferdt so hundert Taler werth/
Hat mir mein Seckel nit beschert/
Zu halten ein groß anzahl Knecht/
Meim Seckel nit will zimen recht/
Vilerley Kost vnd frembden Wein/
Mein Seckhel nit mag Zahler sein/
Groß lust zu Bawen ich wol het/
Ertragen wenns mein Seckel thet/
Vil Rechtfertigung an zuheben/
Meim Seckel wenig gwin thut geben/
Täglich Zehren bey dem Wirth/
Macht meinen Seckel gar verirt/
Mit Frawen treiben Liebes spil/
Mein Seckel zu vil es kosten will/
Zu fangen Kriegen vnd vnruh an/
Mein Seckel nit ertragen kan/
Inn Spil einsetzen grosses Gelt/
Meim Seckel solches gar nit gefelt/
Zu jagen halten vil der Hundt/
Ist meinem Seckel vngesundt/
So auff mein Haußstandt ich nicht acht/
So fellt mein Seckel inn Ohnmacht/
Wann ich mit frembdem Gelt gehe vmb/
Ich vmb mein Gelt vnd Seckel kumb/
Was ich anschaw / das hett ich gern/
Doch kans mein Seckel nit beschern/
Ach das mein Seckel Gelts wer vol/
So zahlt ich meine Schulden wol/
Darumb raht ich ein jeder thue/
Das mit seim Seckel er hab ruh/ꝛc.

Gegen Antwort.

Wann jeder solt bey vnsern Tagen/
Den Seckel sein so thun beklagen/
So wirdt deß Klagens sein kein Endt/
Drumb dich ein wenig zu mir wendt/
Ich will dir sagen auff mein Eydt/
Von deinem Seckel rechten bescheidt/
Wann du inn deinen Jungen Jahrn/
Gelernet etwas vnd erfahrn/
Dermassen gute Künst gestudiert/
Das du drinn hettest promoviert/
Oder sonst vil künstliche Sachen/
Zu brauch deß Menschen lernen machen/
Oder so du inn deinem Handl/
Geführet auffrichtigen Wandl/
Wann du selbst deinem Thun gewart/
Vnd nit auff frembde Leuth gespart/
Fein fleissig alles auffgeschriben/
Das dir nichts wer dahinden bliben/
Vnd alle ding fein wol versorgt/
Nichts vndichtigen Leuthen borgt/.
Oder so du ein Ambts Person/
Demselben recht abwarten thun/
Oder an Fürsten Höfen dich/
Gehalten hettest Ritterlich/
So het dein Seckel dir zuhandt/
Versaget nit das Seyden Gewandt/
Hest einem wol was schencken könden/
Ein Pferdt vil Gelts werth mügen finden/
Künst deinem Standt nach Häuser bawen/
Kurtzweiln auch mit deiner Frawen/
Vnd was dein Hertz sonst het begert/
Dein Seckel dir es hett beschert/
Drumb thue dein Seckel nit anklagen/
Sondern vor von dir selber sagen/
Daß du als vnhäußlicher Gast/
Dein Seckel nit gefüllet hast.

Bey Steffan Michelspacher / Im Jahr 1616.

PLATE I. Sad Lamentation about My Moneybag

Slumped against a tree trunk and in a state of utter dejection is a disheveled man who has seen better days. His doublet is missing buttons on the front and is badly torn at the left elbow; his right stocking is torn and hangs loosely at the knee. His sword rests between his legs, and his hat lies on the ground. In his right hand he listlessly holds an empty moneybag. Confronting him is a fashionably dressed young man, who points out that had the other led a more careful, frugal life, he would not now find himself in such dire straits.

Sad Lamentation about My Moneybag

The wearing of velvet and of silk
My moneybag surely can't endure.
The paying-out of money and means
Disturbs my moneybag terribly.
A horse that's worth a hundred Thalers
My moneybag's never vouchsafed me.
Supporting a mighty servant-staff
Will never suit my moneybag,
Of manifold foods and foreign wines
My moneybag can't the buyer be.
A great urge for building I'd surely bear
If my moneybag could bear it too.
Seeking vindication in courts of law
Gives my moneybag but little gain.
Daily gulosity at the inn
Makes my moneybag all confused.
With women to practice the play of love
Will cost my moneybag all too much.
The starting of squabbles and rackets roused
My moneybag cannot sustain.
To risk much money on a game
Delights my moneybag not at all.
Keeping many hounds for hunting's sport
Is harmful to my moneybag's health.
When I pay my household no heed at all,
My moneybag falls into a faint.
If I'm involved with others' money,
I lose my money and moneybag too.
Whatever I spy and should like to own,
My moneybag can't bestow it on me.
Oh, that my moneybag full could be,
Then I'd pay my debts of a surety.
Thus, I tell all to take this course
That they may live peaceably with their purse.

Retort:

If everyone in present days
Should so lament his moneybag,
Then of laments there'd be no end.
Thus, hearken to me a little while.
I'll tell you now, upon my oath,
The true account of your moneybag.
If you had, in your youthful years,
Learned something, grown experienced,
Studied the liberal arts so much
That you in them had graduated,
Or, otherwise, if you'd learned to do
Many skillful things for mankind's use,
Or if you had, in your transactions,
Pursued the path of honesty,
If you'd given heed to your own deeds,
And not saved it up for other people's,
Painstakingly had recorded all,
So that, for you, nothing was omitted,
And of all things had taken care,
Lent not at all to slippery folk,
Or if, in meeting some official,
You'd waited on him properly,
Or if at princely courts you had
Comported yourself in a courteous way,

Then your moneybag would not suddenly
  Have denied you that silken garb.
You could, indeed, have given gifts,
  And found a horse of excellent worth,
Built houses suited to your station,
  Enjoyed good pleasure with your wife,
And whatever else your heart desired
  Your moneybag would have bestowed on you.
Thus, blame your moneybag no more,
  But rather tell yourself before:
Like an unhousebroken guest or worse,
  That you have failed to fill your purse.

At the Shop of Steffan Michelspacher in the Year 1616.*

* Steffan Michelspacher was active in Augsburg ca. 1614–1620.

Des Seckels Jämmerlich Heulen/ vnnächlessig weh vnd Anklagen vber seinen Herrn.

Mein liber Herr/ Ich kan Wolan/
Mein seufftzen nicht mehr vnterlahn
Dich anzuklagen peinlich schwer/
Nach dems die Noth erfordert sehr:
Du weist wol das die Eltern dein/
Als die Patron vnd Beschemer mein/
Sehr viel Jahr her mich habn augirt/
Mit Golt vnd Silber hoch geziert/
Gemehre/ gebessert/ wie Ich sag/
Von Jahr zu Jahr/ von tag zu tag/
Gefüllt/ erfrewt/ welchs Ich der massen/
Zurühmen nicht kan vnderlassen/
Von Ihnen ward ich gespicket fein/
Mit Rothen gülden groß vnd klein/
Du hast aber nach Ihrem Todt/
Mich bracht in euserst gfahr vnd noth/
Als Ich nun kam in deine Hendt/
Vnd du annambst das Regiment/
Wann du hast wollen Essen/ Trincken/
Oder schönen Jungfrewlein wincken/
Wann du hast wollen Panckettirn/
Mit deiner Gsellschafft dich recreirn,
Wann du hast wollen Tantzen/ springen/
Nach frewden/ lust vnd Kurtzweil ringn
Wann du hast wollen Jagen/ hetzen/
Mit spielen/ Rennen dich ergetzen/
Hast mich allezeit gesprochen an/
Dir aus zuhelffen/ wie Ich dan/
Dir stets willfahret/ vnd der massen/
Dich niemahl habe stecken lassen/
Nun machst es zu grob in den sachen/
Wilst gar ein hädwerck darauß machn/
Ja wann ich wer von lautern stahl/
Mein Boden Von Ertzt vnd Metall/
Mein Riemen von Demanten stein/
So must Ich doch lang löchrig sein/
Dann ich von dir an manchen Ortn/
Vnzehlich viel gebraucht bin worden/
Ins vnuermögen bin ich kommen/
Dann krafft vnd safft ist mir entrunnē/
Dein grosse Gsellschafft hats gemacht/
Vnd dich von hauß vnd hoff gebracht/
Dein zinß vnd Rendt/ auch dein Gültbriff
Sind kommen auf das leichte Schiff/
Deiner Acker vnd deiner Weingarten/
Thut itzunder ein ander Wartn/
Dein schöne Wält dein Schaff vnd wiese/
Thū durchs Gesegn dirs Gott hinfliess
Dein Rind vieh so du gehabt hast/
Das ist nun gantz vnd gar verprast/
Drumb klagt dich an die Bulschafft dein
Das du niemahl verschont hast mein/
Die Schüssel klagt dich an zur frist/
Weil keine Speiß mehr in Ihr ist
Die Flasch wehklagt vnd heület sehr/
Das sie itzund muß sein so lehr/
Die Kanne dich gleichsfalls anklagt/
Kein Wein verhanden ist/ sie Sagt/
Dein Pfert schreyet Rach vber dich/
Hat mangel ann Futder stettiglich/
Dein hundt thut dich anklagen vnd pochē
Dann Er findt weder bein noch knochē
Drumb ist die Schuldt nun aller dein/
Hettstu vorhin geschonet mein/
So wer vber dich wie Ich sag/
Gar nicht ergangen solch Anklag/

Gedruckt zu Franckfurdt am Mayn Bey Conrad Corthoys.

PLATE II. The Purse's Wretched Howling, Ceaseless Lament, and Accusations against Its Master

This illustration divided in half by a large tree depicts a young man's life of pleasure and the resulting downfall. On the right, the young man is spending the inheritance from his parents in the pursuit of hedonistic pleasure. Seated at a table sumptuously set out of doors, he flirts with a young woman, while another couple dances to the accompaniment of a lute player's music. In the background a deer is hunted for sport. On the left side, the inebriated young man slumps against a bank as he is berated by his mistress and growled at by his hungry dog. In the background are the home, the fields, and the herd of cattle that the young man has lost through his profligate lifestyle.

Oh master dear, I can indeed
  No more suppress my sighing now,
Directing at you the gravest charges,
  Since very need does much demand it.
You know full well the way your parents,
  As my protectors and my patrons,
For many years augmented me,
  Adorned me well with gold and silver,
Increased, improved me (as I say)
  From year to year, from day to day,
Filled and rejoiced me, for which I thus
  Can never cease to sing their praise,
So finely I by them was stuffed
  With ruddy Guldens, large and small.
However, after they had died,
  You brought me to peril and despair,
When now I fell into your hands,
  And you assumed authority.
When you have wanted to eat and drink,
  And to fair maidens give a wink,
When you have wanted celebrations
  And, with your fellows, recreations,
When you have wanted to dance and prance,
  And striven for merriment and pleasure,
When you have wanted hunts and chases,
  And amused yourself with games and races,
At every time you turned to me
  To help you out, and I properly
Have always done your will, and so
  Have never left you in the lurch.
Now in these matters you've gone too far,
  And will indeed make them your vocation.
Forsooth, if I were of purest steel,
  My bottom of bronze or some other metal,
My strap adorned with diamond stones,
  I still, long since, would be full of holes,
For I, in many a location,
  And countless times, have been used by you.
To impotence now I've entered in,
  Lost vigor and virility.
Your widespread circle this has done,
  And made you lose both house and home.
Your income, interest, and your drafts
  Have landed on a fragile craft.
Your arables and vineyards large
  Now lie within another's charge.
Your handsome woods, your sheep, and meadows
  Have now (God bless you) fled away.
The herds of cattle you once owned
  Have now been wasted utterly,
And so your harlot charges you
  With never having spared my use.
Your plate accuses you presently
  Because no food upon it lies.
Your bottle wails and howls aloud
  Because it now so empty stands.
Your tankard likewise charges you
  Because (it says) there's no more wine.

Your horse calls vengeance on your head,
  Since it lacks fodder evermore.
Your dog denounces you and growls
  Since neither meat nor bone it finds:
Therefore, the guilt is yours alone.
  If you had spared me in the past,
Then, as I presently have taught,
  At you such blame would not be brought.

Printed in Frankfurt am Main at the Shop of Conrad Corthoys.

Müntzbeschickung der Kipper vnd Wipper.

ES ist jetzt kommn die letzte Zeit/
Von welcher Christus Prophezeit/
Daß grosser Trübsal solte werdn/
Von Angst vnd Noth auff dieser Erdn/
Grosser Furcht vnd Wartung derer Ding/
Die sich noch nie von anbegin
Auff der Welt haben zugetragn/
Darüber die Leut werden zagn/
Es kan auch wol nicht anders seyn/
Denn Trew vnd Glaub ist worden klein/
Barmhertzigkeit wird nicht geübt/
Gott vnd der Nechst auch nicht geliebt/
All Tugenden werden vertriebn/
Gerechtgkeit ist in Himml gstiegn/
Drümb ist jetzt die Eyserne Zeit/
Da all Nahrung zu Boden leit/
Es raubt vnd stilt nur jederman/
Auff was weiß er nur jmmer kan/
Wie öffentlich ist jetzt am Tag/
Drümb ich euch ein Histori sag/
Die sich da vor wenig Tagen
Auff freyer Strassen zugetragn/
Ein Wagen mit vier starckn Rossen/
Fuhre daher auff der Strassen/
Er war beladen also fast/
Daß die Roß an der schweren Last/
Zu ziehen hatten/ daß sie bogn
Ist warlich war / vnd nicht erlogn/
Ein Reuter sah den Wagen an/
Er sprach/ mein Ehrlicher Gespan/
Was führstu da vor eine Last/
Sag mir/ was du geladen hast?
Er sprach / mein lieber frommer Herr/
Es ist eitel altes Kupffer/
Von Kesseln / Blasen / vnd Pfannen/
Küpffern Rinnen vnd Badwannen/
Vbern hauffn zsammen gschlagen/
Das führe ich auff meinem Wagen/
Der Reuter sprach wo dann mit nauß/
Sag mir was wird gemacht darauß?
Eitel Müntz will man drauß machen.
Der Reuter fieng an zu lachen/
Das muß wol werden ehrlich Geld/
Damit betrogen wird die Welt/

Woher kommen die Silberblick/
Damit das Kupffer wird beschickt?
Daß man gute Müntz macht darvon/
Nach des Reichs Constitution?
Daß nemen sie gar nicht in acht/
Dort auff den Boten gebet acht/
Der alßbald folgt meinem Wagen/
Kan eben so viel Silber tragen/
Als man braucht zu der beschickung
Dieses Kupffers / ist gar genung/
Es muß alles zu grunde gehn/
Die lenge kan es nicht bestehn/
Dann es ist jetzt des Teuffels Frucht/
Herfür kommen ein edle Zucht/
Kipper vnd Wipper sind sie genandt/
Das acht man vor grossen Verstandt/
Ob es gleich ist recht Teuffels tück/
Achtens doch für ein Meisterstück/
Damit man vntr des Rechten schein/
Den Armen bringet vmb das sein/
Darzu den Gottlosen ist jag/
Zuverderben Nacht vnd auch Tag
Den Armen/ vnd verschonen nicht
Was sie bekommen ins Gesicht/
Fragen nach keiner Straff der Altn/
Sondern lassens den Teuffel waltn/
Sagen/ wir machens wie wir wolln/
Wie wir nur können vnd auch solln/
Es muß jetzo nur alls sein recht/
Wer daß nicht thut ist viel zu schlecht/
Er taug auch nicht in diese Welt/
Mangelt beydes an Gut vnd Geld/
Solche seind verbunden ohn Zweiffl
Mit jhrm Vater dem leidign Teuffl/
Weil er sie vnter seinem Reich
Gefangen helt alle zugleich/
Auff daß sie sein Leibeigen seyn/
Vollbringen was er jhn bläst ein/
Der wird sie auch kräfftiglich sterckn/
Daß sich mit Worten vnd mit Werckn/
So tieff in diese Sünd verbindn/
Daß er wol keinen lest dahinden/
Von diesen Gottlosen Leuten/
Die in diesen schweren Zeiten/

Vrsach sind daß solch lose Geld
Wird eingeführt in aller Welt.
Denn je mehr der Reichsthaler gilt/
Je mehr der Müntze man abstilt/
Macht leicht groschn vnd schreckenberger/
Achtgroschnstück noch sehr viel ärger/
Es gehet nur vber den Armn/
Gott wol drein sehn vnd sich erbarmn.
Dann das Kippen in dieser Zeit/
Brauchen Kramer vnd Handelsleut
Nicht allein / sondern es ist auch
Bey gelehrten kommen im gbrauch/
Denn mancher fein Erbarer Man/
Der lang studirt, vnd wenig kan/
Vnd führt einen hohen Tittel/
Nehrt sich aber von dem Kippen/
Daß er wol sonsten gar nicht thet/
Wann er so viel studiret hett/
Daß er sich davon könte nehrn/
So könt er sich des Kippen wehrn/
Abr deß Teuffels Geitz vnd Pracht/
Hat die Welt voll Kipper gemacht/
Ob wol keiner allhier genennt/
Darbey aber man sie bald kennt/
Wann sie viel Geld gebracht zuhauff/
Schöne Häuser vnd Garten kauffn/
Landgüter / Wiesen vnd auch Feld/
Vor solch leichtfertig Kippergeld/
Daß sie es bey zeit werden loß/
Auff daß / wenns ein mal kriegt ein stoß/
Das sie keine Handlung mehr treibn/
So könnens auff den Gütern bleibn.

Wie kömpt der Handwercksman darzu/
Der sein sawer Arbeit vnd Müh/
Mit solchem Geld muß bzahlen lan/
Do dargegen der Handelsman/
Alles auff seine Wahren schlegt/
Damits jhm gnug in Kasten tregt/
Er muß es thun / darff er sagen/
Weil die Reichsthaler auffgschlagen.
So geb Gott dem so langs Leben/
Vnd kein gesunde Stund darneben/
Nach diesm Lebn das Hellisch fewr/
Der die Reichsthaler gmacht so thewr.

PLATE III. Coin Arrangement of the Clippers and Whippers*

In a mountainous landscape a heavily laden wagon is being pulled by four horses, straining under the load. A gentleman rider inquires about the driver's cargo and is told that it contains secondhand copper intended for the debasement of coins. Following alongside the wagon is a courier carrying some silver. At the back of the wagon is a soldier, who brandishes a club in one hand and a raised switch in the other as he drives away three woman: the Christian virtues Faith, Hope, and Charity. Languishing in the foreground is a woman with chained hands, who represents the plight of all poor people ruined by inflation. The exploitation of the poor will, however, not remain unpunished, for hovering in the sky is an angel of justice, with scales in one hand and a sword in the other, and in the background gallows stand ready.

The final days have now arrived
Of which Lord Jesus prophesied,
That there would be great misery
With terror and famine on this earth,
Great fear and waiting for those things
Which never since the start of time
Have taken place upon our world.
Therefore the people grow afraid,
Surely it can't be otherwise,
For loyalty and faith grow small,
Compassion's no more practiced now,
God and one's neighbor are loved no more,
All virtues have been chased away,
Justice has gone up to the skies.
Thus the age of iron has come†
When all livelihood has gone to ruin,
Everyone but robs and steals
Whatever he knows that he well can,
As every day is now made clear.
Thus I shall recount for you a tale
Of what only a few days back
Took place upon the open road.
A wagon drawn by four strong steeds
Wended its way along the road.
Laden it was so heavily
That the horses, from the heavy load
They had to drag along, were bent.
It's truly true and not a fable.
A rider, seeing the wagon come,
Spoke out: "My honest wagoner,
What sort of cargo do you pull?
Tell me what you have loaded there?"
He answered: "My dear pious sir,
It's nothing but copper, secondhand,
From kettles, bellows, and pannikins,
Gutters of copper and bathing tubs,
All pounded together in a heap.
That's what I'm pulling in my van."
The rider spoke: "What is your goal,
Tell me, what will be made from it?"
"To naught but coins will it be made."
The rider couldn't hold his laughter back.
"Honest money it will doubtless become,
By which the world will be deceived.
Whence will come the silver coat
With which the copper is alloyed,
So that good coins from it be made,
In keeping with the empire's laws?"

* The German word *kippen* or *abkippen* meant cutting off the edges of good coins, *wippen,* the use of false scales. The basic meaning of *wippen* is "to move up and down," hence "to weigh." *Die Wippe,* or strappado, was a means of torture, and one has to assume that contemporary German speakers were quite aware of this cruel secondary sense of the word pair *Wippe/wippen.*

† See Ovid, *Metamorphoses* 1.127–131 and also 15.260–261.

"They pay no heed to that at all.
Look at the courier coming there,
Who follows my wagon close behind.
He can carry of silver just so much
As one needs for the preparation
Of the copper, just enough.
It all must go to wrack and ruin,
It cannot last for very long,
For it is now the devil's fruit,
And it will bear a noble brood:
Clippers and whippers they are called,
And thought to show great intelligence,
Although it's but the devil's trick,
They think that it's a masterpiece,
Whereby, beneath the guise of right,
They rob the poor of all they have,
These godless folk have as their aim,
In daytime and at night as well
To ruin the poor, and do not spare
Whatever they've set their eyes upon,
Not heeding the ancients' punishments,
But rather letting the devil rule.
They say: We act just as we please,
Just as we can and as we should.
Now everything must be thought right,
Who fails to do it is simple-minded,
And of no value in this world,
And will lack both money and property.
Such people must doubtless be allied
With their father, the devil himself,
Since he keeps them beneath his rule
And holds them captive, all together,
So that they'll be his serfs and slaves,
To do whatever he suggests.
Also, he will give them strength,
That they, by means of words and works,
Will link themselves to this sin so deep,
That he will surely leave none behind
Of all these people without God,
Who in these times of harrowing
Are the reason that such worthless money
Is introduced in all the world.
For the more the Reichsthaler is worth,
The more one pilfers from the coin,
Easily makes Groschens and Schreckenbergers*
(Eight Groschen pieces are even worse).
The poor folk are the victims here,
May God behold it and take pity.
For the clipping in this very time
Is practiced not by tradesmen alone
And merchants too, but has as well
Become the practice of learned folk,
For many a fine, respected man,
Who long has studied, and knows but little,
And bears with pride some lofty title,
Supports himself by clipping and whipping
Which otherwise he'd not do at all,
If he had studied to such degree
That he could support himself thereby,
And could avoid his clipping ways.
But the devil's very greed and pomp
Have made the world with clippers full,
Though none of them will be named here,
They all the same will soon be known,
For they have piled their wealth on high,
Bought handsome houses and gardens too,
Estates and meadows, acres as well,
With such licentious clipping wealth,
But they will lose it in good time,
Since when, one day, it is struck down,
They will ply their trade no more,
And on their properties be left sitting."
  How has the craftsman come to this,
That for his sour work and toil,
With such coin he lets himself be paid?
And the tradesman, on the other hand,

* The Schreckenberger, a small coin of little value, was named after the silver mine and village of Schreckenberg, near the mining center of Annaberg in Saxony's Ore Mountains (Erzgebirge). The coin was in circulation primarily in Saxony and Bohemia.

Drives up the price of all his wares,
So that enough enters his money chest.
He has to do it, so he may say,
Since the Reichsthaler's value has gone up.
May God grant him a lengthy life,
Yet never an hour of healthiness,
And after this life make hellfire sear
The man who's made Reichsthalers dear.

Epitaphium oder deß guten Geldes Grabschrifft.

O du Geitzteuffel auff der Baan/
Was hebstu alls mit dem Geld an/
Ist es noch nicht genug der zeit/
Vnfrid vnd Widerwertigkeit.

WO seynd doch Leut also verflucht/
So arg verschlagen vnd durchsucht/
Als die Gottlose Juden sein/
In den Müntz handel gesetzt ein/
Sein die ärgsten Feind in der Welt/
Die zu grund richten das gut Geld:
Hie kompt ein Christ/
Der ärger ist.
Merck Jud / seh gut Geld bring ich dir/
Was gibstu auff den Wechsel mir?
Auff den Gulden Häller zu lohn/
Jud: Da hastu dreissig Kreutzer schon.
Christ: Was auff den fl. Pfenning im brauch?
Jud: Hier hastu 30. Kreutzer auch.
Christ: Was auff den Gulden Kreutzer her?
Jud: Zehen Patzen gib ich nicht mehr.
Christ: Was auff den Gulden halbe Patzn?
Jud: Hie hast 12. Patzn in dein Tatzn.
Christ: Was gibstu auff ein Gulden Groschn?
Jud: Ein fl. hast nicht hart drumb droschn
Christ: Auff ein Guldn 6. Kreutzer was gibst dar?
Jud: Da hastu einen Gulden bar.
Christ: Auff ein Gulden Drey Pätzner wol/
Jud: Ein Gulden 5. Plappart fürwol.
Christ: Auff 2. Gulden Sechs Pätzner was/
Jud: Vier Guldē dreyssig Kreutzer fürbaß.
Christ: Was gibst auff ein 12. Pätzner gut/
Jud: Dreissig Kreutzer ist mir zu muht.
Christ: Auff ein Reichsthaler was gibst ein?
Jud: 5. Gulden dreyssig Kreutzer fein.
Christ: Was gibst auff ein Goldgulden mir?
Jud: Fünff Gulden 30 Kreutzer dafür/
Christ: Endlich was gibst auff ein Ducaten du/
Jud: Acht Gulden 30. Kreutzer darzu.
Je besser Geld/ je mehr gib ich/
Darauff darnach so richte dich/
Komm bald zu mir wider in samm/
Ich zahl dirs wol bey meiner Scham.
DJß Epitaphium O Christ/
Deß guten Gelds Begräbnuß ist.
Schaw an der Gottloß Christ vorab/
Trägt selbst das gut Geldt zu dem Grab.
Das ist der Juden Tiegl/
Zu lohn solt seyn ein starcker Prügl/
Auff jhren Rucken für ein pahr/
Sag O Leser ist es nicht wahr?
Der Geitz Teuffel ist der rechte Thäter/
Der Wucherer deß Gelds Verräthr/
Die bringens den Juden geflissen/
Wo köndten sie das Geld sonst wissn/
Die werffens in den Tiegel / jhr
Gott werff sie in die Höll dafür/
Ist ob Gott wil nicht lang dahin/
Wird die Höll jhr aller Gwinn/
Wiewol sie dessen nicht besorgn/
Der Vmbhang helt jhr Sach verborgn.
Discordia vns fein andeut/
Diser Welt widerwertigkeit/
In hohem vnd Niederm Stand/
Vnter deß das gut Geld zuhand/
Schreyt vmb Hülff / daß es muß von
Den Juden schändlich zu grund gahn/
Ja es schreyt vber die danebn/
So jhnen den Gwalt haben gebn.
Vnter dem obgmeltem Fürhang/
Hat die Gerechtigkeit kein Gang/
Dann jhr Klarheit will nicht hinnein/
Hie bey den Teuffels Juden sein/
Dieweil sie als der Edel Schatz/
In der schnöden Welt hat kein platz:
Weil die Welt im Vnfrieden steht/
Die zeit der Juden Geldt fortgeht/
Schickt aber Gott guts Regiment/
Der Juden Teuffels Geld sich endt.
Ihr Widerchristische Boßheit/
Mit all jhr Vngerechtigkeit/
Ihr vngerechtes Geld zumal/
Gemacht von allerley Metall/
Wers jetzt nach jhnen schmeltzen thut/
Bringt darvon kaum 2. Pfenning gut.
Solt das nicht zubeklagen seyn/
Gegen dem guten Geld gemein.
Hie spürt man jhren Neyd vnd Haß/
Gegen der Christenheit ohn maß/
Vorzeiten hat man sie erkennt/
Mit jhrem falschen Geldt verbrendt/
Man sicht in aller Welt vmbher/
Daß kein Gerechtigkeit ist mehr/
Warumb sie hat keinen Fortgang/
Das macht der Welt Teuffels vmbhang/
Der in allem nicht schafft das gut/
Biß Gott den Fürhang hinweg thut.
Secht der wigt das Geldt mit Vntrew/
Ey daß es sein letzts wegen sey.
Hinder jhm schlegt der drauff das Präg/
Ach daß sein Seel auch darob leg/
Sampt seiner Müntz tieff in der Erdn/
Daß der Wundsch an jhm war soll werdn/
Daß der Träger/ Gräber/ Todtengräber/
Komm in Höllischen Finstern Nebel/
Was wündsch ich/ sie haben mehr Plag/
Weder man jhnen wündschen mag.
Es ist vmb den Armen zuthun/
Dem thut es vbel darob gahn/
Weil die gut Müntz starck geht zu grund/
O Christ bitt Gott hertzlich jetzund/
Daß er vns laß nach disem Zorn/
Die Himlisch Müntze widerfahrn/
Dardurch vns Christus mit Wolthat/
Erkauffet vnd erlöset hat/
Von der Müntz deß Teuffels die zeit/
Als der verfluchten vnwarheit/
Deß wegen last vns bitten gleich/
Den lieben Gott im Himmelreich/
Daß er abwend diß vngemach/
Das wird gedruckt zu Denck jhm nach.

Zu Augspurg / bey Martin Wörle/
Brieffmaler im Stern-
gäßlein.

PLATE IV. Epitaph or Grave Inscription of Good Money

Oh greed-devil as you go,
Why do you treat money so?
Is there not yet, presently,
Enough discord and adversity?

Depicted in this scene is the full range of activities carried out in the process of minting debased currency. In the room in the foreground a Christian has brought a sack of money, which he wishes to sell to the Jewish money changer, seated at the right. The money changer is in the process of clipping old coins, while his helper on the other side of the table is engaged in weighing the coins to determine their value. In the background workers are smelting the old coins with copper to produce an inferior metal. The man at the left is using this new metal as he hammers debased coins. To his right, two baskets are filled with the coins he has already produced. Covering the window at the rear is a curtain on which is imprinted a battle scene and the word "DISCORDIA," a clear reference to the negative consequence of such immoral activities.

Where's there a people so accursed,
So evil, crafty, and devious,
As are the godless Jewish folk?
Established in the trade with coins,
They are the worst foes in the world,
Driving money to wrack and ruin.
Here comes a Christian
Who is still worse.
See Jew, what good money I bring to you:
What will you give me in return,
As recompense for the Gulden coin?
Jew: For it you'll get thirty Kreuzers now.*
Christian: And what for the Gulden-penny's use?
Jew: Here you'll get thirty Kreuzers too.
Christian: And what for the Gulden-Kreuzer here?
Jew: I'll give no more than Batzens ten.
Christian: What will you give for the Gulden-half-Batzen?
Jew: Here you have twelve Batzens in your paw.
Christian: What will you give for a Gulden-Groschen?
Jew: You'll never work too hard for a Gulden.
Christian: And what for a Gulden and six Kreuzers?
Jew: For that you'll get a Gulden clear.
Christian: And for a Gulden, three Batzners then?*
Jew: A Gulden, five Plapparts indeed.†
Christian: And for two Guldens, six Batzners—what?
Jew: Four Guldens, thirty Kreuzers, to be sure.
Christian: What will you give for twelve Batzners good?
Jew: Thirty Kreuzers are what I have in mind.
Christian: What will you for a Reichsthaler give?
Jew: Five Guldens, thirty Kreuzers fine.
Christian: What will you give me for Gulden of gold?
Jew: Five Guldens and thirty Kreuzers too.

* For the relationship between the various coins, see footnote 16 in the introduction.

* A Batzner is the same as a Batzen.

† A Plappart was an Upper Rhenish coin worth about half a Groschen.

Christian: Finally, what will you give for a ducat?
Jew: Eight Guldens, and thirty Kreuzers besides.
The better the money, the more I'll give:
Hereafter act accordingly,
Come and join with me soon again,
I'll pay you well, though at my loss.
This epitaph, oh Christian man,
Is for good money's funeral.
Behold, first, how the godless Christian
Himself bears good money to its grave.
That's the devil's cauldron of the Jews,
The reward should be a thorough threshing
On their backs for every pair.
Now tell me, reader, is it not true:
The devil of greed's the actual doer,
The usurer the money's betrayer.
To the Jews they bear it zealously.
Where else could they think to place their coin,
They cast it into the cauldron there,
May God cast them into hell for that.
If God so wills, it will not take long,
Hell will be the profit of them all,
Though that does not bother them in the least.
The curtain keeps their business hidden.
Discordia* show us plain and clear
The loathsome nature of this world,
In all classes, high and low,
Meanwhile money presently
Cries out for aid, since shamefully
It's forced into ruin by the Jews.
Yes, it cries out against others too,
Who have given them this power.
Beneath the curtain, named above,
Righteousness has no entryway,
For its clarity will not enter here*
To consort with the devil's Jews.
Because it, as the noble treasure,
Has no place in that vicious world.
As long as the dissention stands,
The age of Jews' money will proceed,
But if God will send good government,
The Jews' devil-money will have an end,
Their anti-Christian evilness,
With all its lack of righteousness,
Their tainted coin especially,
Made of every sort of metal.
Whoever melts it in their wake,
Will get but two pennies in return.
Should that not be lamentable,
Against good money commonly:
Here one detects their envy and hate
Against Christendom, measureless.
In times past, one found them out,
And had them burned, with their false coin.
Now looking all the world about,
One sees that righteousness is no more,
Why it no longer can prevail
Is the work, in the world, of the devil's curtain,
Which in all things does naught of good,
Until God will tear the curtain away.
Behold: he weighs money crookedly,
Oh, that it might be his final weighing.
Behind him, the fellow strikes the die,
Oh, that his soul might lie on it,
Along with his coin, deep in the earth,
And that, in him, the wish came true
That the bearers, engravers, gravediggers,
Would land in the darkling fogs of hell.
What else do I wish? That they have more woe
Than ever one could wish for them.
It's a question of the poor
For whom things go so wretchedly
Since good coin's ruined so forcefully.
Oh Christian, pray God with all your heart
That, after this day of wrath is past,*

* See *Aeneid* VI.280–281. The name of Discordia also appears on the curtain, or shop window, in the picture.

* *Righteousness* is a key word of both the Old and New Testament, whereas *clarity* is found only in the latter (see Rev. 18:1).

He'll let us partake of heavenly coin,
Whereby Christ in his charity
Has purchased us and us redeemed
From the devil's coinage in this age,
And, as well, from his damned falsity,
On this account, let us forthwith pray
To our dear God in heaven's realm,
That He'll avert this misery:
That's printed here in His memory.

Augsburg, at the Shop of Martin Wörle,
Illuminator on Sterngässlein.

* See Rev. 6:17.

Der Wucherische Müntzmeister.

Müntzmeister.

Aufft zu/ laufft zu/ ihr lieben Leut/
In dieser angenämen Zeit/
Kompt her zu mir auff diesen Plan/
Merckt auff/ was ich euch zeige an:
Kompt her zu mir/ seyt arm odr reich/
Ihr Jungen vnd Alten zugleich/
Schawet an/ hört zu ohn beschwerd/
Wie es beschaffen ist auff Erd/
Kriegesgeschrey/ wie ist bekandt/
Erschallet jetzt in alle Land.
Ein jeder dazu Nacht vnd Tag
Sich bemühet/ vnnd dahin tracht/
Wie er möge viel Geldt vnd Gut
Samblen/ vnd haben guten Muht.
Wer viel Gelt hat ist lieb vnnd werth/
Deß Dürfftigen niemand begert.
Wer Gelt hat/ kompt bald zu Ehren/
Arme thut man gschwind abkehren.
Wer Gelt hat/ wird gar hoch geacht/
Welches ich gar wol hab betracht.
Darumb die Müntz bald auff mich nam/
Daher ich bin worden ein Mann.
Ich thet bey meinen Spießgeselln/
Kipper vnd Auffwechßler bestelln
Mit fleiß/ daß sie auß alln Orten/
Die beste Müntz zu mir führten:
Daher mein Tiegl so sehr zunam/
Daß ich bald ward ein reicher Mann.
Vor Zeiten bey vielen Fratzen/
Heller/ Pfenning/ Dreyer/ Batzen/
Wurdn gehalten in schlechtem Werth/
Bißweilen sie niemand begert/
Da solt es alles Thaler seyn/
Odr Golt/ das ander war gemein.
Auch wündschtens in vielen Städten/
Daß sie solch schlecht Müntz nicht hetten.
Ich aber recht betracht die Sachn/
Gedacht/ du solt es anders machn/
Mein Schmeltz Tiegel nam sie gern an/
Daher ich ward ein reicher Mann.
Doch diese Müntze nicht allein/
Sondern auch Groschen vnd Creutzr fein/
Was? Reichsthaler in grosser Zahl/
Wurdn mir zugeführt überal/
Welchen ich gar geschwind vnd bald/
Verändert jhr erste gestalt/
Mit Kupffer ich das weiß abtrieb/
Daß nur schön rot farb überblieb.
Daher ichs auch so weit gebracht/
Daß Kupffer jetzt wird hochgeacht/
Da vor Jahrn das Silber allein/
In grosser Herrn Schatz ward glegt ein/
Thut fürwar an jetzo im gleichn
Kupffer fein mählich mit einschleichn/
Vnd wann ich das nicht hett gethan/
Wer ich nicht geworden ein reichr Mann.

Fräwlein Conscientia.

JA freylich du keinnützer Heldt/
Verschmeltzest viel Silber vnd Gelt/
Was zuvor von Silber gewest/
Für Kupffer sich jetzt sehen läst/
Daher bist wordn ein reicher Mann.
Aber merck was ich dir zeige an/
Du hast betrogn viel grosser Herrn/
Die Kauffleut thust du auch verirn/
Dein schmeltzen macht daß gstigen seyn/
So hoch jhr Wahren in gemein/
Daß/ was man mit müh vnd sorgen/
In vielen Wochn hat erworben/
Vmb ein Eln Zeugs bald zahlen muß/
Solt das nicht bringen groß Verdruß?
Du machest daß dem armen Mann/
Kein Pfenning jetzt man geben kan.
Hiedurch dem Crämer sein Wahrn bleibn/
Kan sein Nahrung nicht weiter treibn/
Das Marck jhm ziehest auß dem Bein/
Drüber er seufftzet in geheim/
Der Armen Thränen übr sich steign/
Werden nicht vngerochen bleibn/
GOtt wird dich stürtzen gar geschwind/
Entgelten wirdts dein Weib vnnd Kind:
Dein Glück wird sich wenden gar bald/
Wirst haben ein viel andr gestalt/
Ob du schon blühst ein gering Zeit/
Wirst bald drauff haben viel Hertzleid/
Drumb schicke dich nur fein darein/
Jetzt muß vnd soll dein Garauß seyn.

Müntz Meister.

ACh/ wie ist mir so angst vnd weh/
Wo bleib jetzt ich/ nicht längr hie steh/
O weh/ weh/ was für ein Gesicht/
Hat mir erschröcklich ding bericht/
Groß ist mein Jammer vnd Elend/
Die gantze Welt ist mir zu eng.
War ists/ gar viel hab ich betrogn/
Vnd sie gar schändtlich außgesogn/
Ihr Kipper vnd Auffwechßler ebn/
Bringet mich jetzund vmb mein Lebn/
Drumb nemet diß gar wol in acht/
Jetzt fahr ich hin zu guter Nacht.

ENDE.

PLATE V. The Profiteering Master Coiner

Standing proudly at the very center and holding several moneybags with his right hand—above which is written "Money must be there"—is a fashionably dressed master coiner. A large medal with the words "I now flourish" hangs prominently from the sash draped across his doublet. In the workshop behind him to the right his helpers are busy melting down old coins of value and producing new, debased coins. The banderole above their heads reads, "Vigorously we pound it out." In a home to the left an aged man laments, "Oh God, protect indeed the deprived," while his daughter consoles him, "It will occur at the proper time." Behind the master coiner a lute-playing putto labeled "Conscience" hovers on a cloud. The impending downfall of the master coiner is assured, for he is already balancing precariously on one foot atop a winged orb, an emblem representing the fickle nature of fortune. Inscribed on the orb are the ominous words, "Fortune and glass, how fast they shatter." The sense of doom is underscored by the presence of ravens—harbingers of ill fortune—perched on leafless branches, from which ropes for hanging dangle.

Master Coiner:

Run hither, run, dear people, do,
In this fair season of the year,
Come here to me, upon this green,
Pay heed to what I'll show you now.
Come here to me, be you rich or poor,
Young people and you old folks too,
Behold and hark, it's easily done,
And learn how things on earth are won.
The cries of war, as is well known,
Sound loudly now in every land,
And everybody, day and night,
Strives and struggles with the aim
Of seeing how much wealth and weal
They can collect and have good cheer.
Who has much money is liked and prized,
But no one wants a needy man.
Who's got money is soon approved,
The poor man's swiftly swept away.
Who's got money is held in high esteem
Which closely I've indeed observed.
Thus I took coins as my pursuit,
And so I've become a very man.
Among my cronies I recruited
Clippers and shifty moneychangers,
Intentionally, so that everywhere
To me they brought the best of coins:
There my melting pot so much increased
That I a rich man soon became.
A while ago, 'midst many a sneer,
Hellers, Pfennigs, Dreyers, Batzens
Were thought to be of little worth,
And sometimes no one wanted them,
For all coins were supposed to be
Thalers or gold, the rest were common.
In many cities they also wished
To have no worthless coins at all.
But I took a careful look at things
And thought: You'll do it differently.
My crucible gladly swallowed them,
And so I became a wealthy man.
But not just with such coins alone,
But also with Groschens and Kreuzers fine.
What? Reichsthalers in great amounts
Came to my hands from every side,
And I quite speedily and soon
Exchanged their first form for another,
With copper I drove their whiteness away,
That only a nice red color stayed.
So that now I've brought it to the point
That copper stands in high esteem,
When years ago it was silver alone
That was put in great lords' treasure chests.
Now, forsooth, in the selfsame way

Copper comes creeping in besides,
And if I had not done it then
I shouldn't have become a wealthy man.

Miss Conscience:

You bootless hero, yes of course,
Much silver and money you've melted down,
And what had silver been before,
As copper now lets itself be seen,
And so you've become a wealthy man.
But mark what I'll announce to you:
Many great gentlemen you have tricked,
And also led merchant folk astray,
Your smelting's made the price of wares
Ascend to such heights generally,
That what's been earned in many weeks
With tribulation and with toil
For a single thing must soon be paid.
Shall that not cause great discontent?
You've fixed it so one cannot give
A single penny to the poor,
The tradesman's wares stay on the shelf,
And he can maintain his trade no more.
You suck the marrow from his bones,
Which gives him cause for secret sighs.
The tears shed by the poor increase,
But this will not stay unavenged.
God will swiftly hurl you down,
For it your wife and child will pay.
Your fortunes soon will be reversed,
And you will take much different form.
Though you may bloom a scanty time,
Soon you will know much grief of heart,
Thus you before your fate must bow,
Your quietus must and shall be now.

Master Coiner:

Oh woe, how terrified I grow,
Where shall I go, I can stay no more,
Oh woe, oh woe, what a vision to see
That foretells horrid things for me.
Great is my misery and pain,
The whole world's closing in on me,
It's true, many people I've betrayed,
And shamefully have sucked them dry,
You clippers and you profiteers,
You now deprive me of my life,
Thus take this matter well to heart,
Now bidding good night, I depart.

THE END.

Ein Newe Rähterschafft.

Raht was ist das ich bitt dich drumb/
Hört sicht vnd greifft nit vnd ist stum̃/
Ist vnempfindlich kan nit schmöcken/
Sein Leib vnd Glider gar nit ströcken/
In der gantzen Welt hin vnd her/
Erzeigt man jhm sehr grosse ehr/

Kan jhm doch selber helffen nit/
Steigt hoch vnd kan doch gehn kein tritt/
Er ist also arm vnd ellend/
Wer jhn angreifft beschmotzt die Händ/
Ist gantz krafftloß allhie auff Erd/
Sein doch die gantze Welt begert.

ES ist kaum ein ding jetzt auff Erd/
Im auffsteigen vnd hohem werth/
Als eben das Geld in gemein/
Es sey jetzt gleich groß oder klein/
Von gutem Gold vnd Silber klar/
Schier in der gantzen Welt fürwar/
Daruon gar vil zu melden wer/
Auß Welschen Landen biß hieher/
Wer doch solches hab angebracht/
Der es hab auffsteigend gemacht.
SEcht wunder wie hoch ist es kommen/
Vnd an der Laitter hinauff klum̃en/
Daß es wol nit mehr weiter kan/
Wie es hie ist zusehen an/
Es seyn die Golguldin genennt
So hoch / daß man sie schier nit kennt/
Freylich ist es jhn wolgerahten/
Sie seynd schier über die Ducaten/
Die waren lang das beste Gold/
In hohem werth vnd reichem Sold/
Die Goldguldin waren Schatz Gelt/
Auch die Ducaten wie gemelt/
Die theten lang gleichsam verschwiegen/
Bey vil Leuten verborgen ligen/
Jetzt aber müssen sie von Hauß/
Weil jhrs gleichen so hoch kombt auß/
Vnd andere Goldstuck darneben/
Die man also hoch thut erheben/
Ja so hoch thut die Laitter zeugen/
Dyß sie nit künden höher steigen/
Vnd ob man sie trieb mit gewalt/
Hat die Laitter kein hinderhalt/
Sie möchten mit solchem bossen/
Den Kopff an dem Himmel zerstossen/

Dann stieß einer den andern rab/
Ein Sprichwort ich vernommen hab/
Wann ein ding kommet gar zu hoch/
So muß es wider fallen doch/
Gott lest sich vbersteigen nicht/
Sein Schlag ist gleich darauff gericht/
Er kan die Laitter bald außrotten/
Sie steht ohn das auff lauter Kroten/
Das Gelt von gutem Silber secht/
Beleibet nicht in seinem recht/
Wie es anfänglich ward geschlagen/
Vor Jahren vnd vor langen Tagen/
Die Königischen Daler werth/
Kommen auch für/hoch an auff Erd/
Die Dölpel vnd die Silberkronen/
Thun alls Edelleut her gronen/
Sie gelten so vil auff der bahn/
Daß mans schier nit mehr leyden kan/
Die Viertl eines Dalers gut/
Selten man einen finden thut/
In summa das gut silber Gelt/
Ist jetzt gar augenem der Welt/
Man wixlet solches ein mit hauffn/
Das böß Gelt thut auch mit einlauffn/
Deß ringsten Gelt muß ich gedencken/
Das man nit vnlangst thet verschencken/
Die Schüsseller vnd Ruffen Haller/
Auch die beschnittenen Jüden Daler/
Die Teschler truckte halbe Batzn/
Thut man jetzt fein zusammen kratzn/
Das war ein so vnwerthes Gelt/
Dessen vns jetzt am meisten fehlt/
Im zahlen übrigem nauß geben/
Thut sich die gröste klag erheben/

Im kauffen vnd verkauffen hewr/
Ist das klein Gelt so mächtig thewr/
Das ist die klag jeder Person/
Welliche da zugegen stahn/
Der Burger/ Handwercksman vnd Baur/
Die sehen zu den sachen saur/
Wer die Laitter bracht auff die Welt/
Daran so hoch steiget das Geldt/
Das ist der Neydig Geitzig Mann/
Der staht hie vor der Laitter an/
Welcher thut seinen Kindern zeigen/
Die hohe Laitter auffzusteigen/
Nach Reichthumb mit hohem nachsinnen/
Groß Gelt in der Welt zugewinnen/
Hie steht sein Geltsack vnd sein Kassen/
Die er voll alt Gelt thet einfassen/
Richt das auff Wucher durch sein List/
Weil es in dem auffsteigen ist/
Der Baur thut sein Maul hefftig bören/
Muß sich mit harter Arbeit nören/
Der Scheffler möcht mit seinen Reiffen/
Das Gelt alls ob der Laitter streiffen/
Der Burger gibt den zweyen recht/
Sein Gut nöhrt jhn vnd sein Geschlecht/
In summa was jetzund auffstaht/
Wider zu grund vnd boden gaht/
Dann Gott richt es also auff Erden/
Daß die Menschen erhalten werden/
Steig nit die Laitter der Welt weit/
Sonder die Laitter Gottes heut/
Welche führt in die Seligkeit/
Dieselbig ist Christus mit Namen/
Die helff allen frommen zusammen/
Dort in die Seligkeit sprecht Amen.

Augspurg / bey Daniel Mannaser / Kupfferstecher / bey Werthabruckerthor.

PLATE VI. A New Guessing Game

Guess what it is: I beg you, do:
  Hears not nor sees nor grasps, is mute,
Is without feeling, cannot taste,
  Neither its body nor limbs can stretch.
In the world entire, wherever one turns,
  He's shown the very greatest honor.
Yet he can never help himself,
  Climbs high and cannot move a step,
Is thus poor and miserable,
  Whoever grabs him, soils his hands,
Here on earth it's wholly impotent,
  Yet the whole world on him is bent.

Against the backdrop of a country landscape a ladder ascends diagonally toward the sky. Below it a farmer, an artisan, and a burgher stand and watch in amazement as six coins of various sizes are being carried skywards on the backs of six children. They are encouraged by their father at the base of the ladder—a man marked as a Jew by the ring on his left shoulder—who is intent on making his fortune through the debasement of money. At his feet are a moneybag and a chest filled with old-style money accumulated through cunning. The prospects for the man are nevertheless not good, for in contrast to Jacob's ladder, which led to divine salvation, this ladder rests precariously on the backs of toads and has only a very limited height.

There's hardly a thing now on the earth
  In climbing up and in high worth,
As money itself, generally,
  Whether it be large or small,
Of excellent gold or silver pure,
  In almost the whole world indeed.
Of it a great deal can be told,
  From Italian lands the whole way hither,
Yet who may have arranged it so,
  And its ascendance has arranged?
Behold this wonder: how high it's climbed
  And clambered up the ladder, so high
That it indeed can go no farther,
  As here can plainly be observed.
They are the coins, Goldguldens called,
  So high they scarce can be recognized.
Of course, it's turned out well for them,
  They've almost risen above the ducats,
Which long were thought the best of gold,
  In value high, giving rich reward.
The Goldguldens were treasured money,
  Quite like the ducats, as we've said.
They stayed, as it were, a long time still,
  Remaining concealed in many hands,
But now they've had to leave their home,
  Since the likes of them so high have climbed
And other golden coins besides,
  Which likewise are lifted thus on high,
So high, just as the ladder shows,
  That they could not climb higher still,
And, though one drove them on with force,
  The ladder has no place to lean,
They might with such buffoonery
  Bump their heads to pieces on the sky,
Then one would knock the other down.
  Now I have heard a proverb say
That when a thing climbs up too high,
  It must at last come to a fall.
God lets Himself not be outclimbed,
  At such His blow is aimed straightway,
Soon He can root the ladder out.
  Besides, it's propped on naught but toads.
Money made of good silver, see,
  Does not stay in its proper form,
As it was hammered out to start,
  Long years and many long days ago.
The Royal Thaler, valuable,
  Also come high up on the earth,

The doubloons and the silver crowns,
Make all the nobles groan aloud,
They have such value in their course
That it can almost not be borne,
The quarter of a Thaler good
One presently but seldom finds,
In sum, the excellent silver coin
Is now quite pleasing to the world.
Such coins are now exchanged in heaps,
And bad money, too, is mixing in,
I have to mention the smallest coins,
Which, not long since, one gave away,
The plate lickers' and the whorehouse pennies,
The circumcised Thalers of the Jews,
The pouchmakers' squeezed Half-Batzens
One now takes care to scrape together.
These were coins, quite valueless,
Which we now lack, most of all.
In paying out what's left of it,
The greatest lament of all arises.
This year, in buying and in sale,
The little coins have grown so dear:
That's the lament of everyone
Who at the present is involved,
The burghers, artisans, and peasants,
Look at the matter sourly,
The one who brought this ladder to earth
On which the coinage climbed so high,
Is that hateful, grasping man
Who stands before the ladder here,
And to his children shows the way
To clamber up the ladder high
For riches and highfalutin plans,
To win much money in the world.
Here stand his moneybag and chest
Which he has filled with old-style coin,
Through his cunning, he aims it at usury,
Since it is in ascendancy.
The peasant opens his maw a-groaning,
Supporting himself with heavy toil,
The cooper with his iron hoop
Would pull all money from the ladder,
The burgher says these two are right,
His funds support him and his clan.
In short: what now is climbing up
Once more will fall down to the ground,
For God's arranged it so on earth
That humankind must be preserved.
Do not climb the world's ladder far,
But rather the ladder of God today,
Which leads up into the blessedness:
That ladder bears of Christ the name,
Let it help all pious folk the same
Into blessedness: So say "Amen."

Augsburg, at the Shop of Daniel Mannasser,
Engraver at Werthabrucker Gate.

Newe Müntzlaitter.

Raht was ist das/ ich bitt dich drumb/
Hort nit/ sicht nit/ greifft nit/ ist stumb/
Ist vnempfindlich kan nit schmecken/
Sein Leib vnd Glider gar nit strecken.
In der gantzen Welt hin vnd her
Erzaigt man jhm sehr groß Ehr

Kan jhm doch selber helffen nit
Steigt hoch vnd kan doch gehn kein tritt
Es ist so arm vnd so elendt
Wer es angreifft beschmutzt die Händt
Ist gantz krafftloß allhie auff Erd
Doch seiner jederman begert.

NIchts ist/ halt ich/ auff diser Erd
Im auffstig vnd so hohem werth
Als eben das Gelt in gemein
Es sey jetzt gleich groß oder klein
Fragt jhr wer es hab angebracht
Vnd so hochsteigend hab gemacht?
Secht wunder wie hoch ist es kommen
Vnd an der Laitter hinauff klummen
Daß es wol nit mehr höher kan/
Wie es hie ist zusehen an/
Es seyn/ die man Goldguldin nennt
So hoch das man sie schier nit kennt
So wol ist es jhn jetzt gerathen
Deßgleichen auch die schön Ducaten
So müssen lang/ gleichsamb verschwigen/
In manchem schatz verborgen ligen
Die müssen aber jetzt von Hauß
Weil man sie gibt so thewer auß
Treibt man sie höher mit gewalt
So hat die Stieg kein hinderhalt
Es möchten die klein vnd die grossen
Am Himmel noch den Kopff zerstossen.
Dann stieß einer den andern rab
Ein Sprichwort ich vernommen hab/
Wann ein ding kommet gar zu hoch
So muß es widerfallen doch
Gott last sich vbersteigen nicht/
Sein Schlag ist gleich darauff gericht
Er kan die Laitter bald außrotten
Sie steht ohn das auff lauter Krotten
Vnd diesem abschewlichen Thier
Den Geitz in gemein vergleichen wir

Dann gleicher weiß als wie die Krot
Nit gnug kan fressen Erd vnd Koth
Also der Geitzhalß ist gesitt
Er kan erfüllet werden nit
Dann je das Gelt gut oder schlecht
Bleibt jetzt nit mehr in seinem recht
Wie es anfänglich ward geschlagen
Das thut der gmaine Mann hoch klagen
Die Königische Thaler werth/
Gelten heur noch vilmehr als ferdt/
Die Dölpel vnd die Silber Cronen
Die lassen sich vil höher spannen/
Vnd steigen also hoch hinan
Daß mans schier nimmer leiden kan.
Die Viertl eines Thalers gut
Man selten nunmehr finden thut
In Summa das gut Silber Gelt
Verkreucht sich allgmach in der Welt
Man wichßlet solches ein mit hauffen
Drumb thut die böse Müntz einlauffen
Deß ringsten Gelts muß ich gedencken
Das man nit vnlangst thet verschencken
Die Schüsseler vnd Rusenhaller
Auch die beschnittnen Judenthaler/
Die Teschler/ truckte halbe Batzen
Thut man jetzt fein zusammen kratzen
Das war ein so vnwerthes Gelt
Vnd dessen jetzt am meisten fehlt
Im zahlen vnd im hinauß geben
Thut sich die gröste klag erheben/
Im kauffen vnd verkauffen heur
Ist das klein Gelt so mächtig theur

Der Burger/ Handwerchsmann vnd Baur
Die sehen zu den sachen saur
Wer dise Laitter bracht auff d Welt
Daran so hoch auffsteigt das Gelt
Das ist der neidig geitzig Mann
Den jhr seht vor der Laitter stahn
Der thut hie seinen Kindern zeigen
Die hohe Laitter auffzusteigen
Lernt sie dem Gelt vnd Guet nachsinnen
Wie es mit vortheil sey zugwinnen
Hie steht sein Geltsack vnd sein Cassen
Die er thet voll alt Gelt einfassen
Richt das auff Wucher durch sein List/
Weil es in dem auffsteigen ist
Der Baur sein Maul thut hefftig böhren
Muß sich mit harter Arbeit nöhren/
Der Schäffler möcht mit seinen Raiffen
Das Gelt alls ab der Laitter straiffen
Der Burger gibt den zweyen recht
Sorgt auch er werd ein armer Knecht
Weil dann die Müntz gestign so hoch
Vnd jmmerdar wil steigen noch
So ist allein die Schuld hiebey
Deß Geitzes vnd der Wucherey
Bleibt jhn die zeitlich straf dahinden
So werden sies dort ewig finden
Vnd steigen so tief vndersich
Als hoch die Müntz steigt vbersich.

Gedruckt im Jahr/ 1621.

PLATE VII. New Coin-Ladder

Guess what it is: I beg you, do:
Hears not nor sees nor grasps, is mute,
Is without feeling, cannot taste,
Neither its body nor limbs can stretch,
In the world entire, wherever one turns,
It's shown the very greatest honor,
Yet it can never help itself,
Climbs high and cannot move a step,
Is thus poor and miserable,
Whoever grabs it, soils his hands,
Here on earth it's wholly impotent,
Yet everyone on it is bent.

Against the backdrop of a country landscape a ladder ascends diagonally toward the sky. Below it a farmer, an artisan, and a burgher stand and watch in amazement as six coins of various sizes are being carried skywards on the backs of six children. They are encouraged by their father at the base of the ladder—a man marked as a Jew by the ring on his left shoulder—who is intent on making his fortune through the debasement of money. At his feet are a moneybag and a chest filled with old-style money accumulated through cunning. The prospects for the man are nevertheless not good, for in contrast to Jacob's ladder, which led to divine salvation, this ladder rests precariously on the backs of toads and has only a very limited height.*

Now there is naught, I think, on earth
In climbing up and such high worth,
As money itself generally,
Whether it be large or small.
You ask: who has applied it here,
And made it so high-climbing now?
Behold this wonder: how high it's climbed,
And clambered up the ladder so high
That it cannot the higher rise,
As here can plainly be observed
They are the coins, Goldguldens called,
So high they scarce can be recognized.
They've prospered now so very well,
And in like wise, the ducats fair,
As it were, they've kept a long time still,
And in many a treasure trove lie hidden,
But now they've had to leave their home,
Since people give them out so dearly
And drive them higher up by force.
The ladder here has no support,
They, both the small coins and the large,
Might bump their heads against the sky,
Then one would knock the other down.
I have heard a proverb say:
That when a thing climbs up too high,
It must at last come to a fall,
God lets Himself not be outclimbed,
At such, His blow is aimed straightway,
Soon He can root the ladder out.
Besides, it's propped on naught but toads,
And we quite commonly compare
Avarice to this disgusting beast,
Because, in like wise, as the toad
Can't gobble its fill of earth and filth,
Just so the miser has the wont
That he can never be satisfied,
For whether the money's good or bad,
It does not stay in its proper form
As it was hammered out to start.
That makes the common man lament.
The Royal Thalers, valuable,
Are worth this year much more than last,
The doubloons and the silver crowns

* This illustration is very similar to the preceding one, whereas the poet's message is more minatory. Rather than offering the hope of God's ladder, ascending into heaven, the poet reminds the reader that the ladder may well lead down to hell.

Can have their worth brought higher still,
And ascend so far on high
That it almost cannot be borne,
The quarter of a Thaler good,
One presently but seldom finds.
In sum, the excellent silver coins
Now gradually from the world withdraw.
Such coins are now exchanged in heaps,
And thus bad money's mixing in,
I have to mention the smallest coins
Which, not long since, one gave away,
The platelickers' and the whorehouse pennies
And the circumcised Thalers of the Jews,
The pouchmakers' squeezed Half-Batzens,
One now takes care to scrape together:
These were coins, quite valueless,
Which now are lacking most of all.
In paying and in laying out
The greatest lament of all arises,
This year, in buying and in sale,
The little coins have grown so dear,
The burghers, artisans, and peasants
Look at the matter sourly.
The one who brought this ladder to earth,
On which the coinage climbs so high,
Is that hateful, grasping man
You see before the ladder here,
He to his children shows the way
To clamber up the ladder high,
Teaches them to ponder wealth and worth,
And how these may with gain be won.
Here stand his moneybag and chest
Which he has filled with old-style coin,
Through his cunning, he aims it at usury,
Since it is in ascendancy.
The peasant opens his maw a-groaning,
Supporting himself with heavy toil,
The cooper with his iron hoop
Would pull all money from the ladder,
The burgher says these two are right
And fears he too will be left poor,
Since now the money climbs so high,
And keeps on climbing more and more.
The blame for this alone belongs
To avarice and usurers
If they're spared earthly punishment,
They'll get it in eternity,
And will descend so deep below
As now the coinage high does go.

Printed in the Year 1621.

Ein newes Gespräch von dem jetzigen vnträglichen Gelt auffsteigen vnd elenden Zustand im Müntzwesen.

Heller.

VOr zeiten war ich lieb vnd werth/
Zum Allmosen man mein begert/
Der Betler mich frölich auffnam/
Wann er mich in sein Hand bekam/
Am Silber war ich noch so gut/
Als man jetzt zu zweyen Pfenning thut/
Der Tiegel hat mich gantz verdorbn/
Ich bin samb wer ich gar gestorbn/
Mein lieber Pfenning sag mir doch/
Bist gstorben oder lebst du noch?

Pfenning.

ACh lieber Heller merck mich eben/
Es geht mir auch hart an das Lebn/
Ich bin ein recht verkauffter Knecht/
Vor Jahren war ich viel zu schlecht/
Daß man mich zun Dreybätznern legt/
Jetzund gar Taler auß mir schlägt/
Dann an mir gibt der Wuchrer Hauff/
Am Gülden gern acht Batzen auff/
Sag an Dreyheller Hochgeborn/
Was machst du mit deim Jägerhorn?

Drey Heller.

ICh hab mich mit meim Jägers Horn/
Auch schier auß Teutschem Land verlorn/
Muß jetzund ein arm Martyr seyn/
Vnd in das glüend Fewr nein/
Wirdt mir mein guter stand veracht/
Wann man die loß Müntz auß mir macht/
Sag dir also mein Pfenning gut
Nun auch klagt wie mirs gehen thut;
Du halber Creutzer sag auch mir
Wie stehet der Handel dann mit dir?

Halb Creutzer.

WAs soll ich viel von mir her sagn/
Du magst Goltschmied vnd Müntzer fragn/
Wie man vns arme Tropffen hat
Auch auffgewechselt frü vnd spat/
Erstlich wolt man vnser nicht achtn/
Jetzt aber thut man vns nach trachtn/
Wie der Fuchs nach der Hennen Lebn/
Thut viel Auffwechsel auff vns gebn/
Was machstu dann du alter Dreyr/
Ich meyn du ligst auch lang im Fewr?

Dreyer.

DEr Handel steht mit mir also:
Wann man mich hat so ist man fro/
Dieweil mein werth am Silber gut/
Mir man dann sehr nachstellen thut/
Muß bald ins warme Bad hinein/
Deßhalben Creutzers Gsellschafft seyn/
Auß vnser eim drey Creutzer wern/
Heist das nicht kommen hoch zu Ehrn/
Dieweil man mich setzt allen für/
Du Creutzer/was machens mit dir?

Creutzer.

MEin Gschlecht war niemaln gar zu groß/
Die halben Creutzer das verdroß/
Daß jhrer soviel sollen seyn/
Vnd müsten doch ins Fewr hinein/
Weil wir waren am Silber reich/
Hielt man vns jhnen am werth gleich/
Vnser keiner kompt mehr an Tag/
Darumb mein Dreyer nun nicht frag
Wir hieltn so wol als jhr die Katzn
Wo seyd dann jhr jhr halben Batzn?

Halber Batz.

WIr sind tretten in Herren Ordn/
vnd gar zu silbern Bechern wordn/
Stehn in Kästen vnd Credentzen/
Dörffn nichts thun dann faulentzen/
Werden gefült mit gutem Wein/
Dörffen nicht mehr beym Bauren seyn/
So wol nicht hart im Land vmbwandern/
Von einer Statt vnd Dorff zum andern/
Sondern sind frey als die Schweitzer/
Wie lebst du dann Freund Dreycreutzer?

Drey Creutzer.

SIe machen mich so loß vnd schlim/
Daß ich gar auff dem Wasser schwim/
Wolten mich etlich zeyhen gern/
Ich kom von einer alten Latern/
Ein Blechin Schüssel sey mein Muttr/
Kupffer oder Messing mein Brudr/
Vexirn mich weiters in jhrm Gspött/
Ich hab das Silber gar verredt/
Habn mich gleichwol gern die Fratzen/
Wie gehts dann euch jhr alten Batzen?

Alter Batz.

WIe solts vns alten Batzen gehn/
Wir werden bald wider aufferstehn/
Wern nur vnser noch viel im Lebn/
Man thät drey Batzen vmb ein gebn/
Wir wurden prägt von Silber gut/
Jetzt ligen wir längst in der Glut/
Selten wirdt einer mehr gefundn/
Nicht anders ob wir seyn verschwundn/
Sag an sechs Creutzer wo bistu?
Geht das Kalb auch jetzt mit der Khu?

Sechs Creutzer.

VOr diesem ward ich so veracht/
Wem man mich gab ward vngeschlacht/
Als wann ich etwas hett gestoln/
Sie heissen mich den schlimmen Poln/
Wer ist jetzund besser als ich/
Weil jederman will haben mich/
Man zahlt mich mehr als zu thewr/
Aber nun lig ich schon im Fewr/
Du zehen Kreutzer mit dem Kopff/
Wie stehts mit dir du guter Tropff?

Zehen Creutzer.

ZV zwölff Creutzern hat man vns gern/
Wir kommen gleich nah oder fern/
Man läst vns aber nicht lang gantz/
Sondern müssen mit zum Finantz/
Vnd lauffen mit dem Judenspieß/
Ehrlichen Leuthen zum verdrieß/
So kompt das gut Gelt mit der zeit/
Ja gantz vnd gar von Land vnd Leut/
Drey Bätzner du bist vber mich/
Mein/was helt man dann jetzt auff dich?

Drey Bätzner.

ICh sag dirs auch mit einem Wort/
Man wechselt mich schon vmb ein Ort/
Wann ich nur zehen Jahr alt bin/
Man gibt mich auch wol thewrer hin/
Da ich viel Silber in mir hab/
Sonderlich die alten vorab/
Doch die drey Bätzner heut zu Tag/
Einer eins Batzens werth seyn mag/
Du sechs Bätzner sag ohn beschwert/
Wie schätzt du dich/was bist du werth?

Sechs Bätzner.

DEin fragen kompt mir seltzam für/
Halt ichs doch allzeit mit dir/
So viel ich gilt/das giltstu halb/
Ich bin die Kuh/vnd du das Kalb/
Mein Vatter gilt jetzt viel auff Erd/
Man helt jhn auff neun Batzen werth/
Ich vnd du seind darzu geschickt/
Daß man mit vns die Pfannen flickt/
Was wird man denn noch auß vns pfoschen/
Nun höret an die Gülden Groschen.

Gülden Thaler.

ICh hab zum Handel still geschwign/
Vnd bin fein allgemach gestign/
Nah bey drey Gülden gilt ich gern/
Hoff aber es soll nicht lang wern/
So wöll ich gar drey Gülden gelten/
Weil ich bin steckend blieben selten/
Weil der Thaler ist mein vortrab/
Den ich allzeit zum besten hab/
Hör Thaler/wie bist jetzt so still/
Mein/steig einmal/vns hilfft es viel?

Reichs Thaler.

BIn ich dann nicht gestiegen fort/
Gilt schon drey Gülden vnd ein Ort/
Die Dölpel gelten noch viel mehr/
Ja alle Thaler steigen sehr/
Sonderlich was gut alte seyn/
Die sperret man auffs fleissigst eyn/
Können gleichwol keine Ruh findn/
Müssen noch im Gefängnuß schindn/
Ihrem Herren dem Mammons Knecht/
Merckt drauff was der Golgülden spricht.

Goldtgülden.

MAn nennet mich das Rheinisch Golt/
Dem Thaler ich nachsteigen wolt/
Dieweil ich fast vier gulden gilt/
Hab auch schon alle weil gezielt/
Folgends vier Gulden zuerlangn/
Drauff hatten mich schon viel gefangn/
Wie könd ich doch nur länger schweign/
Vnd das Silber allein lassen steign/
Ein Wurst wolt ich jhm lassen bratn/
Was wurden sagen die Ducatn?

Ducaten.

ICh bin das beste Golt im Reich/
Drumb ists auch billig daß ich steig/
Dieweiln besonders die Goltschmid/
Meiner können entrahten nit/
Die Goldschlager vnd andere mehr/
Brauchen mich alle viel vnd sehr/
Fünff Gülden gilt ich jetzund gern/
Vnd will mich niemand drumb entpern/
Hab auch schon gut Post vernommen/
Ich wird gar bald höher kommen.

Silber.

WAs wird aber drauß werden mehr/
Wann alle Müntz so steiget sehr/
Was wird sein letzlich der außgang/
Kan auch das ding bestehen lang/
Wann Golt vnd Silber das Metal/
Wirdt so verderbet vberal/
Wo wirdt man endtlich nehmen Gelt/
Welches sein rechte Müntzprob helt.
Ist das nicht eine Sünd vnd Schand/
Daß Jüden müntzen im Teutschland.

Goldt.

NIchts guts auß dem ding werden kan/
Das versicht leichtlich jederman/
Dann dadurch wird der Teutschen Gelt
Verachtet in der gantzen Welt/
Alle ding wird dardurch sehr thewr/
Wie man erfahren ferd vnd hewr/
Wird aber noch viel ärger werdn/
Da man nicht abhilfft den Beschwerdn/
In summ/es prophecey zugleich/
Groß veränderung im gantzen Reich.

Kupffer.

ICh thu mich an ewr klag nicht kehrn/
Das ding geraicht nur mir zu Ehrn/
Allein dem Silber vnd dem Golt/
War man vber all Metall holt/
Das Kupffer must hinden anstehn/
Jetzt aber wirds viel anderst gehn/
Wann Golt vnd Silber vrlaub hat/
So kompt das Kupffer an die stat/
Wie werden gefallen dir die sachn/
Wann man auß Kupffer Gelt wirt machn?

Getruckt im Jahr 1621.

PLATE VIII. A New Colloquy on Money's Present Unbelievable Inflation and the Wretched State of Coinage

Seventeen coins, all minted from the early sixteenth to the early seventeenth century, are arranged in ascending value as if part of an official printed mandate about coinage.* Each laments its loss of value through debasement and inflation. The last three items are the metals used for coinage, and ironically it is copper—used in the debasement of coins—rather than the precious metals gold and silver that stands at the very end.

Heller:

Dear was I once and valuable,
And people wanted me as alms;
The beggar took me happily
Whenever he got me in his hand.
In silver I was rather good.
When now one adds me to two Pfennigs,
The smelting ladle has ruined me entire.
I am indeed as if quite dead.
Oh, my dear Pfennig, tell me, do,
Have you died, what has become of you?

Pfennig:

Oh, dear Heller, look at me.
I too am at the point of death;
I am a fellow sold and betrayed.
Years past, I was much too plain
To be laid beside a Drei-Batzner coin.
Now, they make Thalers out of me,
For with me the usurers' band
Gladly adds three Batzens to the Gulden.
Tell me, Drei-Heller, lofty born,
What do you do with your huntsman's horn?

Drei-Heller:

With my huntsman's horn I've disappeared,
Almost, I, too, from Germany,
And now must be a wretched martyr
Cast into the glowing flames.
My honored class is now despised
Since men make worthless coins of me.
Then, my Pfennig, I bid you farewell.
Now weep at what's befallen me:
You, Half-Kreuzer, tell me true,
How then the trade does stand with you?

Half-Kreuzer:

What much shall I say about myself?
You may ask the goldsmiths and the coiners,
How we poor wretches have been treated,
Raising our value, early and late.
At first, no one would pay us heed,
But now we're very much desired,
The way the fox seeks out the hen.
Much changing upwards with us is made.
What are you doing, old friend Dreyer,
I guess that you too lie in the fire?

Dreyer:

This is the treatment I've received:
When people have me, they rejoice,
Because in silver my value's good,
And so there's much pursuit of me.
Soon to the warm bath I must go,
And be the Half-Kreuzer's company.
From one of us, three Kreuzers come.
Is that not promotion of high estate,
Since before all others I am set.
Kreuzer, what treatment do you get?

* For the relationship among the various coins, see footnote 16 in the introduction.

Kreuzer:

My tribe was never all too large,
Which made the Half-Kreuzers quite annoyed,
That of them there should be so many,
And yet they into the fire must go.
Since we were in silver rich,
People think we're like to them in worth.
None of us sees daylight any more.
Therefore, my Dreyer, do not ask.
Like you, I've had the cat to beat.*
Half-Batzen now, where are you, where?

Half-Batz:

We now have entered lordly ranks,
And have indeed become silver cups,
Stand in chests and cabinets,
Have naught to do but be at rest,
Are filled brim-full with excellent wine,
And stay in peasant hands no more,
Nor wander cruelly about
From one town and hamlet to another,
But rather are free, quite like the Swiss.
How then do you, friend Drei-Kreuzer, exist?

Drei-Kreuzer:

They've rendered me so thin and poor
That I may float upon the water,
And some would like to bring the charge
That I from an ancient lantern come.
My mother was a plate of tin,
My brother was of copper or brass.
With their jeers they keep tormenting me.
I've sworn off silver altogether,
Yet fools desire me all the same.
But, old Batzen, what's your game?

* *Wir hielten so wohl ihr die Katzen*. The idiom refers to a punishment in which the culprit was put on public display holding a cat.

Old Batz:

How now should we old Batzens fare?
Quite soon we shall be resurrected,
And many more of us soon will live.
Three Batzens are given for just one.
From excellent silver we were stamped;
Now we lie on the flames long since,
Rarely a single one of us is found,
Quite as if we all had disappeared.
Speak up, Sechs-Kreuzer, where are you now?
Does your calf also trail the cow?

Sechs-Kreuzer:

Formerly, I was so despised,
Whoever received me grew very rude,
As if I'd engaged in thievery,
And even called me "the evil Pole."
But now who's better off than I,
For everyone wants to get hold of me.
They pay far more than I am worth,
Yet now I'm lying in the fire.
You, Zehn-Kreuzer, with head stamped on,
How are things going, good simpleton?

Zehn-Kreuzer:

For us, twelve Kreuzers are gladly given,
Whether we come from near or far,
But we are not left whole for long.
Rather we must enter skullduggery
And practice Hebrew usury,*
Vexing honest folk for sure.
Thus good money in the course of time
Will vanish wholly from land and folk.
Drei-Batzner, you've gotten ahead of me.
I wonder: what thoughts about you may be?

* *Und lauffen mit dem Judenspieß*. The reference in the German to the "Jewish spear" may have its sources in John 19:34, where at the Crucifixion "one of the soldiers pierced [Jesus's] side with a spear." Since, however, Jews were not allowed to bear arms, the phrase has a strong ironic effect and may allude to usury as a Jewish "weapon."

Drei-Batzner:

I'll tell you briefly, with a word:
They exchange me now for a quartered coin.
But when I'm only ten years old,
They give a dear price for me,
Since so much silver I contain,
Yet the Drei-Batzner of today,
May only be worth a single Batz.
You Sechs-Batzner, speak with impunity,
What's your estimate, what might your value be?

Sechs-Batzner:

Your query seems quite strange to me.
After all, I've always stayed near to you.
Whatever I'm worth, you're worth the half,
For I'm the cow and you the calf.
My father's worth much now, here on earth.
They say he's got eight Batzens' worth.
Both I and you must share the fate
That with us people patch their pans.
Into what else can we be botched?
Now hear what the Gulden-Groschen's hatched.

Gulden-Thaler:

I have kept mum through all this trade,
And slowly have risen very high,
In worth I'm close to Guldens three
But hope it won't stay so for long.
Thus I'd like to have three Guldens' worth,
Since the Thaler acts as my vanguard:
On him I always play a little trick.
Listen, Thaler, why are you so still,
Come, climb a little, won't that fill the bill?

Reichsthaler:

Have I not clambered all the while?
I'm already three Guldens and a quarter worth.
The doubloons are valued at even more.
Yes, all the Thalers are climbing high,
Especially those that are good and old.
Carefully they are confined,
But all the same can find no rest,
And in prison still must labor hard
For Mammon, their master, as his very slaves.
Heed what the gold Gulden says.

Goldgulden:

The people call me Roman gold.
After the Thaler I wanted to climb.
Since I am worth many Guldens indeed,
I've always had that as my aim,
Thusly, to reach four Guldens' worth,
That's why many keep me captive,
Yet how could I stay longer still,
And merely let the silver climb?
I'll roast it a sausage, if I may.*
What would the ducats have to say?

Ducats:

I am the empire's best gold of all.
Thus, it's only fair that I ascend,
Because the goldsmiths especially
Can't do their work if they lack me.
The gold beaters and the others too
Need me, all of them, and sore.
Now I'm worth five Guldens easily,
And so no one can dispense with me.
I've already got good news in the mail
That even higher I shall sail.

Silver:

What, however, will result
If all the coinage climbs so high,
What will the end of all this be?
Can this matter continue long
When gold and silver, these metals all,
Will come to ruin everywhere?

* *Ein Wurst will ich ihm lassen braten.* According to Jacob Grimm's *Deutsches Wörterbuch* (vol. 30, col. 2302) the idiom can mean "to tell someone something," or, in a friendlier interpretation, "to do someone a favor."

Where will money at last be found
Which its true coinage-worth has kept?
Is that not a sin and shame
That in Germany Jews play the coiners' game?

Gold:

From this thing nothing good can come.
That can quickly be grasped by everyone,
For the Germans' money in this way
Throughout the world will be despised.
Thereby all things grow very dear,
As one's discovered, last year and this.
But it will turn out still worse by far,
Because the damage is not redressed.
In short, it's directly prophesied:
Great change in the empire far and wide.

Copper:

I pay no heed to your laments.
The thing vouchsafes honor to none but me.
To silver and to gold alone,
Above all metals, men were well disposed.
Copper had to bring up the rear,
But now matters go a different course.
When gold and silver are on leave,
Then copper has to take command.
How will you like the turn things take
When one from copper coins will make?

Printed in the Year 1621.

Wie der Reich den Armen frißt:

Der Arm der leidt ietzt grosse Noth.
Man nimpt ihm von dem Mündt das Brodt,
Zür Krafft kan er nicht kommen mehr,
Man gönt Jhm weder gab noch Ehr,
Ein jeder dicht nach falschem Sinn,
Das man Jhn außaüg, wie ein Spinn,
Der Armen Kürzen Rücken thüt,
Vnd labet sich mit ihrem Blüt,
Haüt, Fell, wird alles gezogen ab,
Das man Jn bring an Bettelstab:
Als dann geht es nach dem Sprichwort,
Wie man das Offter hatt gehort:
Der Reich frißt ietzünd den Armen,
Das es müß Gott thün erbarmen,
Endtlich der Teüffel frißt den Reichen
Werdens gefreßen alle zügleichen:
Christliche Lieb wird gar veracht,
Den Armen Mann aüch ietzt außlacht,
Erkaltet ist die Liebe güt,
Wie mans im Wertkhe spüren thüt.

PLATE IX. How the Rich Man Devours the Poor*

A poor man, simply dressed, lies helplessly in the clutches of a sumptuously dressed rich man, who is beginning to devour the poor man at the same time that he himself is being devoured by the devil. As the horned devil takes the rich man's head into his maw he uses his left hand to grab a well-dressed woman, the personification of Avarice, who spews forth coins, which she has ingested. In front of her lie an open sack filled with coins and a broken scale used for weighing money.

Great woe the poor man now endures.
The bread is taken from his mouth.
No more can he regain his strength,
Neither gifts nor honor is he given,
Everyone lies, false-mindedly,
So that he's sucked dry, as a spider
Does to poor folk's withered gnats,
And with their blood itself restores.
Their skin and hide are stripped away,
And they are brought to the beggar's staff.
Thus matters go, as the proverb says,
Which people frequently have heard:
The rich man now devours the poor,
So God to pity must be moved,
At last, the devil devours the rich,
They're both devoured, one like the other,
Christian love's indeed despised,
The poor man, too, is now derided,
Good love itself has turned to cold,
As one in this work can behold.

* This sheet was reissued in Augsburg in 1629 by Johann Klockher, whose imprint is printed on a separate strip of paper and pasted on at the bottom.

ACh höchster Gott/von Ewigkeit/
1 Ich hab erlebt ein böse zeit.
Ich bin fürwar ein armer Man/
Vnd weiß auch nicht/wo hnauß/ wo hnan?
Vor wenig jahren/wie ich meld/
Wie stunds doch so wol in der welt.
Die vnderthanen jederzeit
Ehrten/nechst Gott/Ihr Obrigkeit.
Gut Fried vnd ruh war in dem Reich/
Jtzt aber gehts zu gar vngleich.
Einer wil da/der ander dort hnauß/
Was wil zu letzt nur werden drauß?
Plündern/Stehlen/Raub/Mord vnd Brand
Nimbt allenthalben vberhand.
Böse Müntz/Blech vnd Küpperey/
Recht Teuffelswerck vnd schinderey/
Plagt manchen guten Biederman:
Ach Gott/was soll ich fangen an?
Ich steh auff einen Distel strauch/
Vnd bin fast gantz verdorben auch.
Der Krieg/die Müntz/die thewre zeit
Bringt mir fürwar groß hertzeleydt.
Dann ich in grossen sorgen steh/
Vnd auch für Angst schier gar vergeh.
Wann ich gedenck/es soll Frieden sein/
So kompt bald etwas anderst drein.
Ach Gott/thu dich vber mich Armen
Auß Gnaden/vnd vmbsonst erbarmn.
Dann wo ich mich hin wend vnd kehr/
Da stechn mich Dorn vnd Distel sehr.
2 Sih/Schnudelputz/ was klagstu viel/
An dich ich mich nit kehren will.
Klag hin/klag her/sing auff/sing niedr/
Was ich bekomb/ geb ich nit widr.
Tag vnd Nacht thu ich weidlich zehrn/
Mit plündern muß ich mich ernehrn.
Was mir nur kompt in mein Handt/
Sey Geistlich oder Weltlich standt/
Daß muß daran/ohn allen schertz/
Darob frewet sich im Leib mein Hertz.
3 Ach Gott/wie thuts so vbel stehn/
Ich darff nit für mein Hauß hnauß gehn/
Ich werd beraubt vnd bestohln:
Solchs thut man offntlich/vnuerholn.
Vnd hälts darzu noch für ein Ehr/
Wir seind fürwar gepeinigt sehr.
Kauffleut/Burger vnd Bawersmann/
Werden auff der Straß grieffen an/
Ja auch zu Wasser vnd zu Landt:
Ist das Kriegßbrauch/ Pfui an der schandt.
4 Daß du dich klagst der Kriegßleut sehr/
Ich will dich prömbsen noch viel mehr/
Mit meiner Müntz/ in einer Summ/
Die ich thu wider schmeltzen vmb.
Kupffer vnd Blech will ich nit sparn/
Solt ich gleich/ weiß nit/ wohin fahrn.
Darmit kan ich/beydn groß vnd klein/
Die Krafft saugen auß Marck vnd Bein.
Doch wanns solt wissn der gmeine Mann/
Dörffts vns/wie jenen Küppern gahn.
5 Ach Jammer/Noth vnd Hertzeleydt/
Wie sein wir doch so gplagte Leut.
Viel böse Müntz wird vns zubracht/
Ich glaub/der Teuffl habs selbst erdacht.
Reichßthaler/ gute Silbersortn/
Werden verschmeltzt an vielen Ortn/
Daher der Thaler steigt so hoch:
Wehrts lang/ muß ich entlauffen noch.
Mein Seckel ist zerrissen sehr/
Ist ärger als der Krieg vielmehr.
6 Ich aber bin ein dapffer Mann/
Wann ich nichts mehr bekommen kan
Auff freyer Strassen/in dem Feldt/
Alßdann muß mir wol geben Geldt
Der Haußmann/ oder fang an ein Strauß/
Vnd zünd jhm an sein eygen Hauß:
Verbrenn jhn wol mit Weib vnd Kindt/
Deßwegen wir so geartet sind.
Was wir nit haben abgenommn/
Das muß im Fewr vnd Rauch vmbkommn.
7 O grosser Jammer/ O grosse Noth/
Daß es doch mög erbarmen Gott.
Mann hat mir all daß Mein genommn/
Bin drüber vmb Hauß vnd Hoff kommn.
Mann hat mir alles abgebrennt/
Ist daß nit jammer vnd elend?
Mancher kriegt vnbefugter weiß/
Verbränt/ verheert das Landt mit fleiß.
Gott wirds gewiß endlich rechen/
Vnd vber jhn das Vrtheil sprechn.
8 Ich bin ein Soldat/ führ darnebn
Mit fressn vnd sauffn ein wacker Leben.
Bin voll den Abend als den Morgn/
Vnd laß die klein Waltvöglein sorgn.
Was ich seh mit den Augen mein/
Rips/ Raps/ muß in mein Sack hinein.
Solt auch ein ander gar verderbn/
Oder gleich in dem Elend sterbn/
Acht ichs nit/ frag darnach nit viel:
Guraschi/ frisch ichs wagen will.
9 Ach Gott/ich heb auff meine Händt/
Wie hat sich doch das Glück gewendt.
Vor kurtzer zeit/war ich zimlich reich/
An Hauß vnd Hoff/ vieln Geldt zugleich.
Mann hat mir alles abgenommn/
Bin drüber in das Elend kommn/
Darinnen muß ich jtzund sterbn/
Verschmachten vnd auch gar verderbn.
Gott wolle sich vber mich Armn
Vnd meiner btrübten Seel erbarmn.
Daß mancher Tyrannischer weiß
Krieg führt vnd thuts mit allem fleiß:
Vnd verhergt dardurch nur das Landt
Mit rauben/ plündern/mord vnd brandt.
Daß auch die Teuffels Küpperey/
Verfälschung dr Müntz vnd schinderey
Im schwang so gehet Tag vnd Nacht/
Welchs der Teuffel selbst hat erdacht:
Dardurch mancher muß gar verderben/
Vnd in dem bittern Elend sterbn:
Were kein wunder/in gemein/
Daß Donnr vnd Hagel schlüg darein.
Doch wird Gott wol zu seiner zeit
Straffen solch vngerechtigkeit.
Demselben sey es heimgestellt/
Er wirds wol machn/ wies jhm gefällt.
Doch muß es bkennen jederman/
Daß wirs vmb Gott verschuldet han:
Derselb wöll gnädig bey vns stahn.

PLATE X. Prickly Sea Holly, Or the Way of the World at the Present Time

A poor man with staff in hand stands within a thistle patch and bemoans his life of misery: "However I turn myself, to and fro, / Distress and misery deal me a blow." The flower heads of the sea holly (eryngium) are medallions, which depict on the left side the activities of destructive elements in the society versus on the right side the plight of the common man. In number 2, an armed soldier boasts, "With theft and pillage I proceed." In number 3, a man waylaid by two armed men complains, "I am robbed and cannot recover." In number 4, a man busy minting debased coins confesses, "Not copper nor tin by me are spared." In number 5, a man in distress sighs, "My very being is ruined, entire." In number 6, a soldier setting a house on fire admits, "I burn and steal with all my strength." In number 7, a distraught farmer standing in front of a burning building laments, "My house and farm are all burned down." In number 8, a soldier laden with goods and drinking from a large jug proudly admits, "I trick, gorge, and swill both day and night." In number 9, a man lying on the ground with his hands raised toward heaven moans, "In my pain I mortal hunger know." At the bottom left four Jewish moneychangers convene with sacks filled with coins, while at the bottom right three distressed men hold empty moneybags.

Almightiest God of eternity,
1 I have lived through an evil time,
I'm a poor man in very truth,
And do not know where I shall turn.
A few years back, as I now tell,
All things in the world went well,
At all times the subjects gave
Honor to God and their government.
In the empire peace and calm prevailed,
But now it's all turned upside down.
One goes this way, another that,
And what will be the end of it?
Pillage, rapine, murder, fire
Get everywhere the upper hand,
Bad money, tinplate, copper coinage too,
The devil's work, crass dishonesty,
Are many a good man's misery.
Oh God, what shall I try to do?
I stand upon a thistle patch,
And nigh have gone to wrack and ruin.
The war, the coinage, the dear-priced times
Cause me, indeed, much grief and sorrow.
For I am mightily concerned
And close to perishing from fear.
Whenever I think that peace will come,
Then something else gets in the way,
Oh God, have pity on me now,
A poor man, in Your grace for naught,
For no matter where I turn my way,
Thorns and thistles beset me sore.
2 Now, snot-nose, why do you complain?
I'll take no heed of you at all.
Weep hither and thither, sing high and low,
What I've got, I'll not return.
Day and night I gobble heartily,
I must feed myself with pilfering;
Whatever falls into my hands,
Be it worldly goods or churchly wares,
That's gone for good, and that's no jest,
And in my body my heart rejoices.
3 Oh God, how wretchedly matters stand,
I cannot venture from my house,
Lest I be plundered, pillaged too,
Such things are done in public view,
And it's even seen to be an honor.
We are indeed tormented much,
Merchants, burghers, and peasantry
On the open highway are attacked,

Forsooth, on water and on land:
Is that war's usage—what disgrace!
4 Don't complain about the soldiery,
I'll be your gadfly even more
With my coinage, and in sum,
Which I now will smelt anew.
I'll not hold back with copper and tin
Even though I'll go I know not where.
Thereby I can, from great and small,
Suck out their strength from marrow and bone.
Yet, lest the common man should know,
We might go the way these clippers* go.
5 Oh misery, poverty, pain of heart,
How cruelly are we folk tormented.
Much wretched money to us is brought,
I think the devil's worked it out,
Reichsthalers and silver coinage good
Are melted down in many places,
That's why the Thaler climbs so high.
If this continues, I must flee.
My moneybag is torn to shreds.
It's crueler than the war by far.
6 Nonetheless, I'm a doughty man,
Wherever I can grab no more
On open roads and in the field,
The money must surely be given me
By the cottager: I'll start a fight
And set his very house afire,
And burn him up with wife and child,
For that, you see, is the way we are.
Whatever we've not taken away
Must be consumed in smoke and flame.†

* The German word *Küppern* is a subsidiary form, dative plural, of *Kipper* (see Grimm, vol. 11, col. 2770), but it may also contain a suggestion of *kupfern, küpfern* (see Grimm, vol. 11, col. 2765: both a verb, "to copper," and an adjective, "copper"), a metal so important in the mutilation and falsification of coins.

† The word *umbkossen* in the German is a misprint for *umbkommen* (to die). Such printer's errors occur not infrequently in these hasty productions.

7 Oh mighty misery, giant woe,
Would that God had mercy on me,
From me they've taken all I own,
I am bereft of house and home,
And burned to ashes all I possess,
Is that not misery, not distress?
Many pilfer without excuse,
Scorch and ravage with design.
Surely God one day will vengeance wreak
And over them His judgment speak.
8 I'm a soldier and I lead as well
A splendid life with gule and drink,
I'm drunk at evening as at morning,
And let the little wood-birds worry.
Whatever I spy with these my eyes
One-two-three must slide into my bag,
Let someone else go to ruination
Or simply perish in starvation.
I pay it no heed nor ask much about it,
Courage! Without delay, I'll dare it.
9 Oh God, I raise my hands on high,
How have my fortunes been reversed,
A short time back, I was passing rich,
In house and home, in money too,
They've taken all I have from me,
And so I've entered misery,
And now in that state I must die,
Languish away and be destroyed.
Would God have pity on me, poor man,
And pity on my saddened soul.
For many a person in tyrant's wise
Wages war and does it zealously,
And lays waste the land thereby
With pillage, plunder, murder, flame.
And so the devil's coin-clipping too,
Falsifying of coins and trickery,
Spread abroad both day and night,
Something the devil himself's devised:
On that account many a person's ruined,
And must perish in bitter misery,
If now no miracle occurs

And hail and thunder strike the earth.
Yet God indeed in His own time
Will punish such iniquities.
Let it be given to His care,
He'll deal with it as pleases Him.
Yet every human must confess
That we've transgressed against God's ways:*
May He now aid us in His Grace.

* Placing the blame for catastrophes on their allegedly sinful victims was commonplace in the literature of the time. Thus, the war itself and, later in the century, the Turkish advance were perceived by many as divine punishments.

Hie wirdt Fraw Armut angedeut/ Darneben auch vil Handwercksleut/ Nach jhrem Thun vnd Wesen heut.

Söx Tag Arbeitt Ver Richtt dein Ampt..
Sunst Bistu Hie Vnd Dört Ver Dampit..
Vud Kanstt Nemer Kein Sabat Tag..
Hie Noch Dortt Han Vor Armutt Klag..
Dero Wegen lueg Du Auf Dein Sach..
Das du nicht Kumbst In Vngemach..

Hoert zu jhr Armen/ vnd jhr Reichen/
Die jhrer wolfahrt thun nachschleichen/
Vnd jmmerdar hertzlich begehrn
Sich zu nöhren mit Gott vnd Ehrn/
Aber die/ so der Welt nach hoffen/
Die machen täglich jhre possen/
Dann jhrer seynd ein grosses Heer/
Die gleichsamb fahren auff dem Meer/
Vnd sich von jhrem Glück vmbwenden/
Bey der Fraw Armut hie zulenden/
Der Welt Gott Bachus diser zeit/
Täglich zu jhm locket die Leut/
Richt sie fein ab mit jhrem Gut/
Schickt sie darnach zu der Armut.
DJe Apotecker seynd gar klug/
Bekommen wol jhr Geld mit fug/
Vnd köndens wider auch verthon/
Wann er das seinig nicht wil hon.
Der Astronomus in den Tagn/
An dem Gstirn muß sein Gelt erjagn/
Daruon er dann wird schwach vnd matt/
Lobt sich/ biß er kein Geld mehr hat/
Der Procurator deß geleichen/
Sein Gelt thut mit dem Maul erschleichen/
Welches er mit dem/ so jhn schmirbt/
Verthut/ biß ein jeder verdirbt.
Der Schreiber thut auch geleichfalls/
Biß er die Armut bringt an Hals/
Die Reisser vnd Formschneider all/
Brieffmaler vnd Buchbinder zmal/
Die seynd gern frölich alle Tag/
Biß auch die Armut kompt mit klag/
Es seynd noch der Handwercker vier/
Die all auch gerne trincken Bier/
Maler/ Glaser/ Handschuchstricker/
Vnd die verwegne Pfannenflicker/
Die Mawrer vnd die Zimmerleut/
Seynd recht verwegen doch mit bscheid/
Vnd will jhr Lohn auch gar nit klecken/
Weiß vnd braun Bier thut jhn wol schmecken/
Goldschmid/ Steinschneider vnd Bildhawr/
Haben am Zechen gar kein schawr/

Der Kauffman vnd der Jud die zwen/
In eim Handel beysammen stehn/
Der Müntzer/ Goldschlager vnd Kramer/
Verthun jhr Gelde in grossem Jamer/
Die Kartenmaler in gemein/
Die Würffelmacher groß vnd klein/
Thun trewlich auch dartzu mit muth/
Daß einer verspielt Haab vnd Gut/
Die Seckler/ Gürtler/ Nestler gut/
Hausen offt biß an die Armut/
Die Metzger/ Jäger/ vnd der Koch/
Die werffen das jhr in ein Loch/
Der Müller/ Beck vnd auch der Bawr/
Bekommen jhre Nahrung sawr/
Wann sie jhr sach nicht recht nachgohn/
Müssens zu der Armut daruon/
Der Bierbrew/ Wirth vnd auch der Schneider/
Werden in jhrem Thun stets gscheider/
Doch weil das Zechen ist so gut/
Trifft sie endlich auch die Armut/
Die Kürscher/ Ferber/ Huter/ Weber/
Thut nicht beliben die Sewtröber/
Schuchmacher/ Balbierer/ Zanbrecher/
Seynd bey dem Bier auch gute Zecher/
Die Bader/ Kieffer/ Fingerhüter/
Bringen zusammen nit vil Güter/
Die Ledrer/ Loder/ Bürstenbinder/
Seynd recht verbrendte arge Kinder/
Schaffen dem Bacho jhren frommen/
Biß daß sie auch zur Armut kommen/
Kammacher vnd Tuchscheerer beyd/
Thun jhren Weibern vil zu leyd/
Das vberig verstehe man wol/
Jhr viel ich jetzund nennen sol
Die Schmid/ was Arbeit mit dem Hamer/
Derselben seynd ein gantzer Jamer/
Die haben all lust zu dem Zechen/
Lassen jhnen auch nichts abbrechen/
Jhr Weiber zancken ist vmbsunst/
Doch die mit hoffen/ haben gunst/
Die Kargen so jhnen abstohn/
Kein Frid bey jhrer Gsellschafft hon/

Sattler/ Hafner vnd auch Schleiffer/
Singer/ Spiller/ Geiger/ Pfeiffer/
Die Leyrer/ Zitter/ Trummelschlager/
Die Ballenbinder/ vnd Sacktrager/
Die haben all gute vernunfft/
Vnd seynd ins Bachi Bruderzunfft/
Der Steinmetz/ Ziegler/ Zimmerman/
Der Schreiner/ Wagner/ vnd fortan/
Die Schlosser/ Drexler/ Büchsenschäffter/
Seynd aller Zechen possen stiffter/
Die Biramenter/ Siber/ Sailer/
Die machen Wein vnd Bier nicht failer/
Ja man find auch wol vil der Reichen/
Die sich Handwercksleuten vergleichen/
So das jhrig verthun beyzeiten/
Biß sie zu der Armut einreiten/
Floßleut/ Fischer/ Hefftelmacher/
Die Melber/ Hucker/ Kiechelbacher/
Die Weinziehr/ Karnziehr vnd Bergknappen/
Seynd theils recht verthone Bierschlappen/
Die endlich vor der zeit all müssen/
Mit dem Freßnarren all Tag büssen/.
Dann werdens Schalcksnarren darauß/
Ja recht Stocknarren in dem Hauß/
Die sich nit lassen weisen/ lehrn/
Sich lieber zu der Armut kehrn/
Die werden rechte Hungerleider/
Täglich mit jhrem Schaden gschelder/
Lufftschlicker/ Nachtarbeiter grob/
Korscheußler/ Stattlumpen ohn lob/
Die alle muß Fraw Armut nöhren/
Könden sich jhr nit mehr erwöhren/
Es geht also/ wer nicht wil hausen/
Denen muß man mit Kolben lausen/
Aber ein recht Häußlicher Mann/
Jst bey Gott vnd Menschen wol dran/
Wer Gott förcht/ vnd wart der Arbeit/
Der hat den Segen Gotts allzeit/
Leidt kein Armut in ewigkeit.

Zu Augspurg/ bey Daniel Mannasser/ Kupfferstecher/ bey Werthabrucker Thor/ 1621.

PLATE XI. Here Dame Poverty Is Indicated, together with Many Artisans, according to Their Activity and Existence Today

In a clearing before the walls of a town a host of artisans and laborers of various types while away their time drinking, singing, and gambling. Utensils needed for their normal daily activities lie unused on the ground. In the background a procession of other workers is leading Bacchus—seated triumphantly upon a barrel of wine—to join the revelers. This carefree merriment takes place on the train of a cloak worn by Dame Poverty, an indication of the dire consequences of such foolish living. Attired in rags and with her left breast exposed—as would be that of Caritas—she supports a young child with her right arm as she extends her left to summon the revelers. A second child holds an empty bowl in one hand and clutches Dame Poverty's dress with the other. Verses engraved below read:

Take of your labor six days' good care,
Else you are damned, both here and there.
And never you'll have a Sabbath free
Here or there, from cruel poverty.
Thus to your business pay close heed,
Lest you shall land in dreadful need.

Hearken, you poor and rich men too:
There are those who creeping pursue what's good,*
And always try their best
To keep themselves with God and honor.
But there're also those who pursue the world,
Who daily carry on their tricks,
And they comprise a mighty host
Who travel, as it were, on the sea,
And turn their backs on their true fortune,
And land at last with Dame Poverty.
Bacchus, the worldly god, in this time
Daily entices people to him,
Cleverly robs them of what they own,
And afterwards sends them to penury.
Apothecaries are smart indeed,
And rightly rake their money in,
Yet could swiftly waste it again
When they no longer wish to keep it.
The astronomer, these very days,
Must gather his money from the stars,
But he grows feeble and tired thereby,
And soothes himself till he has no money.
The overseer, the selfsame way,
Earns his money with his mouth,
Yet, by what affords him pleasure,
Wastes his money, till everyone's ruined.
The clerk does very much the same
Till he gets poverty on his neck.
The draftsmen, the block cutters as well,
The illuminators and bookbinders too,*
Have happy hours the whole day through
Till poverty arrives with woe.
And there are artisans, four in number,
Who all of them love to quaff their beer:
Painter, glaziers, glove knitters too,
Pot menders in their impudence.
The masons and the carpenters,
Are quite bold too, yet within bounds,
And do not wish to waste their wages.
White beer, brown beer, suit their taste.

* *Die ihrer wolfahrt thun nachschleichen.* This line contains two scriptural references of a positive nature. See Ps. 106:5 for mention of the "good" and Eccles. 14:22 for reference to the word *pursue.*

* These as well as other artisans connected with the production of books are depicted and described by Hans Sachs in *Eygentliche Beschreibung aller Stände* (Frankfurt am Main, 1568).

Goldsmiths, gem cutters, sculptors too
  Are not at all afraid to drink.
The merchant and the Jew, those two,
  Are together in a single trade.
The coiners, gold leafers, shopkeepers too
  Waste their money to harmful ends.
The playing-card painters generally,
  The dice makers, great and small,
Set faithfully about this task,
  Wasting whatever they may own.
Sack makers, belt makers, makers of bindings
  Act in this way, until they're poor.
The butcher, huntsman, and the cook
  Throw their money down a hole.
The miller, baker, and the peasant
  Have to work hard to earn their wage,
But if they don't tend it carefully,
  They too must enter poverty.
Brewers, innkeepers, tailors
  Grow ever smarter in what they do,
But since it's so much fun to drink,
  Poverty strikes them at the end.
The furriers, dyers, hatters, weavers
  Will take no pleasure in the swine-husks.*
Shoemakers, barbers, drawers of teeth
  Are also mighty topers of beer.
Bath masters, coopers, thimble makers
  Never can put much money aside.
Leatherers, woolers, binders of brooms
  Are naughty children when they drink,
And faithfully serve the Bacchus cult
  Until they too are indigent.
Comb makers and cloth cutters both
  Inflict much grief upon their wives.
And all the rest is understood,
  Which I'll directly catalogue:
The smiths who do their work with hammers,
  They're the cause of endless misery.
They take all pleasure in their drinking,
  And never deny themselves a gulp.
The scolding by their wives is vain,
  Yet they with harlots are in favor.
The skinflints who do not take part
  Get no peace from their company.
Saddlers, potters, scissors grinders,
  Singers, gamesters, fiddlers, fifers,
Harpers, drummers, zither players,
  Bale binders and bag carriers,
They have good minds, the lot of them,
  And yet join Bacchus's brotherhood.
The stonemasons, bricklayers, carpenters,
  The joiners, wagoners, and so forth,
The locksmiths, turners, armorers
  Are the prompters of all drunken pranks.
The parchmenters, sieve makers, makers of rope,
  Make not wine or beer the cheaper.
Indeed, there're many among the rich
  Who're like unto the artisans
And waste their riches early on
  Until they ride into penury.
Raftsmen, fishermen, hasp makers,
  Flour dealers, hucksters, cookie bakers,
Vintners, wood gatherers, and miners
  Are partly beer swillers, quite undone,
Who at length and prematurely
  Must with food loonies do atonement.
Then all will turn into buffoons,
  Verily, sheer and utter fools,
Those who'll not let themselves be taught
  And rather turn to poverty.
They will end as starveling wretches,
  Learning each day more of their harm.
Air lickers and crude sewer-cleaners,
  Shit shovelers, town dregs without praise,
They all by Dame Poverty are nourished
  And can no longer ward her off.
That's the world's way: who won't be careful
  Has to be thrashed with heavy cudgels.

* *Thut nicht gelieben die Sewtröber.* The scriptural reference is to a verse in the parable of the prodigal son (Luke 15:16).

But a true and settled man
Will be well off with God and man.
He who fears God and tends his task
Will have God's blessing perpetually,
And suffer no want in eternity.

Augsburg, at the Shop of Daniel Mannasser,
Engraver at Werthabrucker Gate, 1621.

Zweyerley Supplicanten an ihre Herren.

IHr groſſen Herren/
nemt in acht/
Wir haben einen Fund
erdacht/
Das Ewr Genad wird
viel eintragn/
Geb vns Vrlaub/ daß wir aufſſchlagn
Viel Müntzen/ wir wolln alle Jahr
Euch geben ſo viel tauſent paar/
Welche gut in die Kammer ſeyn/
Wenn jährlich ſo viel kömmet ein/
Welchs wir gedenck'n hinaus zu führn/
Das wird man im Effecte ſpürn.

Die Gemein vnd Vnterthanen bitten.

ACh hoch vnd liebe Obrigkeit/
Seyd vns zu hören auch bereit/
Mit Lügen habn ſie euch bericht/
Darumb wollt jhnen gleuben nicht.
Es iſt nicht allein vnſer Schad/
Sondern noch mehr Ewer Genad/
Denn ob Jhr von dem Pacht viel han
Der Müntzen/ ſo weis jederman
Daß alle Wahren ſchlagen auff/
Vnd werden ſo gar thewr am Kauff/
Nun bedenckt wie viel man das Jahr
Zu Hoff mus kauffen immerdar
Halte gegn einander dieſe Summn/
Vnd ſchawt/ welche höher wird komn/
Das iſt nur ein Schad/ aber mehr
Wil ich jetzund noch zehlen her:
Die Vnterthanen werden arm/
Daß es Gott im Himmel erbarm/
Vnd ſehe drein. So frag ich noch/
Wie können ſie was geben doch

Dann ſolch falſch Gut hat ſo viel fluch/
Helt wie Wein im zerbrochnen Krug/
Der Geldgott ders jhnn hat gegebn
Wirds jhnn ſegnen in jenem Lebn.

DIs ſey genung von jhnn geſagt/
Nun mus vbr vns auch ſeyn geklagt/
Daß wir dis alls mit vnſer Sünd
Haben verdient/ vnd Gottes Bund
Vielfeltig vbertreten hie/
Drumb iſts noth gweſt zu beten jeh
So iſts hohe zeit jetzunder/
Ach HErr hilff/ ſonſt wir gehn vnter/
Das Waſſer geht vns an die Seel/
Wir haben der Landſtraffen viel/
Krieg/ Thewrung/ Peſtilentz vnd Sterbn/
Noch iſt das ſchädlichſte Verderbn
Die böſe Müntz vnter allen/
Wir ſind in Menſchen Händ gefalln/
Löß vns HErr aus dieſem Elend/
Wir ergebn vns in deine Händ/
Denn dein Barmhertzigkeit iſt gros/
Zerſtör die böß Pracktické loß/
Dem edl Gab/ Gold vnd Silber fein
Miſchens mit Kupffr/ wie Gifft in Wein/
Das krigt der Landmann für ſein Korn/
Sein ſaure Arbeit iſt verlohrn/
Dein Segn iſt weg von allm Handel/
Ach HErr du nicht von vns wandel/
Bleib bey vns/ es wil abend werdn/
Verlaß vns nicht auff dieſer Erdn/
Hol vns bald in dein Himmelreich/
Denn alle Zeichen ſind faſt gleich
Erfüllt/ die du haſt prophezeyt/
Darumb iſt dein Zukunfft nicht weit/
Denn dieſe letzte Müntzenplag
Iſt ein Zeichen fürm Jüngſtentag.

Dann es wol auff dem Waſſer ſchwam/
Darumb iſt euch ein jeder gram.
Er hat auch ſolche Warnung nicht
Gehabt wie jhr/ ſolchs widerſpricht
Der ſchwartze Kipper/ der die Kunſt
Euch hie gelernt hat/ wird ſein Gunſt
All ſeinen Dienern dort beweiſn/
Vnd ſie mit Pech vnd Schwefel ſpeiſn/
Die böſe Müntz auch auff das Hertz
Drucken vnd pregn/ ohn allen ſchertz
Die fewrich roth küpfferig Schlang
Wird euch nicht in die Verſen lang
Stechen/ ſondern immer nagen/
Das Gwiſſen allezeit plagen/
Dieweil jhr wol wiſſt was jhr thut/
Das koſt der Armen Schweis vnd Blut /
Jhr kalter Herd wird ſeyn ewr Eſch/
Jhr Angſt vnd Noth/ ewr harte Preß/
Jhr ſeufftzen iſt der blaſend Wind
Der dort das Helliſch Fewr anzünd/
Jhr Thränen ſind das Waſſer heis/
Darinn zu ſieden ſolch Geſchmeiß/
Ich wil geſchweigen all der Fluchr
Vber ſolchen gar groſſen Wuchr.
Noch mehr ſchadt euch jhr ernſts Gebet/
Halt mir zu gut mein ſcharffe Red/
Es iſt bewärt aus Gottes Wort/
Jhr habts doch ſelber offt gehort/
Es wird in ewigkeit nicht liegn/
Drumb thu dich ſelber nicht betriegn/
Himmel vnd Erde wird vergehn/
Sein Wort aber wird bleiben ſtehn/
Der reiche Mann hat es erfahrn/
Er hats ſo grob in ſeinen Jahrn
Nicht gemacht/ dann man lieſet zwar
Daß er Armen nichts geben dar/

Ihrt Obrigkeit/ wenn sie nichts habn
Können sie weder reitn noch trabn
Wer kein Pfert hat. Das Sprichwort gut
Sagt/ das ist ein Schelm/ der mehr thut
Als er kan. So ist auch eben
Ein Dieb/ der andern mehr wil gebn
Als er selbst hat/ er muß stelen/
Wie jener Schustr/ mus erzehlen:
Ders Leder stal/ vnd gab die Schu
Vmb Gotts willn/ sein Macherlohn zu.
Wann Obrigkeit von der Gemein
Nichts krigt/ vnd trägt die Last allein/
Wie kan jhr Stand lange bestehn?
Mich dünckt/ er mus zurücke gehn/
Ob sie schon hette Crœsus Schatz/
So heist es bald/ ein ander hats/
Ihr gute Müntz die kömpt hinaus/
Dagegen Kupffr vnd Blech ins Haus/
Aristoteles schreibt ein Verß/
Ein falscher Freund ist was ärgers
Als ein falsch Müntzer/ doch zu letzt
Kommen sie beyd ins Teufels Netz.
Syrach saget: Ein Lügner ist
Ergr als ein Dieb/ voll arge List/
Doch kommen sie an Galgen beyd/
Auch sagt man offt mit gutm bescheid/
Weist mir ein Lügner/ ich weis euch
Einn Dieb/ sind beyd von einem Zeug/
Wobey wird jetzt am meistn gelogn/
Gefährt/ beschmissen vnd betrogn/
Als bey dem kippn vnd wippen falsch/
Loben vnd liegn aus einem Hals/
Das eilfft Gebot habn sie gelernt/
Fuchsschwentzen die Herrn heur vnd fernd/
Für Augen schön/ hinter rück feind/
Ihr keiner ders mit trewen meynt/
Wers jhnn vmbs Herrn Nutz zu thun/
Was dörffen sie so grossen Lohn
So viel tausent in kurtzer zeit
Zu gewinnen/ vnd gehn gekleidt/
Sie vnd jhre Weiber prächtig/
Das pravirn macht sie verdächtig/
Daß sies nicht gut mit der Herrschafft
Meynen/ denn jhre groß Barschafft
Zeugt/ daß sie sich nur selbst laben/
Als Herren auff schönn Rossen drabn/
Ihr Weiber als die Edelfrawn
Prangen daher/ sagt mir in trawn/
Wer mus alles bezahlen doch?
Der gmeine Mann bis dato noch/
Wann derselbige nicht mehr hat/
So kömpts endlich auff jhr Genad/
Manch ehrlicher Mann mus entlauffn/
Denn sie die Güter zu sich kauffn/
Das machts/ daß sie bald werden reich/
Dadurch verderbn so viel zugleich/
Dann so kans ja nicht lenger stehn/
Das Römisch Reich müst vnter gehn/
Ist dann an jhnn so viel gelegn/
Wer diese Sach recht thut erwegn/
So sind sie wie die Jüden loß/
Die krigen alls in jhren Schoß/
Sie solten nur als Knechte seyn/
So wolln sie seyn als Herren fein.
Weltkindr sind klügr in jhrm Geschlecht
Als Kindr des Liechts/ vnd Gottes Knecht.
Der vntrew Haußhalter macht sich freund
Mit dem vngrechten Mammon heunt/
Damit er komm in jhre Hütten/
Er wirds aber noch hie verschütten.

Noch wil mans nicht für böß erkenn/
Sondern einn freyen Wechsel nenn/
Prediger vnd Lehrer sie schmehn/
Die es straffen/ jhr Wort jhnn drehn/
Ja ein gantz Vniversitet
Lestern/ als wenn sie vnrecht hett/
Daß sie Kippern die Beicht versagn/
Vnd jhnn des HErren Tisch abschlagn/
Ist wippn nicht gut/ thun sie vnrecht/
Ist kippen falsch/ warumb verfecht
Ihrs/ vnd heist gut/ was doch böß ist/
Vnd böß/ das gut/ zu jeder frist/
Vber welchs Gott selber schreyt weh/
Drumb hütet euch/ vnd thuts nicht meh.
Sondern bekehret euch je eh/
Oder jhr vergeht wie der Schnee.

An alle Kipper vnd Wipper.

ACh liebe Leut/ nemt doch in acht/
Ich glaub/ jhr wist nicht was jr macht/
So jhrs wisst/ ists desto schlimmer/
So last ab/ vnd thut es nimmer/
Eh euch das ewig Weh/ Weh/ Weh
Betrifft/ denn solch Gut wie der Schnee
Verschmeltzen wird auff einen hauff/
Es ist fürwar ein thewrer Kauff
Den man bezahlet mit der Haut/
Noch thewrer ists/ sags vberlaut
Was die Seele bezahlen mus/
Drumb bitt ich euch/ bey zeit thut Buß/
Ehe denn es euch rewt zu spat/
Hie ist noch zeit/ Gott vmb Genad
Zu bitten. Wer zur helffte kehrt/
Irrt nicht alzeit/ wie Syrach lehrt.
Wer aber fort geht auff dem Weg
Des Verderbens/ vnd krumme Steg/
Da findet er auch einen sitzn/
Der eine Wag helt bey der Spitzn/
Dann wird er euch da einlegen/
Vnd euch wie das Gold thun wegen/
Die Gerechtigkeit darneben/
Vnd also zugleich auffheben/
Vnd wenn jhr hett noch so viel Geld/
Bey euch/ dazu die gantze Welt/
Werdt jhr da zu leicht befunden/
Fahrt in die höh/ wie der vnden/
Die Schnur bricht/ die rechte Wagen
Kan kein Vngerechte tragen/
Gott kippt sie aus/ vnd wippts ins Fewr/
Da müssen sie bezahlen thewr
Den letzten Hellr/ solch vntrew Knecht/
Welch jhren Mitknechten thun vnrecht/
Die krigen da jhrn rechten Lohn/
Weil sie alhie kein gut gethan/
Denn Geld/ dadurch andre verderbn
Kömpt selten auff den dritten Erbn/
Was hilfft denn alls schinden vnd schabn/
Lauffen/ rennen/ auff Pferden trabn?
Mit grossen Federn auff dem Hut/
Verbrennen bald in Fewers glut/
Denckt/ wenn jhr hie fürm Fewer heis
Steht/ bald vom Leib absleust der Schweis/
Wie heis es in der Hell mus seyn?
Wie jhr hie Gold vnd Silber fein
Durch das Fewr sieben mal probirt/
Nicht zu leutern/ daß feiner wird/
Sondern machts je länger je ärgr/
Man speyt fast an die Schreckenbergr/
Sie haben jhren rechten Nam/
Daß eim schreckt solch pecuniam.

Aber das steht nicht/ daß er sein
Armut genommen/ vnd da ein-
Gebrocket hat/ durch kippn vnd wippn/
Oder leichtfertiges Müntztippn/
Hat er gefressen vnd gesoffn/
Noch ist er darumb nicht entloffn/
Daß er andrn Leutn das jhr verthan.
Hat er sich köstlich kleiden lan/
So hat er kein schwer Seidn gemacht/
Noch Welsche practica erdacht/
Die man wol teutsche Schelmstück nennt/
Wissens zu bedecken behend/
Daß sie Staub vntr die Würtze mischn/
Auff falsch Saffran sind sie geflissn/
Thun roth Fleisch darbey verborgen/
Vnd dieses ohn alle Sorgen/
Darzu alls mit ehrlichem Schein/
Drumb wird ewr Gricht nicht ferne seyn/
Judas verkaufft das beste Gut
Vmb gering Geld/ seht was jhr thut/
Ihr gebt für Gold vnd Silber fein/
Kupffer/ Blech/ oder Schaum/ ich meyn/
Damit wolt jhr den Himmel kauffn/
Ja der Hell werdt jhr nicht entlauffn/
Doch wündsch ich euch die Seligkeit/
Drumb euch zu wahrer Buß bereit/
Daß jhr nicht denckt ich bin euch feind/
Sondern habs gut mit euch gemeynt/
So wil ich auch Gott für euch bitten/
Daß er euch aus den bösen Sittn
Helffn woll/ denn viel bekandte Leut
Darunter seyn/ ach daß sie heut
Die Stimm des HErren wolten hörn/
Vnd sich von dem Vbel bekehrn.
Ander gestalt wirds besser nicht.
Denn wenn jhr komt für Gottes Gricht
Da werdt jhrs erfahren vnd sehn
Wie Kipper vnd Wipper bestehn/
Da sie selbst werden außgekipt/
Vnd auff die lincke Seit gewipt/
Als stinckende Böck abgesondrt/
Darumb euch nicht so sehr verwundrt
Mus man von jedm vnnützen Wort
Rechenschafft geben/ wie gehort/
Von diesem Laster noch viel mehr/
Da so viel Leut vmb Gut vnd Ehr
Werden gebracht/ ja vmb das Lebn/
Denn viel sich hart bekümmern ebn/
Daß sie vmbs jhrig kommen sind/
In so gar kurtzer zeit geschwind/
Denn der zuvor ist reich gewest/
Der sitzt jetzt in eim schlechten Nest/
Vnd hat wenig zu beissen hie/
Vnd so es ja nutz jemand/ sieh/
So sinds nur Kipper vnd Müntzer/
Vnmüglich ists/ daß es lang währ/
Werdens in kürtzen außspeyen
Müssen/ vnd zu spat gerewen.
Dann Witwen/ Wäysn vnd arme Leut
Seufftzen vnd trawren auch noch heut
Vber jhren grossen Schaden/
Da Wipper sie mit beladen/
Vnd brauchn jhr Geld zur Kipperey/
Krigen dafür Kupffer vnd Bley/
Die liebe Geistligkeit mus auch
Entgelten diesen newen Brauch/
Edel/ Vnedel/ Bürgr vnd Baurn
Müssn all entgelten dieser Laurn/
Ich warn/ daß jhr nicht werdt erschlagn/
Ich wolts allzeit mit euch nicht wagn.

PLATE XII. Two Kinds of Supplication to You Gentlemen

In an audience hall on the left a ruler sits at the end of a long table and accepts petitions from citizens concerned about the inflation in Germany. Many more wait at the door to be allowed to enter. Scribes at the table are making note of the petitions. The sword and scales of justice hover in a cloud above the petitioners, while from a cloud on the other side of the room a finger points to a menacing prophecy on the wall (Dan. 5:25), which foretells the destruction of the perpetrators of the inflation. On the right, a moneychanger—aided by the devil—and his cohorts are busy weighing and counting old coins and minting new, debased ones. A moneychanger having been weighed on the scales of justice has been found guilty; the cords on the scales have broken, and the moneychanger is plummeting directly toward a fiery end in hell.

Take heed, you highborn gentlemen,
We've thought out a discovery
Which will bring your graces profit,
Grant us permission, that we may
Stamp many coins, each year we will
Give you so many thousand pairs
Which into your chamber enter well.
When yearly so much has accrued,
As we are planning to produce,
You'll know that by the very effect.*

Common People and Subjects Plead:
Oh Government, so high and dear,
Be ready, too, to hear us out.
They've stuffed you full with false reports,
It's not just the damage done unto us,
But even more unto your graces.
For whether you get much from management
Of coins or not, everyone well knows
That all the wares will rise in price,
And grow dear indeed when they are sold.
Now consider how much one every year
At court must purchase constantly,
Compare all these sums, one to the other,
And see which will emerge the higher.

* The German word *Effecte* is from the French *effet* (negotiable paper).

That's but one harm done, but still more
I wish now to enumerate.
The subjects all become so poor
That God in heaven's moved to pity
And understanding. Thus I still ask
How can they give more, after all,
To your government, if they have naught?
Neither can he ride nor trot,
Who has no horse. The proverb says
That he's a scoundrel who does more
Than ever he can. And that one, too,
is a thief, who will give others more
Than he himself has, he must steal,
Like that shoemaker (so I've heard)
Who stole the leather to make the shoes,
For God's sake and his payment too.
When the government from the community
Gets nothing, and bears the load alone,
How can its standing long be maintained?
It seems to me it must decline,
Even though it has a Croesus's treasure:
Thus it's soon claimed that another has it.
The valid coin goes on its way.
Instead, tin and copper enter the house,
Aristotle's written in a verse:*

* The source of the statement cannot be identified; no verse by Aristotle is extant.

A false friend is something worse
Than a false coiner, yet at the end
They both land in the devil's net.
The book of Sirach says that a liar*
Is worse than a thief, with cruel cunning filled.
Yet both will end on the gallows tree.
It's often said too, and with good sense:
Show me a liar and I'll show you
A thief: both are cut from a single cloth:
Just where can there now be more lying,
Skullduggery, trickery, and cheating,
Than in the falseness of clipping and whipping,
They praise and lie from a single throat,
The eleventh commandment they have learned:
Flattering gentlemen this year and last,
Pleasing when present, hostile behind,
Not a one of them acts loyally,
If they wanted to be at your graces' service.
How come they win such great reward,
So many thousands in so short a time,
And stroll about, so finely dressed,
They and their women, splendidly,
Their display gives them a suspect air
Of not meaning well with their gentle
employers,
For the sum of ready cash they possess
Betrays that they help themselves alone:
They trot like lordships on handsome steeds,
Their women, like ladies of quality,
Look very fine. Now tell me in truth:
Who must pay for it in the end?
The common man, till this very date,
And when he has no more to give,
Then it falls on your graces, finally.
Many an honest man must run away,
Because they buy up properties,
That means that they grow swiftly rich,
Driving many to ruin simultaneously,
But it can no longer continue so,

* See Eccles. 20:27.

The Roman Empire would have to perish.*
Is that, for them, of such importance?
Whoever considers the matter aright
Sees that they act like wanton Jews,
Who gather all into their bosom.
They should be nothing but menials,
But they want to be like masters fine.
Worldlings are wiser in their tribe
Than children of light and servants of God.
The unjust steward becomes the friend
Of unrighteous Mammon this very night,†
That he may enter into their dwellings,
But here too, he will, spilling, waste it.‡
For such false winnings are much accursed,
And keep like wine in a broken jug,
The money god, who's given it to them,
Will bless it for them in the life beyond.

But let it be enough talk of them
Now a lament must be raised against us too:
That we all this, by having sinned,
Have earned it in many a manner and wise,
Transgressing against the laws of God.
Therefore it's needful forever to pray,
And now, at last, it is high time.
Help us, Oh Lord, lest we perish,
The water creeps up to our soul,
We are much punished, countrywide,
War, inflation, plague, and death.
But still the most harmful cause of ruin,
Among all others, is evil coin.
We have fallen into the hands of men§
Release us, God, from our distress.
We submit ourselves into Your hands,**
For Your mercifulness is great.
Destroy these evil practices:

* The reference here is to the Holy Roman Empire of the German Nation.

† See Luke 16:8–9.

‡ See Matt. 9:17.

§ See 2 Sam. 24:14.

** See again 2 Sam. 24:14.

Into noble gifts, gold and silver fine,
They mix copper, like bane in wine.
That's what the countryman gets for his grain,
His bitter toil is thrown away,
Your blessing from all trade is gone,
Oh Lord, turn not from us away,
Abide with us, for evening comes,*
Desert us not upon the earth,
Soon take us to Your heavenly realm,
For almost all the signs are now
Fulfilled, as You have prophesied.
Your future, thus, is not far away,
Because this final coinage-plague
Is a signal for the Judgment Day.
Yet men will still not grasp its evil,
But rather call it free exchange,
They scorn the preachers and the teachers,
Who censure it, their words perverting,
Indeed, a university entire†
Is slandered, as if it had gone wrong,
Because to the clippers it denies confession,
Nor lets them take the Lord's communion.
If clipping's not good, then they do ill.
If clipping's false, why do you defend it,
Calling it good when it's plainly wrong
And evil what's good, at every turn.
At this the Lord Himself cries woe.
Thus guard yourselves, do it no more,
But forthwith to conversion go,
Or you will vanish like the snow.

To the Clippers and the Whippers:

Oh dear people, now pay heed,
I think you know not what you do,
And if you know it, that is worse.
So stop, and do it never more,
Before the eternal cry, woe, woe, woe
Befalls you, for such treasure like the snow

* See Luke 24:29.

† The university cannot be identified.

Will melt into a little heap.
Indeed, it is a bargain dear
Which one must pay for with his skin,
And dearer still (say it aloud)
The payment that the soul must pay.
Therefore I beg you, atone in time,
Before repentance comes too late,
Here there's still time to beg of God
His grace. Who turns around halfway
Does not always err, as Sirach teaches,*
But whoever proceeds along the path
Of ruin, on the crooked way,
There he'll encounter someone sitting
Who holds a balance by its top,
And then he'll cast you into it,
And weigh you, as we do with gold,
Balanced against righteousness,
And so directly you'll be raised,
For even though you'd have much coin
In your pockets, and the whole world besides,
You will be weighed and found too light.†
You'll fly aloft, finally
The cord will break, the bowl of right
Can carry no unrighteous men.
These God tips out, whips them in the fire,
Where they must pay exceeding dear
The final penny. These unjust fellows
Who to their co-fellows have done wrong,‡
At last will get their just deserts,
Since here on earth they've done no good.
For money, by which others are ruined,
Seldom descends to the third generation.
What good is all this skinning and swindling,
Running, racing, trotting on horses
With splendid plumage on your hat?
It will all be consumed in the flame of fire,
Think, when you stand here before the blaze,

* See Eccles. 17:20–23.

† See Dan. 5:27.

‡ See Rev. 19:10.

And sweat soon from your body pours:
How hot then must it be in hell?
Just so, both gold and silver fine
You've run through the fire some seven times,
Not to purify it, to render it finer,
But to make it, the longer you melt it, the
    worse.
One almost spits on the Schreckenberger,*
They've been given the proper name,
Such *pecunia* causes people fear,
For it indeed swam on the water,†
That's the reason everyone detests you.
But he has not such a warning received‡
As you have: that is refused
By the black clipper, who has taught
You his art, his favor will be shown
To all his servants down below,
And he'll feed them there on pitch and sulfur,
And stamp bad coins upon their heart,
And emboss them there, it is no jest;
The fiery serpent of the copper red
Will not long sting you in your heels,
But instead will gnaw eternally
At your conscience, torturing you forever,
So that you'll know well what you have done:
It's cost the poor folk's blood and sweat,
Their cold hearth will your ashes be,
Their fear and terror your hard-edged mold,
Their sighing is the raging wind
That there ignites the fires of hell,
Their tears the water, scalding hot,
In which such rabble will be boiled.
I shall not mention the curses all
They've hurled at such great usury,
Their earnest prayer will hurt you still more.

* See note on page 37. The name of the village and mine means literally "terror mountain."

† See 2 Kings 6:5–10.

‡ One assumes that the person referred to is the black clipper or the devil, depicted in the lower right-hand corner of the engraving.

Forgive me now my sermon sharp,
It can be proven by God's word
Which you yourself have often heard,
It will not lie, forever more.
Therefore yourself do not deceive,
Heaven and earth will pass away,*
His word however will remain.
The rich man's found it to be true,†
He had not in his years on earth
Behaved as cruelly: one reads indeed
That he gave nothing to the poor,
But it's not written that he took
Their poverty and crumbled it,
By means of clipping and whipping
Or by light-fingered coinage clipping.
To be sure, he gobbled and drank,
Yet he did not go so far
That he took others' property;
Though he dressed himself quite splendidly,
He did not make a heavy silk,
Nor devised Italian practices,
Which one well may call German roguery.
They know cleverly to conceal
How they've blended dust into the spice,
With false saffron they are skilled,
So that red meat's age may be concealed.
They do all this without a care,
And with false honesty besides.
Therefore your judgment's not far off,
Judas sold the greatest good
For little money, see what you do:
For gold and silver fine you give
Copper, brass, or dross, I think.
You mean to purchase heaven thereby,
But you will not escape from hell.
Yet I wish blessedness for you:
Thus, ready yourself for atonement true:
That you'll not think I am your foe,

* See Matt. 24:35.

† See the parable of the rich man and Lazarus (Luke 6:19–31).

But rather have meant it well with you,
Thus I shall pray to God for you,
That He will help you to escape
Your evil ways, for many well-known folk
Are involved in them. Oh, that they today
Would hear the message of the Lord
And from this evil turn away,
Otherwise, things will not improve,
For when you come before God's court
There you will learn and there will see,
How clippers and whippers meet the test:
There they themselves will be clipped out,
And whipped to the left-hand side away,
And shunted off like stinking goats.*
Therefore be not much surprised:
One must for every worthless word
Give an accounting, as is right,
And of this vice so much the more,
Because so many by it are robbed
Of honor and goods, yes, life itself.
For many are beset by care
That they will lose all that they own
In a very short time, and speedily.
For he who has been rich before,
Now sits in a nasty nest indeed,
And has but little on which to gnaw,
And if it profits anyone, behold!
It's the clippers and coiners.
It's impossible that it long will last;
In a short time they will have to be
Spat out, repenting their deeds too late.
For widows, orphans, and the poor
Still sigh and moan this very day
About the terrible injury
With which the whippers have burdened them,
By using their coins for the clippers' trade,
For which they get but copper and tin.
Our dear clergy too has been forced
To suffer from this novel crime,
Nobles, commoners, burghers, peasants
Must suffer from these miscreants.
I warn you, that you'll not be slain,
I'd never dare to share your game.

* See Matt. 25:32 and 41.

Geitz- vnd Wucher Spiegel.

In welchem sich die jenigen wol zubeschawen haben/ so mit dem abschäwlichen Laster deß vnersättlichen Geitzes vnd Wuchers behafftet/ zur trewhertzigen Warnung für Augen gestellet.

Wje können jetzt zu dieser Zeit/
Mehr fortkommen die gmeinen Leuth?
Dieweil es gibt der Wuchrer viel/
Die alls auffkauffen in der Eil/
Korn vnd Wein mit grossen Summen/
Das man schier nichts kan bekommen.
Es sey dann vmb vierfaches Gelt/
Drauff ist deß Wuchrers Sinn gestelt.
Wann aber kombt der liebe Gott/
Vnd den Armen errett auß Noht/
Den Reichen fordert bey seim Gwissn/
Ob er auch hab an jhm bewissn/
Das gut Werck der Barmhertzigkeit/
So wirdt kommen ein andrer Bscheidt:
Anders als hie auff dieser Welt/
Dieweil es jedem so gefelt/
Zu wucheren mit Korn vnd Wein/
Dann es vilen so geht hein:
Denen soll man aber zur Hauben
Greiffen/ vnd die Zecken wol klauben/
Vnd rupffen die Flugfedren auß:
Wer hinder sich kaufft in sein Hauß/
All Wein vnd Korn im gantzen Land/
Vnd förchtet weder Sünd noch Schand/
Damit ein armer Mann nichts findt/
Bald Hungers stirbt mit Weib vnd Kindt:
In dem er jhm als ein Bößwicht/
Sein Leibs Narung vnd Krafft entzeucht/
Welchs jhn auffhalt in seinem Lebn/
A. Da Moses jhm doch die Lehr gebn/
Daß er seins Nechsten Ehr vnd Gut/
Soll lieben als sein eigen Blut.
Er aber acht keins Armen Noht/
B. Vnd streit muthwillig wider Gott.
Ist also sein gantzes Gedicht/
Nuhr auff den Mammon abgericht.
Demselben dient er Tag vnd Nacht/
Vnd seines Schöpffers wenig acht.
Dieweil er nuhr nach seinem Willn/
Alhie mag Kastn vnd Keller fülln.
C. Darumb sicht er ins Gbürg hinein/
Ob auch die Rebn tragen viel Wein:
Vnd gibt dem Rebman gern Gelt drauff/
Daß er bekom deß Weins vollauff.
Verläst sich/ obs schon nicht geht ab/
Daß er doch guten Eßig hab:
D. Der wirdt jhm gnommen auß dem Faß/
Wa er nicht vom Wucher ablast.
Sondern verhart im bösen Wesn/
Da jhm doch Moses das Gsetz glesn/
Vermeint er hab gleich gnug daran/
Die Seel mag fahren wa Sie kan.
Derhalben braucht er ohn Verdrieß/
Sein wolgebutzten Judenspieß.
Sticht mit demselben vmb sich her/
Vnd wirdt jhm gantz kein Reiß zu schwer.
Ja/ sein mit Wucher gwonnen Guth/
Jhm selbst den grösten Schaden thut:
Macht jhn zu einem Sünden Knecht/
E. Daß er von Lastern börsten möcht.
Er ist ein solcher träger Gsell/
Zu gutem faul/ wie ein Esel.
Gut Speiß macht jhn so schleckerhafft/
Zu Marckt er alles zu sich rafft:
Empfindt gar nichts in seim Gewissn/
Meint/ er müß alles zu sich reissn.
Das macht sein Neid/ sein Geitz vnd Zorn/
Daß er nicht denckt heut oder morgn/
Werd sein Seel von jhm genommen/
Wa wirdt hernach Sie hinkommen?
Die gute Kost macht jhn so geil/
Daß er versuchet all sein Heyl.
Mit Gelt vnd Gaben auch verführt/
Wa er die gringste Armuht spürt.
F. Der Hochmuht treibt jhn auch dahin/
Daß er jhm nimbt in seinen Sinn/
Zu thun alles was jhn nuhr glust/
Dann der Wucher wärmbt jhm sein Brust.
Vnd weil sein Sinn in Lüfften schwebt/
Er gar ohn ein Gewissen lebt/
In Geitz/ Finantz darzu Hochmuht/
Aber es selten lang gut thut.
Dann Gott von Himmel stürtzen thut/
Der Engel hoch- vnd stoltzen Muht.
Also auch solcher Leuhte Pracht/
Gott der HErr bald zu schanden macht.
Da jhn Gotts Straff solt schrecken ab/
Kühlt er sich mit dem Gwinn fein ab/
Vnd sticht mit dem Schindmesser sein/
An alle Ort vnd End hinein/
Ob er schon manchen Fählstich thut/
Dann Gott offt rächt des Armen Blut:
Vnd kombt der Fluch mit grossem Spott/
Daß er muß spilen Bancheroht.
In das Schiff sitzen vnd falliren/
G. Sich plöchen lassen vnd Thurniren.
Da ist dann gfallen sein Reichthumb/
Vnd groß Credit ist kommen vmb.
H. Gleich wie der Habich alls außspeit/
Was er sein Lebtag hat gebeut.
I. Endlichen er dann auch wird kranck/
Vnd fährt stracks in der Höllen gstanck.
Damit der Teuffl das Spiel gewonnen
K. Im Brett/ weist jms/ weil er vnbsonnen/
Sein zeitlich Heyl nicht wol betracht/
Vnd sich vmbs ewig auch gebracht.
L. Da spert die Höll den Rachen auff/
Vnd kommen jhm all Sünd zu hauff/
Daß er mit Leib vnd Seel zugleich/
Dem Teuffel dient in seinem Reich.

Warnung.

Die lieben Alten vor viel Jahren/
So nicht viel Ränck haben erfahren/
Von Wucher/ Geitz vnd auch Finantz/
Die haben solchen Gsellen gantz/
Die Sacramenta nicht spendirt/
So ein solch gottloß Leben gführt.
Jetz gehn Sie all zum Tisch deß Herrn/
Ja trutz/ der jhn solches solt wehrn.
Aber das gschicht zu jhrem Gricht/
Weil kein Besserung drauff geschicht.
Darumb du Christ zu jeder Zeit/
Den Geitz vnd losen Wucher meidt/
Der in der Schrifft/ wie jeder list/
Bey Seelen straff verbotten ist.
Auff daß dir das nicht widerfahr/
Davon ich jetz gantz offenbahr/
Nach meinm Verstandt/ gar vnverzagt/
Auß Gottes Wort hab geweissagt.

E N D E.

PLATE XIII. Mirror of Greed and Usury, in Which Those Are Put on Display Who Are Infected with the Revolting Vice of Insatiable Greed and Usury, Placed before Your Eyes as an Earnest Warning

Flanked to his left by the maw of hell and to his right by Moses with the Ten Commandments, a Janus-faced figure in strange clothing stands defiantly at the center. His doublet is a wine cask bearing the name "Wine-Jew." The lid of the cask is his hat, and upon it sit two small demons, who are tapping wine through his head. His baggy pants bear the name "Grain-Jew," and from them hang the attributes of various vices; peering out from behind his right leg is an ass, symbolizing sloth. While brandishing a sword in one hand and a flayer's blade in the other, the Jew, who has accumulated his wealth through profiteering and usury, pays no heed to Moses, who admonishes him to love his neighbor and to honor his neighbor's property. In the background is depicted the outcome of the Jew's ill-conceived desire for wealth. Along the shore two ships wait to take on the casks of wine that the Jew (G) has obtained through bribery. All is, however, for naught, for just as the hawk on top of the cliff (H) disgorges all that it has eaten, the Jew lies on the shore on the right and bewails the loss of his riches. The fall from heaven of the goddess Ate—with the mirror of vanity in her hand and the clawed foot of a devil—underscores the sinful pride of the Jew. The devil flips over a backgammon board to indicate that the game the Jew has played is finished. At the far right the Jew now lies sick and suffering on a bed that is entering the maw of hell. The money, which he accumulated, lies in sacks of diminishing size at the feet of Moses.

How now can, in the present time,
   Ordinary people get ahead?
At fault are the many usurers,
   Who buy up everything in haste,
Grain and wine in great amounts,
   That next to nothing's to be had,
Unless it's bought with fourfold coin.
   That's what the usurer intends,
But when will our dear God arrive
   To save the poor folk in their need
And ask the rich man, on his conscience,
   If he has drawn into account
The good work of sweet charity.
   Another answer then will come,
Different from that upon this earth,
   Because it pleases everyone
To profiteer from grain and wine,
   For it's the practice many follow.
However, these will, by their crests,
   Be seized, their ticks be picked away,
Their flying feathers all plucked out:
   The one who hoards inside his house
All grain and wine throughout the land,
   And fears not sin nor his disgrace,
So that a poor man nothing finds
   And starves to death with wife and child,
Because that person, like a rogue,
   Has robbed him of the food and strength,
Which give him succor in his life.
A. For Moses has given him this rule:
As though it were his own blood, that he
   Love his neighbor's honor and property.*
But he does not heed the poor man's need,
B. And against God fights wantonly,
And therefore all his thoughts and deeds
   Have only Mammon as their guide,
The god he serves both night and day,

* A reference to Lev. 19:18.

And his Creator little heeds,
Because he solely, by his will,
His cellar and his chest may fill.
C. Therefore he goes into the hills
To see if the grapes will bear much wine,
And gives the vintager a bribe
To let him have the wine entire,
And depends (although it's not a need)
On getting good vinegar besides.
D. But it will be taken from his vat
If he does not leave off usury,
But rather persists in evil ways,
Though Moses has read his law to him,
And thinks he's done enough thereby,
His soul may go wherever it will.
Thus he employs, without dismay,
His nicely polished Jewish spear,*
Thrusts it about him, right and left.
For him, no campaign is too hard.
Yes, his money won with usury,
To him will do the greatest harm:
Turn him into a slave of sin,
E. That he from vices well might burst.
But he is such a lazy fellow,
Slothful in goodness, like an ass;
Good food makes him lickerish.
At markets he grabs all for himself,
In his conscience he feels naught at all
And thinks he must get everything.
His envy, greed, and anger make
Him forget that, tomorrow or today,
His soul will be taken from him away:
In what's to come, where will it land?
His splendid food makes him so lewd
That he will venture all his luck.†

With coin and gifts too, he seduces
Where the least poverty he suspects,
F. His pride does drive him to the point
That he gets notions in his mind
To do whatever he may please.
Profiteering heats his very breast.
And since his mind floats in the air,
Without a conscience he exists,
In greed and trickery, pride besides,
But it will seldom last long or well.
For God from heaven did cast down
The angels' arrogance and pride.
Likewise, the Lord God swiftly turns
Such people's splendor to disgrace.
When God's punishment should give him pause,
He soothes himself with what he's won
And plunges in his flayer's blade
At every nook and every cranny,
Though many a misaimed thrust he makes.
God oft avenges the poor man's blood,
And the curse strikes 'midst great mockery,
So that he must play the bankrupt's game
And sit on the ship in insolvency,
G. Crying and raging, be put in the stocks,
Because his riches have collapsed,
And his great credit is swept away.
H. Just as the goshawk must disgorge
All it has swallowed, its whole life long,
I. At length he too will then fall ill
And go straightway to the stench of hell,
Because the devil's won the game.
K. On the game board it's shown him, since foolishly
He paid no heed to his earthly weal
And robbed himself of that in heaven.
L. Then hell opens its maw up wide,
And all his sins on him descend,
So that he, with body and soul together,
Must serve the devil in his realm.

* *Derhalben braucht er ohn Verdrieß / Sein volgebuttzen Judenspieß.* See note at bottom right on page 61.

† *Daß er versuchet all sein Heyl.* The phrase *sein Heil versuchen* (to try his luck) is an idiom that exists in modern German, but *Heil* also has the primary meaning of "salvation."

Warning:

The dear ancients, long years ago,*
  Who not so many tricks did know
Of usury, avarice, and fraud
  Refused to give the sacraments
To wretched fellows such as these,
  Who such a godless life had led.
Now they approach the altar rail
  Defying those who'd deny it to them,
But that will happen at their judgment,
  Since no improvement has occurred.
Therefore, oh Christian, always shun
  Foul avarice and usury,
Which in Scripture, as all men know,
  By penalty of soul is banned,†
So that this will not be your fate,
  Of which I presently relate
After my judgment, unafraid,
  And from God's word prophecy have made.

THE END.

* *Die lieben Alten vor viel Jahren.* The intended reference is to the Church Fathers.

† See Ezek. 18:13 for the condemnation of usury.

Tantali fames, Das ist:

Beschreibung der vnersetlichen vnd gantz schädlichen Natur vnd eygenschafft der hefftigen Kranckheit der Geldtsucht.

Darinn so wol auß H. Schrifft als andern Prophan vnd Weltlichen Authorn kürtzlich probiert wirdt/ daß ein vngerechter Pfennig/ vermög deß gemeinen Sprichworts/ zehen andere auffresse.

Melius est modicum justo, super diuitias peccatorum multas, Psal. 36.

WAs ist diß für ein Wunderthier
Mit offnem Rach/ vnd flügen vier/
Auch grausamlichen Greiffn klawn/
Damit thuts greulich vm̄ sich hawn/
Zerreist vnd frist was es erwischt/
Goldt/ Silber/ Kleyder/ Bänck vnd Tisch/
Auch Brot vnd Wein/ Gült/ Zins vnd Rint/
Durch diß Thier alles gehling verschwindt/
Gleich wie das Fewr brents als hinweg/
Nichts ist daß jhm den hunger legt/
Es ist kürtzlich vnrechtes Guet/
Entsprungen auß deß Geitzes Bruet/
Dann diß hat dise aigenschafft/
Verzehrt allgmach Golt/ Guet vnd krafft/
Wo vnrecht Guet eingwurtzet hat/
Da hat guet Glück kein bleibent stat/
Diß ist ein geitzig Egel Bruet/
Saugt auß Gelt/ Guet/ Fleisch/ Marck vñ bluet/
Wer will doch disen Hunger stiln/
Wer will doch den Wolffsmagn fülln?
Was gnueg wer einem Volck vnd fleck/
Frist dises Thier allein hinweck/
Schreyt allezeit zufressen her/
So man jhm gibt/ will es noch mehr/
Ist gleich deß grossen Meeres Rach/
Ein gfrässig Wurm/ verzehrent Trach/
Wer Reich will werdn ohne schandt/
Verjag vnrecht Guet auß dem Landt/
Dann diß Thier vmbgestürtzet hat/
Vil grosse Reichtumb vnd Haußrath/
4. Reg. 4. Woher kombt Giezi der Aussatz/
Als auß Betrug/ vnd falschem Schatz/
Was hat das Volck vor Jerich gschlagn/
Iosue. 7. Als Achans Geitz/ wie d Schrifft thut sagn?
Das vnrecht Guet hat jhn verbrent/
Verstainigt mit Viech/ Weib vnd Kindt/
Nabal im Zorn Gottes starb/
Diß alles durch den Geitz erwarb/
1. Reg. 25 Versagt dem Dauid hülff vnd Speyß/
Sich selbst verdambt auff dise weiß/
Diß Thier trowt denen nuer Armuth/
So setzen allen sinn vnd Mueth/

Prou. 25. Nach gschwinden Reichthumb vnd groß Gelt/
Habac. Nur ellendt bringt es in die Welt/
Isai. 15. Es sambler nichts als Laimb vnd Koth/
Den Schatz geneust ein freche Rott.
Diß Thier bringt Væ, Væ, ach vnd wehe/
So zvil vertrawn auff Geltes Ehe/
Amos. 6. Diß Thier macht alles herb vnd saur/
Vergifft ist diser grausam laur.
Es ist wie ein verzehrent feur/
Wer es nit meidt/ dem wirds lachn theur.
Diß Thier hat gschwecht gar grosse macht/
Der Reich ist worden offt verlacht/
Vnd worden zu eim Bettelman/
Diß alles vngerecht Gueth kan.
Dann es frist Goldt/ Gelt/ Gueth vnd Hab/
Vnd gibt nichts als den Bettelstab/
Man schindt vnd schabt bey tag vnd nacht/
Man tobt vnd wüth/ man sorgt vnd wacht/
Kein gfahr man acht/ ist alls gering/
Damit man Reichthumb zwegn bring.
So mans zuwegen hat gebracht/
Mit viler sorg/ vil müh vnd wacht/
So rindts hindurch waiß niemandt wie/
Als ob mans hett gesehen nie.
Wer Reich will werdn rechter gstalt/
Derselb diß grausamb Thier nit bhalt.
Die Obrigkeit vrthaile frey/
Leuit. 24 Wies Gwissen vnd Recht bringt herbey.
Der Vnderthan sey allezeit/
Epist. Gehorsamb seiner Obrigkeit/
Paul ad Der Kauffmann geb nit böse Wahr/
Rom. 13 Vmb doppelt Gelt/ mits armen gfahr/
Der Handtwercksmann sein arbeit recht/
Mach Herrn/ Burger/ Paurn/ Knecht/
Der Wirth brauch nit die doppelt kreydt/
Vermischung böser Weinen meydt/
Der Diener richte fleissig auß/
Was jhm der Herr beuilcht im Hauß.
Kein platz soll haben böse kunst/
Dardurch man suech der Herrn gunst/
Durch schmaichln/ loben/ schendtlich liegn/
Daß sich die Balcken möchtn biegn/

Ein jeder seh in seinem standt/
Daß er leb ohn betrug vnd schandt/
Vil zittern wans Gelt nemen ein/
Wanns geben auß/ so brings jhn peyn/
Empfinden also toppelt straff/
Wers Gelt liebt/ wirdt ein solcher Aff.
Cic. 2. Den halt ich für ein rechten Man/
lib. Offi. Der Gelt mit maß verachten kan/
Wirffts nit vergeblich in das koth/
Halt es auch nit für seinen Gott/
Wer als verthut wirdt mangel habn/
Der Geitz kan sich im Gueth nit labn/
Hier. de Was hilfft dann dich ein voller Kast/
Ver. do. Wanns Gwissen hat kein ruh noch rast?
ser. 12. Die Reichthumb stehn nit in der hab/
Senec. Sie stehn im Hertzn/ vnd Gmüth vorab/
Ep. 16. So einer hett die gantze Welt/
Sen. ibi. Das Gmüth noch durstig wer nach Gelt/
So wers noch ein groß armuthey/
Wie Seneca diß bezeuget frey/
Wer der Natur gemäß lebt ist reich/
Wer dient dem Wohn verdirbet gleich/
Der Narr vom Gelt wirdt vmbgeführt/
Der Weiß wirdt erst daruon geziert/
Das Golt ist ein Tyrannisch Heer/
Es helt kein thraw vnd glauben mehr/
Verkaufft offt manchen hinderruck/
Macht offt geschwindt ein grosse luck/
In freundtschafft hat auch offt zerstört/
All starcke Schloß vnd Maurn hört.
Es richt an vil verrätherey/
Vil Krieg vnd Zanck/ vil Mörderey/
Es ist ein Blitz vnd Donnerstral/
Ein Schaur der wüetet vberal/
Zu Velt vnd Hauß/ zu Wasser vnd Landt/
Kein Grewel ist jhm vnbekandt/
Derwegen sehe ein jeder zu/
Daß jhm sein Haab mach kein vnruh/
Daß er behalt nichts vngerecht/
Vnd bleib also deß Mammons Knecht.

E N D E.

PLATE XIV. *Tantali fames,*[*] That is: Description of the Insatiable and Utterly Harmful Nature and Quality of the Violent Illness of Avarice in Which Both from Holy Scripture and Profane and Worldly Authors It Is Briefly Demonstrated That an Ill-Gotten Penny, as the Widespread Proverb Says,[†] Will Devour Ten Others. *Melius est modicum justo, super diuitias peccatorum multas,* Psalm 36.[‡]

A monster with four wings, dangerous talons, and coins for scales devours with an insatiable appetite any material objects within reach: silver goblets, a bench, a book, a sword, a money chest, wares of various types, and so on. The avaricious beast already has hold of the cloak of a man, who tries in vain to free himself. In the background a ship at sea sinks as a village on a hill burns to the ground.

What sort of wondrous beast is this,
With gaping maw and pinions four,
And awful griffin-claws to boot,
Which horribly it hacks about,
Rips up and gulps whatever it's caught,
Gold, silver, garments, benches, tables,
And bread and wine, profit, interest, kine.
Through this beast all vanishes, one-two-three.
Like a fire, it burns all things away,
There's naught that can its hunger sate.
In short, it is ill-gotten gain,
Born straight from out the brood of greed.
For it has this special quality,
It gobbles gold, wealth, strength gradually.
Where ill-gotten gain has taken root,
Good fortune there cannot remain:
This is a grasping leech's spawn,
Sucking money, property, flesh, marrow, and
  blood.
Who will indeed this hunger still?
Who can this wolfish belly fill?
What would suffice for a people and town,
This beast, by itself, can swallow it down,
Forever crying out for fodder.
Whatever it gets, it wants still more.
It's like the great mouth of the sea,
A gluttonous snake, a devouring dragon.
Whoever wants riches without disgrace,
Let him drive ill-gotten gain away from the land,

[*] These two words refer to the hunger of Tantalus, who betrayed the secrets of the gods to mortals and was punished, in Hades, by being placed in a river that receded when he bent down to drink; a tree filled with fruit, which he could not reach, was just above his head. Horace, in *Satirae* I, 1.68–71, asks, "Tantalus, thirsting, seeks the waters fleeing from his lips—why do you laugh? With a change of name, the story tells of you. You sleep gaping with moneybags piled up on all sides."

[†] K. F. W. Wander, *Deutsches Sprichwörter-Lexikon: Ein Hausschatz für das deutsche Volk,* vol. 3 (1873), p. 1269, lists under "Pfennig," no. 108: "Ein ungerechter Pfennig frisst zehn andere (hundert gerechte)" (An ill-gotten penny devours ten others [a hundred honestly earned]) and no. 109: "Ein ungerechtfertiger Pfennig nimpt zehen rechtfertige weg" (An ill-gotten penny takes away ten honestly earned). The scriptural basis is Prov. 10:2.

[‡] Here, as elsewhere, the author refers to the Vulgate, using its numbering, 36:16. This corresponds to the Luther Bible's 37:16.

Because this beast's turned upside down
Many great fortunes, households galore.
What source has Giezi's leprosy*
Save his tricks and treasure, falsely won?
What smote the folk at Jericho
Save Achan's greed, as Scripture says.†
Ill-gotten gain has made him burn,
Stoned him to death, cows, wife, and child.
In the wrath of God did Nabal die,‡
The wages gained by greediness,
Refusing David aid and food,
And thus he did himself condemn.
To those this beast gives poverty
Who all their sense and soul bestow
On rapid riches and great wealth:
It brings the world but misery,
It garners only birdlime and shat,
The treasure a brazen band enjoys.§
This beast brings woe, woe, groans and grief
To those too trustful of money's troth.
This beast makes all things tart and sour.**
This cruel knave is filled with bane.
It's like unto a raging blaze,
He'll laugh but little who fails to shun it.
This beast has made great power weak,
The rich man made a mockery,
Transformed into a mendicant.
All this ill-gotten gain can do,
For it gobbles gold, money, estate, effects,
And gives naught but the beggar's staff.
You hurry and scurry night and day,
You rant and rave, you worry and ward,
You heed no peril, all seems quite small,
So that you can find your way to wealth.

* See 4 Kings 4 (2 Kings 5 in the Luther Bible). The author employs marginalia for his citations "from Holy Scripture and Other Profane and Worldly Authors."

† See Josh. 7.

‡ See 1 Kings 25 (1 Sam. 25 in the Luther Bible).

§ See Prov. 25, Hab. 1:3, and Isa. 15.

** See Amos 6.

When once to wealth you've found the way,
'Midst worry aplenty, much trouble and care,
Then it all runs away, you know not how,
As if you'd never beheld it at all.
Let him who'll grow rich righteously
Not keep this cruel beast's company.
Let authority, frankly and freely, tell*
How conscience and right can this goal attain,
And let its subjects forever be
Obedient to that authority.†
Let not the merchant sell shoddy wares
For a double price, jeopardizing the poor.
Let the artisan do his work honestly,
Masters, burghers, peasants, farmhands the same.
Let the innkeeper not double the bill;
Let him shun the admixture of miserable wines.
Let the servant carry out zealously
What the master's commanded in his house:
Those evil arts shall have no place
By which the master's favor is sought,
Flattery, praise, and such infamous lies
That they'd make the very roof beams bend.
Let each man in his place attend
To living without deceit and shame.
Atremble they rake the money in,
When they pay it out, it gives them pain,
Thus reaping doubled punishment.
A monkey's made thus of the money lover.
I deem him a goodly man and true‡
Who despises money moderately,
Casts it not into the mud in vain,
Yet does not worship it as his god.
Who squanders all will suffer need,
For fortune is not a balm for greed:
What good do bulging coffers do

* See Lev. 24.

† See Rom. 13.

‡ Cicero's *De officiis* (Concerning Duties), letters to his son Marcus on moral obligations, contains the discourse on moderation as defined by the Stoics (I.40).

When conscience knows no peace or rest,*
For wealth lies not in ownership,
It lies, first of all, in heart and mind.†
If someone owned the world entire,
His spirit for money still would thirst,‡
And a great poorness would still prevail,
As Seneca attested, openly.
    He who lives by nature's rule is rich;
He who serves delusion is ruined straightway.
The fool by money is led about,
By it the wise man is but adorned.
Gold is the troop of tyranny,
Respecting neither troth nor faith,
Often selling a man behind his back,
Often swiftly digging a mighty hole.§
In friendship too it's often wrecked
All sturdy locks and hardy walls.
    It gives rise to much treachery,
Much war and strife, much slaughtering.
It's lightning and a thunderbolt,
A tempest raging far and wide,
Indoors and out, on land and sea.
To it no horror is unknown.
Therefore, let every man take care
That he not keep ill-gotten gain
And so a thrall to Mammon remain.

THE END

* The author uses Chapter 12 of St. Jerome's series of miniature biographies, *De viris illustribus* (Concerning Illustrious Men), to introduce Seneca the philosopher and (presumed) proto-Christian.

† See Seneca, *Ad Lucilium Epistolae Morales,* Book II, Chapter 16, 7.

‡ See in the same passage, section 8.

§ This line may echo Job's description of the calamities pressing upon him (30:14).

Der Gelt Siech.

Das Aussetzig verderbt böse Gelt/
Wirdt vns hiemit fürgemelt/

Wie es den schaden hat bekommen/
Vnd wie gar wenig es bring frommen

Der Leser.

WAs muß bedeuten diser Mann/
So Arm/ Ellendt auff der ban/
Wie vbel ist er zugericht/

Das verderbte böse Gelt.

Ach Freundt kennst du mich dann nicht
War ich doch gar dein guter Freundt/
Sihest du mich an für ein Feindt/
Wie so/ das du nicht kennest mich/
Vnd ich thu so wol kennen dich.

Der Leser.

O Ich weiß gar nicht wie du mir/
So wunderbarlich kommest für/
Ich kan dich ja nicht kennen recht/
Wie zeichst auff so Ellendt schlecht/
Sie in einer Schlaffhauben weiß/
Als ein Aussetziger mit fleiß/
Was hast in deiner rechten Hand/
Ein Bettelbrieff ist je ein schand/
Was deut der Klepper den du hast/
In der lincken Hand also fast/
Auch das du dich mit deinem ruggen/
Hie so starck steurest auff dein Krucken/
Ey/ er wie thust du so hart gehn/
[illegible] stehn/
Auch sag mir nur was insonderheit/
Die Ketten an dem Füß bedeut/
Mein wer thut dir so köstlich beltzen/
Deinen rechten Füß auff die Steltzen/
Hat ein rechten Siechenrock an/
Mein sag was bist du für ein Mann/
Gib dich doch zu erkennen mir/

Das Aussetzige verderbte böse Gelt.

So merck ich will es sagen dir/
Ein sehr fürnemer Mann war ich/
Von gutem geschlecht gar vermöglich/
Schön/ starck/ frisch vñ gsund anzuschawẽ
Kundt wol gehn/ raisen all Meß bawẽ
Trib allerley Gewerb fürnem/
Reichen/ Armen war angenem/
Einsmals wolt ich hin von Franckfort/
Auff Leipzig zu/ vnder diß wurd/
Es sich also mit mir begeben/
Das etlich hoche Häupter eben/
Mit fürnemen Landherren theten/
Ohneins wurden/ grossen streit hetten/
Als ich damals war auff der Strassen/
Da hette mich das Glück verlassen/
Es haben mich schnell vnuerhoffen/
Strassenrauber/ Geltmörder antroffen
Hielten mich gefangen/ theten hinlauffen
Mich den Hebreern verkauffen/
Dann jhrer mehr dann zu vil warn/
Vbel sein sie mit mir gefahren/

Dann ich hett gar ein schönen Hüt/
Darum ein Schnur von Gold sehr gut
In meiner rechten Hand het ich/
Ein Wag gemacht sehr köstlich/
Die ein Schüssel gantz guldin war/
Die ander gut von Silber klar/
In meiner lincken Hand ich hett/
Ein scharpffes schwert von Golt gestet
Durchzog mit vil Königreich/
Ich hett frade Glieder zugleich/
Ein gestickten Rock von Gold ich trug/
Bin frey ledig mit gutem füg/
In allen Landen herumb zogen/
Mein handel trib ich vnbetrogen/
Als die Juden mein Wahr genommen/
Fro warens wo sie mich ankamen/
Mein Hüt von Gold namen sie mir/
Gaben mir die Hauben darfür/
Mein Waag sie mir genommen haben/
Den Bettelbrieff mir darfür gaben/

Mein gulden schwert namen sie mir eben
Den Klepper mir darfür han geben/
Wie einem Siechen auff der bahn/
Sie raubten mir auch zuuor an/
Meine gesunde Glider hinwegk/
Die Lauren waren also keck/
Zogen mir auß mein Rock Goldfarb/
Mein schöne gestalt gleich verdarb/
Gaben mir dises Siechenkleyd/
Ja schlügen mir zu grossem leyd/
Die Ketten an meim lincken Füß/
Ach das ist mir ein herbe Büß/
Mein rechter Schenckel ist kein nitz/
Bin nichts wert ich stand oder sitz/
Solt ich nit zu erbarmen sein/
Kenst mich noch nit O Freunde mein/
Ich gib dir zu erkennen frey/
Welcher jetzunder ärger sey/
Der Jud oder der mich vorab/
Jhm schändlich zu verkauffen gab/

Ob er hab recht daran gethan/
Deß will ich Gott vrtheilen lahn/
Vnd weil du mich wilt kennen nicht/
So hör doch meines Namn bericht/
Das gute Gelt war geheissen ich/
Der lange zeit ist gewest vmb dich/
Hoff du werst dich meiner nit schemen/
Dich meiner getrewlich annemmen/
Villeicht kan ich dir dienstlich sein/

Der Leser.

Ja in dem grossen Ellend dein/
Wirst du mir nit vil gutes thun/
Weil du nit kanst ohn Krucken gehn/
Dein ankunfft mich gar nicht erfrewd/
Ach wer sein die trewlose Leut/
Die dich hond also zugericht/
Sie bleiben gewiß ohn gestrafft nicht/
Jetzt ist nichts mehr an dir zu gwinnen/
Es heist mit dir jetzt weit von hinnen/
Der Goldtschmidt achtet dein nit mehr/
Du bist Siech von den Juden her/
Ihr Flüch hat dich getroffen hart/
Dein inwendigs ist böser art/
Verkert/ es ist schand vnd spott/
Vor ehrlichen Leuten bey Gott/
Kein Artzet hilfft dir mehr auff Erdt/
Du bist dir selb nichts nutz noch werdt/
Der Teuffelsiechen Judenhauß/
Hat dich gantz verderbet durchauß/
Du müst dein Pfennig weiter zehrn/

Das Aussetzig verfälschte Gelt.

Du kanst dich mein nit wol erwehren/
Hab ich dir vor gefallen wol/
Laß mich mit dir hinkommen vol/
Es wird ein mal schon besser werden/
Wann der vnfried kompt ab der Erden
Vnd Pax der Fried wird kommen an/
Dann weil ich selber ob der ban/
Thu nur dieweil das best mit mir/

Der Leser.

Ich kan es nicht abschlagen dir/
Zu thun an dir all mein vermögen/
Gar in ein Chur muß ich dich legen/
An ein sonders ort gar allein/
Sonst wird mir von dir als vnrein/
O Pax du edler Gast thu kommen/
So müssens all zu dem erstummen/
Dann wird dein gestalt verendert werden
In ein gut Gelt auff gantzer Erden/
Das ist mein wunsch von hertzen grund/
Vnd mein Gebett zu aller stund/
Vmb Fried/ Lieb vnd Einigkeit/
Diser hochen betrübten zeit/
Amen das geb vns Gott mit frewd.

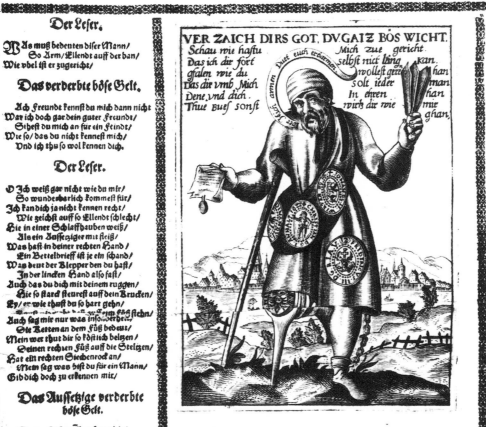

Getruckt zu Augspurg/ in verlegung Daniel Mannasser Kupfferstechers/ beim Klenckerthörlein.

PLATE XV. The Leper Money

The leprous money, bad, debased,
  Is proffered to us in this space,
How it received this injury
  And how small profit there will be.

Standing alone far from the city on the other side of the river is a humpbacked leper, who personifies debased money and who laments his sorry state: "Have mercy on poor me." Having caught his disease from Jews, he now holds in his right hand a beggar's license and in his left a leper's rattle to warn people of his approach. His left leg is chained, and his right one is a peg leg, so that he requires a crutch to walk. Attached to a sack slung across his chest as well as to his robe and peg leg are coins, one of which is dated 1622. The verses in the illustration read as follows:

MAY GOD FORGIVE YOU, VILLAIN OF GREED.
Behold how you have ruined me indeed,
So that I can no more pleasing be
To you, as you liked it formerly,
When all should serve you slavishly
For me, and honor me praisefully.
Do atonement besides, for you as for me.

The Reader:
What must this man's meaning be,
  So poor and wretched as he goes,
How terrible is his condition.

The Debased, Bad Money:
  Oh friends, do you not know me now?
Why, I was once your special friend.
  Do you regard me as a foe?
How is it that you know me not,
  When I know you so very well?

The Reader:
Oh, I know not why you appear
  So very peculiar to my eyes.
I cannot recognize you at all.
  Why do you point at such misery,
Here in a nightcap, all in white,
  And, quite on purpose, like a leper?
What do you have in your right hand?
  A beggar's license is always disgrace.
What means the rattle that you hold
  In your left hand so firmly clutched,
Also, that you with your hunched back,
  Are propped so heavily on your crutch,
Oh, oh, why do you have so stiff a gait?
  You can walk no more than on one foot,
And tell me what, especially,
  The fetters on your foot signify.
My goodness, who's clothed you so oddly
  And put right foot on that wooden stilt?
You wear a genuine patient's garb.
  Please, tell me what sort of man you are.
Go on, reveal yourself to me.

The Leprous, Debased, Bad Money:
  Pay heed, and I shall tell you true.
Betimes, I was a splendid man indeed,
  Of good family, well-to-do,
Handsome, strong, blooming to behold,
  Could journey well, attend all fairs,
Practice all sorts of excellent trades,
  Was welcome to both rich and poor.
Once from Frankfurt I meant to go

To Leipzig, and at this very time
It came to pass thuswise with me
That just then some lofty potentates,*
Involved with mighty heads of state,
Fell out, had great hostilities.
As I was just then under way,
That's when my luck deserted me.
Quite quick and unexpectedly,
I met highway robbers, money-killers,
They held me prisoner, made me run
To sell myself to the Hebrew tribe,
Since they far outnumbered me.
They treated me in evil fashion,
For I then had a handsome hat,
Around it a cord of excellent gold,
And in my right hand I did hold
A scale, produced with special care,
One of its cups was all of gold,
The other made of silver pure.
In my left hand I held a sword,
Sharp and beaten out of gold.
I went with it through many a realm,
In those days all my limbs were straight,
I wore an embroidered garment of gold,
I freely passed and fittingly
In all the countries round about,
And followed my calling undeceived.
When the Jews had taken note of me
(They were happy where they came on me)
They took from me my hat of gold
And gave me this nightcap in its place.
My scale they also took away
And gave me this license to beg instead.
My sword of gold they stole from me too,

* An oblique reference—perhaps intentionally vague—to the beginning of what would become the Thirty Years' War: the election, by the Protestant Estates in Prague, of Frederick V, Elector Palatine, as King of Bohemia (August, 1619), and the defeat of Frederick's disorganized troops by much superior forces of the Catholic League at the Battle of White Mountain (November 8, 1620).

And gave me this rattle in its stead,
As to a sick man under way.
Before they'd also plundered me
By stealing my healthy limbs away,
These villains were so very bold,
They stripped me of my gold-hued coat,
And likewise ruined my handsome form,
And gave me this hospital gown,
And hammered, to my awful pain,
The fetters onto my left foot.
Oh, that is a terrible penalty.
My right thigh is no good at all,
I'm worthless, whether I stand or sit.
Should I your pity not receive?
Don't you know me yet, oh friends of mine?
I'll tell you in all candor now
Which one's the more evil of the two,
The Jew or he who previously
Passed me to him for shameful sale.
Whether he acted right thereby,
Of that I'll let God be the judge.
And since you'll not acknowledge me,
Then hark to the story of my name:
Good money I was titled once,
Who long was in your company.
I hope you'll not be ashamed of me,
And accept me now in goodly troth.
Perhaps I can be of service to you.

The Reader:

Indeed, in your great misery
You will not be much good to me.
Since you can't walk without a crutch,
Your coming gives me no joy at all.
Oh, who may those treacherous people be,
Who have ill-used you in this way?
Surely, they'll not unpunished stay.
From you, now, nothing more's to gain.
Now you must hide yourself away.
No more the goldsmith pays you heed,
You've caught your sickness from the Jews.

The curse they bear has struck you hard,
Your innards are in evil wise
Transformed, a scandal and a mockery
To honest people in God's fold.
No doctor on earth can help you more.
Yourself, you have no use or worth.
The Jew-house, devilishly diseased,
Has utterly ruined you, through and through.
You must keep gnawing on your penny.

The Leprous, Falsified Money:

You cannot shove me thus away.
If I have pleased you in the past,
So let me follow with you now.
Someday, things will have improved,
When discord disappears from earth,
And *Pax,* called Peace, will then arrive.
Since I myself am under way,
Do presently what's best with me.

The Reader:

I can't refuse you what you ask.
For you I'll do all in my power,
In fact, I'll put you in a cure
At a special place, left all alone.
Otherwise, I'll grow unclean from you.
Oh *Pax,* you noble guest, do come:
Thereby must everyone fall mute,
Then you will have your shape exchanged
Into good coins through all the earth.
That's my wish, with all my heart,
And that's my prayer in every hour,
That peace and love and unity
In this much-troubled age will be.
Amen, God grant us this, joyfully.

Printed in Augsburg and Published by Daniel Mannasser, Engraver, near Klencker Gate.

Der hochschädlichen Wipperer vnd Kipperer/ als Gelt/ Land vnd Leuts verderber Lehrmaister.

Jch trag allhie wie jhr secht wol/
Der Lehrenbrieff ein Rugkorb vol/
Vnd gib eim jeden ein/ der bey
Mir das Handwerck hat glernet frey.

Hërbey merckt auff jhr Wipperer/
Jhr Wucherer vnd jhr Kipperer/
Jhr Geltsüchtige hie auff Erden/
Vnd all die bald Reich wöllen werden/
Es seye gleich Herr oder Knecht/
Jch kan euch alle lehren recht/
Jch bin ein Maister abgeriben/
Hab diß Handwerck schon lang getriben/
Es ist mancher Mensch in der Welt/
Der dem Handwerck mit fleiß nachstelt/
Aber es will sich schicken nicht/
Das macht er ist nicht abgericht/
Derhalb folgt mir/ das bitt Jch euch
So will ich euch bald machen Reich/
Vnd solt deß haben grossen gwin/
Dann ich ein alter Maister bin/
Hab schon vil das Handwerck gelehrt/
Jhnen auch Lehrenbrieff beschert/
Vil Königin vnd Potentaten/
Jst bey mir die sach wol gerathen/
Das sie bekommen Gut vnd Gelt/
Ja gantze Länder in der Welt/
Deß habens längst die Lehrenbrieff/
Dort vnden in der Höllen tieff/
Bin eben jetzt gleich auff der strassen/
Mein Lehrenknechten gleicher massen/
Die bey mir außgelehrnet eben/
Jedem ein Lehrenbrieff zu geben/
Damit sie ewig bey mir leben.

Vermahnung vnd Warnung.

Gewarnet sey ein jeder Christ/
Was Stand vnd Würd derselbig ist/
Laß sich disen Maister verflucht/
(Der nur der Leut verderben sucht)
Nicht bethören oder verführen/
Oder euch ewer Hertz berühren/
Dann er ein falscher Lugner ist/
Steckt vol Betrug vnd arger List/
Darmit er die Weltkinder gschwindt/
Vberlistet sacht vnd verblindt/
Vnd sonderlich in diser zeit/
Da sich dem Wucher gar vil Leut
Ergeben vnd gantz ärgerlich/
Mit Kippern bereichen sich/
Als einem Laster gantz verrucht/
Welches Gott selber hat verflucht/
Das solche Leut seyen verdampt/
Die solches treiben vnuerschampt/
Drumb bitt ich euch last daruon ab/
Sonst wirdt gewiß die Höll ewr Grab/
Last ab weil jhr noch fliehen kündt/
Vnd nicht verderbt in solcher Sünd/
Ehe euch ewr Lehrmaister betrieb/
Den Lehrenbrieff in Büsen schieb/
Vnd darmit in die Hölle weiß/
Ewig mit Pech vnd Schwefel speiß/
Deß jhr denn habt ein schlechten preiß.

Gedruckt zu Augspurg/ Jn verlegung Daniel Mannassers Kupfferstechers/ beim Klenckerthörlein.

PLATE XVI. The Mentor of the Most Pernicious Whippers and Clippers as Despoilers of Money, Land, and Populace

Disguised as a peddler of certificates for apprentices, the devil—with horns, a clawed foot, and a serpent's tail—makes his way in open country. His certificates—looking very similar to indulgences—are actually intended for all who are involved in the debasement of coinage, for in his left hand he holds one of these certificates, which reads, "Certificate of Clippers and Whippers, ordered into the depths of hell." The basket on his back is filled with additional certificates for the aristocracy, the clergy, Jews, tradesmen, and merchants. Above are four lines of verse:

I carry here as you can see
A basket full of certificates
And present one to one and all
Who have learned their craft from me.

Now pay heed, you money-whippers,
You usurers, you money-clippers,
You money-cravers here on earth,
And all who want to get rich quick.
Be you master or serving man,
I can instruct you all quite well:
I am a master skilled and sly,
And long since have plied this craft.
There's many a person in the world,
Who's zealously pursued the craft,
But for them it's not turned out aright;
The cause is that they've not been trained.
So follow me, I beg of you,
And quickly I shall make you rich,
And great will be the gains you get,
For I'm a master and veteran.
To many I have taught the trade,
Awarding them certificates.*
Many a queen and potentate
Have had their plans succeed with me,
So that they gather goods and gold;
Indeed, whole nations in the world
Long since have won certificates
Deep down below in hell itself.
Just now I'm passing down the road
To give my apprentices in like fashion,
Each one of them, a certificate,
Now they've absolved their course with me,
So they'll live with me eternally.

Admonition and Warning:

Now shall each Christian soul be warned,
No matter of what class and rank.
Let not this master much accursed,
(Who only seeks mankind's ruination)
To diddle you or to seduce you,
Or touch your very heart within you,
For he's a liar, perfidious,
Full of deceit and cruel artfulness,
By means of which he swiftly dupes
The world's children, nets them, makes them blind.
And in this age, especially,
When many unto usury
Surrender themselves and vexatiously
Grow rich in the clippers' company,
As with a vice all infamous,
Which has by God Himself been cursed,
Saying that such folk shall be damned

* The German word *Lehrbrief* refers to the certificate awarded to an apprentice (*Lehrknecht*) by his master (*Lehrmeister*) at the end of the former's apprenticeship, entitling him to set out as a journeyman.

Who follow such practices without shame.
Thus I implore: from them leave off,
Or surely your grave will be in hell.
Leave off the while you still can flee,
And are not ruined in such sin,
Before your master's business
Can shove your diploma into your breast,
Show the way straight into hell to you,
Feed you pitch forever, brimstone too,
From which bad profit will accrue.

Printed in Augsburg and Published by Daniel Mannasser, Engraver, near Klencker Gate.

Ein Erschröckliche Newe Zeittung so sich begeben vnd zuegetragen In disem 1621 Jar mit eim Geldt wechsler wie Er von Gott so Erschröcklich gestrafft, gibt die Zeittung gnuegsam berücht. 25.

Hört Zue der Erschröckliche Newe Zeittung so sich begeben mit eim Geldt Wechsler In Eim Marckht flecken genant Warendorff nit weit von Klage: fürt sein Nam Caspar Schadtman welcher Gott vnd des Menschen fluech auf sich ge: laden Dann Er In der Landtschafft das guete geldt mit list auf gewichselet dasselbig verschmeltzt, bös nichts wert geldt daraus gemacht vnd die landtschafft dar: mit betrogen also das ein Erschröckliche Teürung daraus eruolgt In allem was der mensch Zue erhaltung seines lebens notturfftig were deswegen die Arme Zue Gott schreyen vnd Zuefften das er wölle die straff von Inen abwenden, welche bitt der güettig Gott erhört vnd disen verfluechten geldt wechsler aus welchem die grosse teürung entsprungen sichtbarlich vnd erschröcklich gestrafft also das er bis öber die Knoden seiner fies In die Erden sunck vnd Im das wilde feur vnd dampf der höllen Zue mundt Nasen vnd ohren ausschlueg das es schröcklich ward an Zue schauen man tett In fragen wie Er die straff verschuldt vnd ob Im nicht Zuehelffen were gab er Zur Antwort Nein dann Er die Arme hefftig betrogen vnd Gott hab in Zue ein: em Exempel daher gestelt auf das alle die Jenigen an Im spieglen die seinem fues: stapffen nachvolgten das Jedem also ergehn würt wa sie nit daruon abstön, würden sie hie da Zeittlich biessen vnd dort die Ewige qual vnd pein leiden, da das Volckh dise wort hördten würden s hoch erschröckhen vnd mit grosser forcht von Im abwich: en Was Gott durch das Erschröcklich Spectackel will andeüten Ist wol Zue merckhen lieber leser weil der verfluecht Geitz Teüfel fast die gantz Welt Regiert, getrückt Im Jar. 1621

PLATE XVII. A Dreadful News Account of What Happened in This Year 1621 to a Moneychanger; This Newspaper Gives a Complete Report of How He Was Suddenly Punished by God.

A moneychanger, who has deceived people with debased coinage, stands at the center as an example of divine punishment. The men on either side look on in horror and cover their noses as the moneychanger sinks to his ankles into the ground, from which the smoke and stench of hell rise. Smoke also emanates from the moneychanger's mouth, nose, ears, fingertips, and moneybag.

Listen to the dreadful news of what happened to a moneychanger in a small market town called Waresville, not far from Moanford. Casper Damageman is the name of him who has brought upon himself the curse of God and man. Because he has bought up good money in the country, melted it down, made worthless money out of it, and deceived the country with it, a dreadful inflation came about in everything that people need to sustain their lives. Therefore, the poor cried out to God and begged that He take this affliction from them, which prayers God graciously heard and punished this accursed moneychanger, who had caused the high inflation, publicly and so dreadfully that he sank into the ground over his ankles, and the fierce fire and smoke of hell poured from his mouth, nose, and ears, so much so that it was dreadful to observe. People asked him how he had incurred such wrath and if he might not be helped. His answer was no, because he had mightily deceived the poor, and God therefore had made an example of him, so that all those who wanted to follow in his footsteps would see their reflection in him; if they were to succumb to what he could not resist, here they would suffer temporal penalty and there eternal torture and pain. When the people heard these words, they became very frightened and turned away from him in great terror. What God wants to show through this dreadful spectacle is clear to see, dear reader, because the accursed devil of avarice has control over almost the whole world. Printed in the year 1621.

Wan der Notig vnd Geitzig zusammen kombt so ist der Teuffel vnderkeüffler.

IM Sprichwort sagt man dz wan der
Notig vnd Geitzig vngefähr/
Zu handlen kum da fehls nit vil/
Der Teuffel sey auch mit im Spil/
Oder wol vnderkaüffler gar/
Dann er weist/ daß im immerdar/
Von solchem Kauff sein theil auch wirdt/
Derhalben beede Parthey anschirt/
Daß keiner dem andern nach geb/
Den Geitzigen macht er so geheb/
Daß er der Noth deß gmeinen Mann
Sich im wenigsten nichts nimbt an/
Er hab dann Vierfach nutz darvon/
Vnd alberait im Seckel schon/
Acht per Cento wil nicht mehr klecken/
Vom Capital mueß man herstrecken/
Vorein zum Zinß ein guet Schmieral/
Vnd ein Pfand daß jhm woll gefale/
Damit wan jemer zum schelmen wur/
Diser Dieb an jhm nichts verlur/
Welcher doch mit dem Juden spieß/
Verderbt von dem haubt biß auff d' Fieß/
Den gmeinen Mann der sich mit Ehren
Noch wol het kūnen länger nehren/
Wann er nicht in die händ gerathen/
Solchem Geitzhals vnd hellen prathen/
Der vmb sich wie der Wurm frist/
Mit Geitz betrug finantz vnd list/
Treibt sein Nechsten von guet vnd hab/
Hin ins Ellend an Bettelstab/
Derdann so ohnwert macht den Armen
Ein Stein solt sich seiner erbarmen/
Meinst nicht daß von solchen Rappen/
Der Teuffel werd sein theil erdappen/
Intgegen sich auch wider find/
Manch verschlagen Mutter Kind/
Wan es verspirt des Reichen sin/
Daß all Hoffnung der hilff ist hin/
Die er doch ohne schaden macht/
In Noth reichen dem Armen Recht/
So gedenckt er doch gewiß auff weg/
Wie er jhm zu letst den Seckel feg/
Dann wan der Geitzhals an der stätt/
Hundert Augen wie Argus hett/
Wirt er doch so manchem anschlag/
Vnd Bueben stuck so alle Tag/
Im schwang gehen/ auff gelt gericht/
Gwiß gar ohn propff entkommen nicht/
Liegen triegen ist jetzt gemein/

Böß kauff vn̄ d guete wort zum schein/
Manicher verpfind leib vnd Seel/
Nur daß jhm der Anschlag nicht fehl/
Gibt sein Nechsten ein blinden kauff/
Da reist die Höll den Rachen auff/
Wilt du dann mit gwalt sein blind/
Du Geitzige Krott der zerrene/
Die erdt/ daß du den Handwercksman/
Mit gwalt zum betrug leitest an/
Will er anderst daß täglich Brodt/
Erhalten mit jammer vnd noth/
Dann alles mueß gerichtet sein/
Beim Geitzteuffel nur auff den schein/
Kein war darin wie bey den alten/
Ja wann es nur so lang thuet halten/
Biß daß es kombt auß meiner gwahr/
Wirt doch nicht zalt hat kein gefahr/
Waß darff man dann vil fragen mehr/
Nach redlichkeit Kunst trew vnd ehr/
Weil alles auff den beschiß ist gericht/
Vortheil in Elen Maß gewicht/
Vnd wer besser kan besser thuet/
Damit sich vermehre daß guet/
Per fas vel nefas gilt als gleich/
Dann jetzt der brauch wer nur ist reich/
Der wirt gar werth vnd thewr gehalten/
Von Reichen Armen jung vnd alten/
Vnnd alles was er thuet vnd sagt/
In allen gefalt vnd wol behagt/
Tuet sich auch fleissig zu jhm fiegen/
Dieweil sie sein geniessen migen/
Wans aber kombt zur bössen zeit/
So steht er allein in dem laid/
Zu schönen Heüsern mit groß sommen/
Alzeit vil tauben gflogen kommen/
Einem alten Hauß zerreissen dach/
Dem fliegen nicht vil tawben noch/
Im leren then frisch gworffen auff/
Find man selten ein Ameyß hauff/
Kein Freind sich bey dir finden last/
Wann du dein guet verlohren hast/
Die Sonn geht auff mit grossem pracht/
Mit jhrem glantz vil schatten macht/
Baldt sich ein wolck legt vber zwer/
So sicht man auch kein schatten mehr/
So thun die leut weil sie daß liecht/
Deß glicks beim Freünden scheinen sich/
So bestehens/ wan daß liecht verlescht/
Ein tropff Wasser all lieb abwescht/
Vnd der mit Freind war vor vmb ringt/
Vmb den sich jetzt keiner mehr tringt/
Solches betracht jeder vor sich/
Vnnd setzt sein Seel ehe in den stich/
Als daß er sich in Armut geb/
Vnnd gantz verachtlich darin leb/
Dem Teuffel gefelt die sach recht/
Vnnd frewet sich der getrewen/ Knecht
Jhn dauert kein mühe Tag vnd nacht/
Dardurch er sein Reich grösser macht/
Geht wie ein prülendt Läw herumb/
Sicht fleissig wo er ein bekum/
Darumb solt sich Arm vnd Reich/
Nicht also lohn betriegen gleich/
Den Geitz der daß zeitlich vermehrt/
Darneben daß Ewig verzehrt/
Hin laufft die zeit/ her kombt der Todt
Der alles jrdisch macht zu kodt/
Dem strengen vnd letsten gericht/
Mag auch kein Mensch entrennen nicht/
Ein jeder diß halt wol zu rath/
Damit die Rew nicht kom zuspat/

PLATE XVIII. When the Needy and the Greedy Meet, the Devil Is the Middleman

This illustration is inspired by a German proverb, which teaches that the interaction of needy and greedy people is fertile ground for the activities of the devil. In front of a leafless tree a barefoot beggar with folded hands kneels before a well-dressed young man, who casts a condescending glance at the shabbily dressed beggar (who desires to be wealthy himself). Hovering above the two is the devil, who has placed his right hand on the head of the greedy young man.

A proverb says that when the needy
And the greedy by some chance
Do business, not much is lacking
For the devil, too, to play the game,
Or be indeed the middleman.
For he knows that from the affair
He evermore will get his share,
Therefore he eggs both partners on,
So that neither to the other cedes:
He makes the greedy man so sharp-set
That for the poor man's penury
He feels not the slightest sympathy,
Unless from it he gets fourfold use
Gone straight into his moneybag,
Eight percent interest will not suffice.
And one must lay out the capital,
And a bribe on top as lubrication,
And a security, to please him well,
So that, when the other's become a rogue,
From him this thief endures no loss,
Who after all with his usury*
Has reduced to ruin, head to foot,
The common man, who honestly
Could have fed himself a longer while,
If he'd not fallen into the hands
Of such a niggard (and roast meat for hell).

* *Welcher doch mit dem Juden spieß.* See note at bottom right on page 61.

Who gnaws, just like a worm,
With greed, deception, tricks, and guile,
He drives his neighbor from what he owns
Into misery on the beggar's staff,
And strips the poor man so of worth
That a stone to pity would be moved.
Don't you think that, from among such ravens,
The devil will carry off his share?
On the other hand, there does exist
Many a clever mother's child
Who, when it reads the rich man's mind
And knows that all hope of help is gone,
By which the rich with impunity
Might do right by the poor man in his need,
Then surely he will ponder ways
At last to scour the rich man's bag,
For though the niggard in his place
Like Argus might have a hundred eyes,
This fellow, with so many a scheme
And roguery, will every day
Be in full swing, at money aimed,
Of course, he'll not escape unharmed,
Lying and cheating are everywhere,
Bad bargains, good words put on display,
Soul and body many a man will pawn
If only his project does not fail,
He offers his neighbor a sale that's faked,
Then hell opens its maw up wide.
Will you then with intent be blind,

You greedy toad, who rages through
The earth, who with intent misleads
The artisan into deceit,
That otherwise his daily bread
Must earn with misery and need.
For with the greed-devil everything
Must at sham alone be aimed,
Now nothing lasts as in the past:
"Indeed, if it holds just long enough
For it to get outside my ken,
And does not grow too old, I'm clear."
How then may one ask any more
For honesty, skill, frankness, and honor,
Since all at dupery is aimed,
Advantage measured by the yard,
Who can do it better, does it better too.
So that his fortune will increase,
*Per fas et nefas,** it's all the same,
For now it's custom that only he
Who's rich is considered worthy and dear,
By rich and poor, by young and old,
And everything he does and says
Pleases them all and suits them well,
They busily join his company,
Wanting the while to enjoy his favor.
But when it comes to evil times,
He'll stand alone in his misery.
To handsome homes 'midst much fluttering,
Many doves will always come aflying,
To an old house and its broken roof,
Not many cock-doves will ever fly.
In empty barn floors, fresh shoveled out,
A tribe of ants one seldom finds,

* "By right and wrong."

No friend will ever be found with you
When you have lost your solvency.
The sun comes up with splendor great,
And with its shine much shadow makes,
As soon as a cloud appears or two,
One no more for the shadow begs,
Thus people act when they behold
Fortune's light aglitter on their friends,
And so they behave when the light goes out:
A water drop washed all love away,
And he who once was by friends surrounded,
Around him now no friends are crowded.
Now each may judge it for himself,
If he'd rather leave his soul in the lurch
Than enter into poverty.
And quite despised therein abide.
This thing will please the devil well,
In his faithful servants he takes much joy,
He spares no effort, night and day,
By which he makes his realm increase,
He roams like a raging lion about,*
Seeking zealously to catch some prey.
Thus neither poor nor rich should let
Themselves by avarice be tricked,
Which makes what's temporal increase
But meanwhile devours what is eternal.
Time flees away and death will come,
Which turns all earthly things to dung.
From that stern and final judgment day
No human being flees away.
Let all men bear this well in mind,
Lest repentance lag too far behind.

* See 1 Pet. 5:8. See also the prayer to St. Michael the Archangel at the end of the Tridentine Mass: "And do thou, O prince of the heavenly host, by divine power thrust into Hell Satan and the other evil spirits who go about in the world seeking the ruin of souls."

Traurige Klage der Armen/ wegen der vberauß grossen Thewrung vnd betrübten Zeit.

ACh Gott das ist jetzt zu erbarmen/
Der Reiche frist das Flaisch der Armen/
Sauget jm auß marck/ schweiß vnd blut/
Zuerhalten sein grosses Gut/
Sanctus Paulus hat wol bedacht/
Weil wir nichts auff die Welt bracht/
Werden wider nichts nemmen mit/
Auß diser Welt das geringste nit/
Sollen vns darumb gnügen lan/
Wenn wir das täglich Brot nur han/
Denn wer gern reich werden will/
Felt in strick vnd anfechtung vil/
In vil thöricht schädliche lüst/
Die der Menschen verderben ist/
Denn sie werden versenckt in grund/
In Sünd vnd Schand zu aller stund/
Dann der Geitz eine Wurtzel ist/
Der manchen Mann mit arger list/
Vom Glauben in den jrrweg führt/
Wie man an vilen Leüten spürt/
Vnd bleibt doch war wie man da singt/
Obs manchem nicht in Ohren klingt/
Es ist kein Brüderliche lieb/
Die gantze Welt ist voller Dieb/
Es ist kein Trew noch Glaube mehr/
Betriegen/ Liegen ist ein ehr/
Ein jederman jetzunder vbet/
Was jhm in seinem Hertzen geliebet/
Wie wirdt aber ein solcher bestehn/
Wenn er vor Gottes Gericht soll gehn/
Klärlich wirdt hie gezeiget an/
Wie es jetzt treibet jederman/
Damit das nur der Arm allein/
Mit seinem Weib vnd Kindern klein/
Muß leyden Hunger/ Durst vnd Noth/
Hat er gleich Gelt/ kein Bier noch Brot/
Kan er darvor bekommen nicht/
Weil es an kleinem Gelt gebricht/

Denn die gantzen Schreckenberger/
Die Thewrung machen so vil ärger/
Weil gantze Groschen vnd Pfenning/
Gefunden werden so gar wenig/
Obs mancher hat/ jhm nicht gefelt/
Das er drauff wider geb klein Gelt/
Lest jhn ehe vngekaufft gahn/
Wann er nicht will vor alles han/
Der Reich der nun Reichsthaler hat/
Der kan alles mit guttem rath/
Kauffen/ vnd ist jhm nichts zu thewer/
Weil jhm das alte Gelt gut stewer/
Von Tag zu Tag in Kasten bracht/
Drumb wann er seine rechnung macht/
Vnd halt es gegen dem alten werth/
Die Thewrung jhn gar nicht beschwert/
Dann er hat in sehr vil Jahren/
Nicht wolfeyler kaufft die Wahren/
Dargegen dann dem Handwercksmann/
Alls fünff mal thewer kommet an/
Denn ob er noch so vil erwirbt/
Bey seinem Handwerck doch verdirbt/
Weil jederman wie man denn spürt/
Mit schlechtem Gelt bezahlet wirdt/
So man aber als nach altem werth/
Bezahlete/ wurdt niemandt gferdt/
Würde auch die Thewrung nicht gespürt/
Die jetzt das leidig Gelt einführt/
Ein jeder thut das seinig sparen/
Getraid/ Güter vnd andere Wahren/
Wills vor solch Gelt verkauffen nicht/
Daher alles/ wie ich bericht/
Hinterhalten wirdt/ vnuerkaufft bleibt/
Keiner mehr gern Handlung treibt/
Sondern sicht/ wie er mit muth/
Den Armen schinden vnd schaben thut/
Das er in diser Thewren zeit/
Groß Armuth vnd auch Elend leid.

Mit seinem Weib vnd seinem Kind/
Vnd auch alle sein Haußgesind/
Der Reich kaufft alls ohn alles ziel/
Weil er hat altes Geltes viel/
Vnterstehet sich auch auffs new/
Vnterzutrucken ohn alle schew/
Den Armen/ welcher sehr betrengt/
Zu Gott rufft/ das er hülffe brengt/
Er rufft biß er endtlich gewehrt/
Was er von jhm habe begert/
Hoff in dem will ich gar nicht jrren/
Will keinem schmeichlen noch hofieren/
Vil weniger krawen ober schmieren/
Die Warheit darff man so nicht zieren/
Wie denn die gmein Practick zmal/
Sich mercken lesset vberal/
Vnd wer dauon vil zusagn/
Aber es darff es niemandt wagn/
Dieweil der alten warheit Geigen/
Die Seiten gsprungen/ muß sie schweigen/
Dems auch wol thut im Hertzen weh/
Sicut vult mittere vadere.
Wirdt auch darauß kein anders nicht/
Sicut vult vadere vadit,
Darumb soll kein Christ erschrecken/
Gott wirdt als mit der zeit entdecken/
Denns kompt ein Tag der ist gewiß/
Deß sollen wir warten ohn verdrieß/
Da kommen wir denn all zu hauff/
Vnd höret alles Ellendt auff/
Da wirdt denn recht noch bleiben recht/
Es verdrieß Herrn oder Knecht/
Denn wer da hie veracht muß sein/
Der lieb nur in dem Hertzen sein/
Warheit die Edle Tugendt schon/
Die Gott blohnet inns Himmels Thron.

Getruckt im Jahr/ *M. DC. XXII.*

Zu Augspurg/ bey Christoph Greutter/ Kupfferstecher/ wonhafft bey Barfusser Thor auff dem Graben.

PLATE XIX. Melancholy Lament of the Poor concerning the Exceedingly Great Inflation and the Afflicted Time

In a desolate landscape in which trees are only stumps and a home stands in disrepair, a poor man dressed in rags is trying to escape from the clutches of a well-dressed man, behind whom is the money he has accumulated. The poor man is trying to reach his wife—similarly poorly dressed—who sits on a box and cradles a young child as an older one flees to her for protection. Observing all of this helplessly from the side is an elderly man, also poorly dressed. Although the rich man is taking advantage of the poor man, he himself is in grave danger, for a monstrous beast on his back holds his head in his jaws and grasps his shoulders with his front paws. The rich man's demise is to be seen in the hellish head at the far right. Roasting in the flames in its gaping mouth are those who have been damned, and in the smoke spewing from the top of the head are the "souls" of these people—devils and beasts.

Oh God, things now are in piteous state,
The rich man devours the poor man's flesh,
Sucks out his marrow, sweat, and blood,
To keep his own excessive fortune.
Saint Paul has reflected well:
Since we bring naught with us to the world,*
We'll take naught with us when we leave,
From this world not the slightest thing,
Therefore we should be satisfied
If we but have our daily bread,†
For he who wishes to grow rich
Falls prey to many lures and snares,
To many foolishly hurtful lusts,
Which are humanity's ruination,‡
For men are plunged down utterly
In sin and shame at every hour,
Since love of money is a root§
Which many a man, with cruel deceit,
Will lead astray from his belief,
As we in many a man perceive,
A song that's true and often sung,
Though it does not ring in many ears.

* See 1 Tim. 6:7.

† See 1 Tim. 6:8.

‡ See 1 Tim. 6:9.

§ See 1 Tim. 6:10.

Brotherly love does not exist,
The world entire is full of thieves,
Constancy and faith exist no more,
Deceit and lying are an honor,
Presently every man commits
What gives him pleasure in his heart.
However, how will such folk pass
When they go before the court of God?
It's shown here, in all clarity
How everyone does now behave,
So that the poor man, he alone,
With wife and band of children small
Must suffer hunger, thirst, and need.
Though he has money, he cannot
Buy bread or wine with what he's got,
Since there's a lack of little coins,
For the whole tribe of Schreckenbergers*
Makes the inflation all the worse,
For whole Groschens and Pfennigs
Are very seldom to be found.
Though many have them, they don't want
To pay out small coins in return,
But let the buyer go unserved
If he will not take everything.
The rich man, having Reichsthalers now,

* See note on page 37.

Can purchase all with peace of mind,
And nothing costs too much for him,
Since the old money has brought good profit,
From day to day, into his chest,
Therefore, when doing his accounts,
He compares the worth it had before,
The inflation bothers him not at all;
For he, in the course of many years,
Has not looked for cheaper goods to buy,
On the other hand, the artisan
Finds everything five times the dearer,
For no matter how much he may earn,
He does but poorly in his craft,
Since everyone, as now one sees,
Is paid with miserable coin.
However when in value old,
The payment came, there was no peril,
And the inflation would not be felt.
Of those who float this wretched coin
Each one now saves what he possesses,
His grain, his goods, and other wares,
And will not sell them for such coin.
Thus everything, as I report,
Is held back and remains unsold.
No longer do they practice trade,
But rather look for ways that they
The poor man may boldly fleece and flay,
So that he, in this inflation's time,
Must suffer great poverty and need,
Together with his wife and child,
And all the members of his house.
The rich man buys all, without all aim,
Since he's got old money in plenitude,
And also makes so bold, anew,
All unashamed, to batter down
The poor man, who, so much beset,
Cries out to God to send him aid.
He cries until at last he's given
What he from Him may have desired.
In this I hope I do not err,
I'll flatter no one, nor will fawn,
Still less use ointment or massage.
One may not so adorn the truth
As to how this common trickery
Can be detected everywhere,
And much more could be said about it,
But no one dares to speak it out,
Since on the fiddle of ancient truth,
The strings are snapped, it must be mute,
Though one indeed feels heart's dismay:
*Sicut vult mittere vadere,**
And nothing else will come of it,
Sicut vult vadere vadit,†
Therefore no Christian shall know fear,
God will reveal all in good time,
For a day will come, so much is sure,
Which we'll await without dismay,
When we'll foregather, all at once,
And all the misery will end.
For what is right will right remain,
Though master or man may be dismayed,
For him who here must be despised,
Let him within his heart desire,
That noble virtue, truth, alone,
Which God rewards at heaven's throne.

Printed in the Year MDCXXII.
Augsburg, at the Shop of Christopher
Greutter, Engraver, near Barfüsser Gate
next to the Moat.

* Professor Vassily Rudich proposes that the ligature at the end of *vadere* indicates a *t*; thus, *vaderet:* "Even as he wishes to send, he would go."

† A translation of this line is, "Even as he wishes to go, he goes." The source of these two Latin lines cannot be determined; the sense seems to be that nothing can be changed. They may suggest the words of the centurion to Jesus at Capernaum (Matt. 8:9).

Der Jüdische Kipper vnd Auffwechßler.

ALso geht es zu in der Welt/
Ein jeder strebt nach Gut vnd Gelt/
Schinden vnd schaben ist ein Kunst/
Wers wol kan/der erlanget Gunst/
Das alte Weib Betriegerey/
Ist jetzt wider geboren new.
Caligula viel hinder sich
Gelt-Würmer gelassen/spür ich.
Nero schon längst ist auffgeflogn/
Welcher viel Leut sonst hat betrogn:
Dannoch sind seiner Folger viel
Gebliebn/welche treiben das Spiel.
Dieser erdenckt new faction,
Davon er habe grossen Lohn.
Ein andr räyset in ferrne Land/
Kompt bald wider mit reicher Hand.
Die KauffLeute wissen gar ebn/
Dem Kauffer süsse wort zu gebn/
Damit sie gar nach jhrem Willn/
Die lären Seckel können fülln.
Bald kompt einer auffgezogen/
Bringt herfür welchs gar erlogen/
Leidet er noht/vnd hat kein Gelt/
Zum Narren er sich gar verstellt.
Singer/Springer/Gauckler übral/
Findet man jetzt in grosser Zahl.
Vmbs Gelt durch viel vnnütze Thand/
Werden betrogen Leut vnd Land:
Vnter diesen thut man spüren/
Wie jetzund das Fähnlein führen/
Die Kipper vnd Auffwechßler sein/
Ihr Orden ist groß vnd gemein:
Es ist kein Stadt/es ist kein Land/
Da man nicht mercket jhre Hand/
Kippern vnd wechseln Tag vnd Nacht/
Sie habens schon dahin gebracht/
Daß gute Müntz ist weggeführt/
Dafür man jetzt nur Kupffer spürt.
Ihr kippen bringt in grosse Noht
Viel Leut/darzu in Hohn vnd Spot.
Ihr kippen Nahrung auffhebt gar/
Wie jederman ist offenbar.
Ihr kippen Gott im Himmel hoch
Erzürnt/viel wenger gefällt noch:
Die lieben Engel auch nit bleibn/
Wo man solch Handthirung thut treibn/
Sondern gar bald an alln Enden/
Thun sie sich von jhnen wenden.
Justitia mit jhrer Wag/
Führt über sie gar grosse Klag/
Weil sie nicht achten/wie bekandt:
Thu recht/förchte Gott/schew niemand.
Fraw Avaritia mit Macht/
Hat sie bald in jhr Netz gebracht/
Diesem Weib/nach jhrem begehr/
Folgen sie nach ohne beschwer.
Aber was man erworben hat/
Mit jhr fleugt hin/vnd nimbt bald ab:
Alles endtlich den Krebsgang geht/
Ist nichts gewiß bey jhr/vnd steht
In Schand vnd Laster mit gewalt
Bringt all/die jhr nachfolgen bald/
Erzeiget sich erst lieb vnd fein/
Gleich wie ein schönes Jungfräwlein/
Hernach sticht sie nach Schlangen Art/
Groß Schmertzen vnd Pein sie gebärt/
Führt zum Verderben vnd groß Noht/
Ins höllisch Fewr vnd ewigen Todt.
Drumb ist mein raht sih dich jetzt für/
Laß kippen fahren weit von dir/
Ernehr dich redlich bleib im Land/
Deß hast du Ehr vnd keine Schand/
Sonsten dir wie deinem Geselln
Dem Müntzer/bald werden nachstelln/
Schand/Spot/Jamer/schmertzen/Elend
Allhie/vnd künfftig ohne End.

ENDE.

PLATE XX. The Jewish Clipper and Profiteer

At the center a Jewish money-clipper—on whose clothes are written "Skinning and swindling are the best thing about me"—faces a crucial decision about how to lead his life. With a rope tied around each arm he is being tugged to his right by Lady Justice and to his left by Lady Avarice, both of whom exhort him, "Follow me." Lady Justice—above whom is written "I lead to the good"—holds in her right hand the scales of justice, which are inscribed with the essence of moral living: "Do right, fear God, and dread no one." She stands firmly upon a raised stone slab labeled "Righteousness." This stone rests in turn upon a larger base, on which is written, "This virtue contains all other virtues." Three Doric columns on the base bear inscriptions about the proper way to lead one's life: "Live honorably, insult no one, and leave to each one his own." Despite all of this advice, the enticements of Lady Avarice are stronger, and the money-clipper, standing on the back of a crayfish—under which is written "It's all going in reverse"—is drawn to her as the crayfish creeps backwards. Lady Avarice holds her young child Usury by the arm and says encouragingly to the money-clipper, "I bring riches." She is, however, wearing a belt of snakes and standing on a skull, a symbol of the vanity of earthly goods. The skull rests on a devil lying on the inscription "Greed leads to ruin" and grasping toward the money-clipper's coat. Behind them an emaciated dog chews on a sausage, but to no avail: "I devour and never grow full." The broken moneybag—from which coins are dropping and next to which is written "What becomes of it"—underscores the money-clipper's misplaced desire for wealth. (In contrast, in his hand on the side of Lady Justice he holds a coin encircled by the inscription "Things honestly contracted endure.") The money-clipper's desire for ill-gotten wealth is not only temporally foolish; it also leads to his eternal damnation. Two angels in the sky flee from him, saying, "We wish to turn away from him." An arrow from above points directly at the money-clipper's head, and the words written there leave no doubt about the man's fate: "God sees and punishes it."

This is what happens in the world:
Each person strives for goods and gold,
Skinning and swindling are an art,
He who can master it, wins favor.
Fraudulence, the ancient crone,
Is presently reborn, like new.
Caligula has left behind*
Many money-worms, I do believe,
Nero long since has exploded,*
Who formerly many a man defrauded,
Nonetheless, many of his band
Are left, to carry on his game.
The one invents new double-deals,
By which he great rewards does reap,
Another travels in distant lands
And so returns with wealth in hand.
The merchants are aware, full well,
Of how to cozen their customers,
So that they, indeed, just as they please,
Can fill their empty moneybags.
Soon someone will come along

* Suetonius devotes several chapters (*De vita Caesarum, Caligula* XXXVIII–XLIII) to the emperor's avarice. By "Geld-Würmer" (money-worms), the author of the broadsheet may mean either the cause of Caligula's death or imitators of his behavior. In fact, Caligula was assassinated by a tribune of the Praetorian Guard. However, Herod Agrippa I (who had the apostle James the Greater put to the sword and imprisoned Peter) was—in the murky account of Acts 12—smitten by an angel of the Lord and "eaten of worms and gave up the ghost." According to hostile reports, a similar fate befell other despots: the dictator Sulla and King Philip II of Spain are said to have been eaten by fleas, i.e., they suffered from phthiriasis or morbus pediculosus.

* Although lightning, thunder, and an earthquake preceded Nero's death (Suetonius, *Nero*, XXXVIII), he committed suicide, aided by Epaphroditus, his private secretary.

And tell what's clearly a barefaced lie,
That he suffers need and has no money,
Indeed pretends to be a fool.
Singers, acrobats, mountebanks everywhere
In mighty numbers one now finds,
People and countries alike are done
Out of their money for useless trash.
Among such tricksters one detects
That those who presently lead the van
Are money-clippers and profiteers.
Their order is spread out far and wide.
There is no town, there is no land
Where one does not detect their hand,
They clip and change both night and day,
They've already brought matters to the point
That valid coinage is swept away,
And for it now copper alone is found.
Their clipping to great penury
Brings many, to shame and mockery,
Their clipping, as everyone can see,
Puts an end to our very economy.
Their clipping angers God on high,
Much less does it afford Him joy,
The angels dear will not remain
Where such manipulations pertain,
But rather they soon turn away
From those that do them, everywhere.
Lady Justice with her pair of scales
Brings charges against them, loud and long,
Since they pay no heed, as is well-known,
To the rule: Do right, fear God, dread none.
Lady Avarice with all her might
Has swiftly caught them in her net,
This woman, in their lubricity,
They follow voluntarily,
But whatever they from her have gained
Flies off with her and soon grows less.
At last all things go crab-wise.*
Nothing is safe with her and lands
Perforce in shame and ruin, to which
She soon brings all who follow her.
At first she seems quite fine and dear,
Quite like a little maiden fair,
But then she bites, in serpent's wise,
Gives birth to agony and pain,
And leads to ruin and great despair,
To hell's fire and eternal death.
Thus my council is: take care,
And far from you let clipping fare,
Support yourself honestly, stay at home,†
And you'll have honor and no shame.
Otherwise, you and your comrade too,
The coiner, soon will be pursued
By shame, scorn, woe, pain, misery
Here and in future, eternally.

THE END.

* *Alles endtlich den Krebsgang geht.* To walk like a crab, or crayfish, is to go backwards.

† See Ps. 37:3.

Christliche Trewhertzige Warnung

An die Gotts- vnd Gwissenlose Geltwucherer: daß Sie doch jhrer Seelen Ewig Seeligkeit besser in acht nemmen wöllen/ rc.

Kom̃ her du Verdambte Rippers Rott/
Die du achtest weder Schand noch Spott/
Du abgöttisch Gottsvergeßne Burscht/
Mit deim vnersettlichen Geldurst.
Weil grosse Herrn dein Handtwerck treiben/
Meinstu wöllest vngestrafft bleiben/
Kom̃ Jch will dir erzehlen wol/
Was endlich dein Lohn werden soll/
Dieweil du hast dein Nächsten betrogen/
Jhm gut Gelt außm Seckl gelogen/
Dem Armen das seinig abgestohlen/
Das sag ich frey gantz vnuerholen/
Dardurch groß Theyrung bracht ins Land/
Welche Jetzundt gar nimbt vberhand/
Ja deß vil Hundert Tausendt Seelen/
Sich Martern müssn ängsten vnd quelen/
Nicht anderst wie die Schlangen stechen/
Wann sie sich im Zorn wollen rechen:

Also du dein Nechsten gstochen hast/
Dardurch er kom̃en in Angst vnd Last/
So solln dich die Höllische Schlangen/
Verfolgen beissen vnd betrangen/
Fährstu noch fort du Teuffelsbrut?
Denckstu nicht an die Höllisch glut/
Wie wirdt es dir einmal ergehn/
Wann du vor Gottesgricht solt stehn/
Weh alßdann deiner Armen Seelen/
Daß Gelt wirdt dich Martern vnd queln:
Ey wirdt dich alßdann frewen dein gut/
Welchs war der Armẽ Schweiß vnd Blut
Das jetzundt starck vbersich schreit/
Biß es Gott fordern wirdt zur Zeit/
Thu Büß vnd steh daruon bald ab/
Mit ehrn vermehr dein Gut vnd Hab:
Wa nit so bleib in Gotts Namen Arm/
Bessr: als zum Teüffel also warm:

Dann was kan der Mensch doch geben/
Zu retten sein Seel vnd Ewigs Leben/
Vnd wann er gleich die gantz Welt gwon/
Wann es heißt einmal auff vnd daruon/
Was wirdt es dich dann helffen könden/
Ey soll ein das schnöd Gelt so blenden/
Hastu Jemandt vnrecht gethon/
So gib jhm darfür zwifach lohn/
Hastu gsündiget mit Zacheo/
Sthe auff mit Jhm/ vnd Mattheo.
Wolan es ist dir gsagt was gut/
Selig ist der Mensch so darnach thut:
Wilt du mir aber volgen nicht/
Erschrickst nicht vor Gottes Gericht:
So fahr ins Teuffels Namen hin/
Schwefel vnd Bech wirdt sein dein gwin/
Du seyest groß Hanß oder klein/
Dem Beelzebub gilt alles gemein.

Getruckt im Jahr/ 1622.

PLATE XXI. Sincere Christian Admonition to the Godless and Conscienceless Usurers, That They Nonetheless May Pay Better Heed to the Eternal Salvation of Their Souls, etc.

Three scenes printed from four different woodblocks depict the activity of money changing and its consequences. At the far left a shabbily attired peasant approaches a moneychanger's shop. Inside the shop the moneychanger sits on a high-backed chair. On either side of the table in front of him stand two finely dressed men, one of whom has placed coins on the table. On the shelf along the back wall is a collection of decorative metalware such as goblets, candlesticks, and small bowls. On the floor are two large money chests, which are open to receive coins. In the room on the right sacks filled with money line the back wall, while a scribe carefully enters the amounts in a ledger. Overseeing all of this activity is Beelzebub, who sits enthroned with sacks of money at his feet.

Come hither, you damned clippers' band,
Who care naught for mockery or shame,
You idolatrous, godforsaken tribe,
With your insatiable money-thirst.
Since mighty lords perform your craft,
Do you think that you'd get off scot-free?
Come, and I'll recount for you
What finally your reward will be,
Since you've deceived your fellow man,
Lied good money out of his purse,
And stolen what the poor man has
(I say it freely, quite unconcealed),
Brought great inflation into the land,
Which presently gets the upper hand,
Indeed made many hundred thousand souls
Suffer tortures, torments, anxieties,
No different from those that serpents cause
When they in wrath will take revenge:
Thus you have stung your fellow man,
So that he's made prey to dismay and fear.
Hell's serpents will the selfsame way
Pursue you, bite you, and beset you.
Will you keep on, you devil's spawn?
Do you not remember the fires of hell,
And how you one fine day will fare,
When you stand before God's judgment seat?
Then woe betide your wretched soul,
Money itself will pain and torment you.
Oh, will you then enjoy your gain,
Which was the poor man's flesh and blood,
And presently cries out aloud,
Till God demands it in good time?
Atone, forego it even now,
Increase your ownings honorably.
It's better than warming with the devil:
For what can a man give, after all,
To save his soul and life eternal,
Even though he's won the world entire,*
When one day the order is up and away,
How then will it be of help to you?
Oh, that base money blinds people so!
If you have cheated anyone,
Then pay him back for that twofold;
If you have sinned in Zacchaeus' way,†
With him and Matthew now arise.‡
Well then, you've been told what's good to do.
Blessed the man who thus behaves,

* See Mark 8:36.

† See Luke 19:2 and 8.

‡ See Matt. 9:9.

But if you will not follow me
And do not fear God's judgment seat,
Then keep on in the devil's name.
Brimstone and pitch will be your gain,
Be you a bigwig or a scrub.
It's all the same to Beelzebub.

Printed in the Year 1622.

Eigentliche andeutung Menschlicher liebe gegen dem Geld / Sampt dessen Nutz vnd Schaden.

AVARITIA EST RADIX OMNIVM MALORVM.

Ephes. 5.

Ein jeder Christ betracht das wol/
Das der Geitz aller vntrew vol.
Seye nichts dann Abgötterey/
Wie Paulus daruon meldet frey.

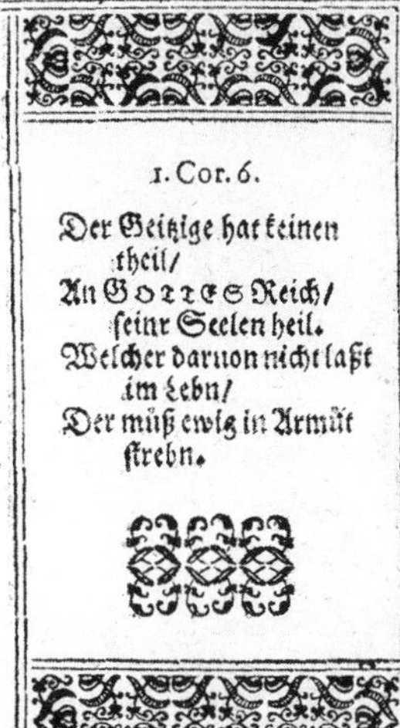

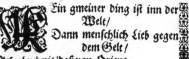

1. Cor. 6.

Der Geitzige hat keinen theil/
An GOTTES Reich/ seinr Seelen heil.
Welcher daruon nicht laßt im Lebn/
Der müß ewig in Armüt strebn.

Kein gmeiner ding ist inn der Welt/
Dann menschlich Lieb gegen dem Gelt/
Ich glaub nit/ daß von Orient
Ein Volck leb biß in Occident/
Welches nicht hertzlich das Gelt lieb/
Vnd es zuerwerben sich üb/
Gelt gliebt den Juden vnd auch Heiden/
Die Christen mögens auch wol leiden/
Wann sie haben deß Geldes gunst/
Dann man gibt keinem vil vmbsunst/
Wann er nit Gelt hat bey der Hand/
In keinem Flecken/ Statt noch Land/
Hört man niemal das Gelt vertreiben/
In aller Welt hat es zubleiben/
Das Gelt lieben die grosse Herren/
Gelt gliebt/ vnd helt es hoch in ehren
Der kauffmañ/ Handwercksmañ vñ baur
Laßts jhm darumb offt werden sawr/
In dem Ehstand/ Mann vnd auch frawen
Vil auff deß Geltes Lieb thun bawen/
Das Gelt gliebt beydes Mägd vñ Knecht/
Kein Stand ich nit erdencken möcht/
Der nit hett liebe zu dem Gelt/
Ob ich gleich vil laß vngemeldt/
Gelt gliebt so gar dem kleinen Kind/
Ja wann gleich einer ist stockblind/
Dannoch ers Gelt in ehren helt/
Vnd sein liebe zu jhm gesellt/
Amor, Amor, O liebes Gelt/
Ist ein gmein Gsang in aller welt/
Dem Gelt gibt menigklich das lob/
Das Gelt in mancher gfahr schwebt ob/
Wann ich Gelt hett/ o hett ich Gelt/
Wird bey den Leüten offt gemelt/
Vnd ist auch solliches nicht ohn/
Ob man sich wol thüt vnderstohn/
Zu erlangen deß Geldes huld/
Dañ mit Geld kan mancher ein schuld
Richten/ die jn noch lang thet plagn/
Wol gar von Weib vnd Kindern jagn/
Das Geld macht eim ein frölichn müt/
Gelt macht vil böse Händel güt/
Das Gelt macht offt ein ding wol richtig/
Das sonsten noch lang blib vntüchtig/
Das Gelt bringt manchem gunst vnd ehr/
Der sonst ein Schalck im Hertzen wär/
Das Gelt hilfft manchem ohn verdruß
Auß einer schweren gefängknuß/
Gelt hilfft manchem auß not vnd gfahr/
Durchs Gelt wirt manch ding offenbar/
Das sunst noch lang zeit blib verschwign/
Wol ewig müst verborgen lign.
Gelt ist also ein kostlich Werth/
Als man kaum finden mag auff Erdt/
Vmbs Gelt findet man einzukauffn/
Darum̃ man sonst noch weit müßt lauffn/
Was not ist zu menschlichem Lebn/
Thüt man vmbs Gelt zukauffen gebn/
Essen/ Trincken/ Kleyder/ Wohnung/
Vnd was zur jeden Handthierung
Man braucht/ ist alles zubekummen/
Vmb das lieb Gelt/ vnd ist in summen
Am Gelt alles allein gelegen/
Drauff thüt sich mancher gar erwegen.
Doch daß jhr vil in diser Welt
Rechtmässig lieb haben das Gelt/
Zeitlicher Armüt zu entladen/
Vnd dort an jhrer Seel nicht schaden/
Darzu sag ich/ O nein/ nein/ nein/
Weil dasselbig je nicht will sein/
Dann mancher liebt es zu vnmässig/
Zu grossem geitz vnablässig/
Biß daß er sein Seel gantz verderbt/
Vnd der Him̃lischen schätz enterbt/
Mannicher liebet es mit füg/ Eph. 5. v. 5.
Zu Finantz/ Wucher vnd Betrüg/
Darmit schind vnd preßt er den Armen/
Dessn wird sich Gott auch nicht erbarmen. Iac. 2. v. 13
Mancher deß Geldes Huld auch sucht/
Zu fressen/ sauffen/ gantz verrucht/
Biß Gott der speyß bauch (sampt der speyß 1. Cor. 6. v. 13.
Deß Bauchs) zerstöhret gleicher weiß/
Mannicher liebet es ohn schey/
Zur Vnzucht/ Schand vnd Büberey/
Vnd in solcher befleckung schwer/
Verfehlt deß heiligen Steigs er. Isa. 35. v. 8.
Mancher helt es in hohem acht/
Zu weltlichem Wollust vnd Pracht/
Zur vppigkeit/ stoltz vnd Hochmüt/
Biß jhn der Höchst ernidern thüt. Syr. 10. v. 16.
Ein jeder mag gut achtung haben/
Daß er Gottes Geschenck vnd Gaben
Nicht brauch jhm selbs zum widerspil/
Vnd dem Geld nicht vertraw zuvil/
Sondern mit Lob vnd Danckbarkeit/
Von dem/ der es jhm gibt/ die zeit
Annim̃/ vnd darvon theile mit/
Dem Dürfftigen/ der kompt vnd bitt/
So mag er hie zeitlich entgehn/
Der Armüt/ vnd dort wolbestehn/
Wers Geld also recht braucht allzeit/
Hinderts nicht an der Seligkeit/
Yb Lieb/ förcht Gott/ vnd halt sein wort/ Mich. 6. v. 8.
Das ist (hie zeitlich/ vnd auch dort)
Der beste Schatz/ vnd höchste Hort.

M. R.

Augspurg/ bey Mattheo Rembold/ Kunstführer. 1622.

PLATE XXII. Genuine Interpretation of Mankind's Love of Money, together with Its Usefulness and Harm

AVARITIA EST RADIX OMNIUM MALORUM.*

Situated in the open area between two towns is a circular covered temple. Resting on the altar is an overstuffed sack of money, from which individual coins are falling to the floor. A Jew, a Turk, and a Christian kneel on the steps at the base of the temple as they give homage to Mammon. To the left are four verses based on Ephesians 5:5:

Let every Christian ponder well
How greed is filled with faithlessness,
Is nothing but idolatry,
As Paul declares it openly.

To the right are four verses from 1 Corinthians 6:10:

The greedy man does not partake
Of God's kingdom and His spirit's weal.
Who does not give up greed in life
Must struggle in poverty eternally.

Nothing's more common in this world
Than the love of humankind for money.
I do not think a people lives
From Orient to Occident
Which does not love money ardently,
And practices ways of winning it.
Money's dear to Jews and heathens too,
And Christians gladly suffer it
When money's favor they possess,
For no one's given much for naught,
When he has no money close at hand.
In nary a village, town, or land
One never hears that money's expelled;
It persists throughout the world entire.
Money by mighty lords is loved,
Just as it's held in high esteem
By merchants, artisans, and peasants,
Who for its sake often let life sour.
In marriage, husbands and wives too
On money's love do much depend.
Servant girls and farmhands love it well.
No class might come into my mind
Which love for money never knew,
Though many will remain unnamed.
Why, little children hold money dear,
Yes, though someone be stone-blind,
He honors money in his mind,
And keeps it as dear company.
"*Amor, Amor,* oh money dear,"
Is a song spread through the world entire.
Many sorts of people give money praise;
Over many a peril money soars.
"If I had money, were money mine."
Is often repeated by everyone,
And such, too, fails not to occur,
Though one must daring be indeed
To win the favor money brings,

* See 1 Tim. 6:10.

For many a man with money can
Fix a debt that's been his constant plague,
Estranging him from wife and child.
Money gives people a happy heart;
Money often puts things in a proper way,
Which otherwise would improper stay.
To many a man, money brings honor and praise,
Who else in his heart would be a rogue.
Money aids many without dismay
To make an escape from durance vile.
Money helps many from peril and plight,
Through money many a thing's revealed
Which otherwise long would be kept concealed,
Indeed would stay hidden forevermore.
Thus, money has a precious worth
Whose like can scarce be found on earth,
For money one finds, for purchase ready,
What otherwise must be pursued afar.
Whatever's required for human life,
With money one can go and buy it:
Food, drink, clothing, and dwelling place.
And what for every operation
Is needed, is wholly to be had
For dear money, and so, at the end,
On money alone all things depend:
This many a man indeed has pondered.
Yet that there are many in this world
Who love money fittingly
For easing poverty on earth,
And in the next do their souls no harm.
To that I say: "Oh no, no, no,"
Since the same will never come to pass,
For many love it too excessively
To the point of greed, unceasingly,
Until they ruin their souls entire
And from heaven's treasure are disowned.*
Many men love it, and with good reason,
For deals, profiteering, and deceit,
By which they skin and oppress the poor.

* See Eph. 5:5.

To such God will extend no mercy.*
Many, too, seek out money's favor
For gorging and swilling quite heinously,
Till God the potbelly (and the food
That's in the belly) likewise destroys.†
Many love money unashamed
For lechery, lewdness, and rascality,
And in such terrible defilement they
Will miss the path of sanctity.‡
Many hold money in high regard
For worldly pleasure and display,
For luxury, arrogance, and pride,
Until the Highest casts them down.§
Let every man pay careful heed
That he does not, to his own harm,
Employ God's presents and His gifts,
Nor put in money excessive trust,
But rather, with thankfulness and praise,
Let him accept the time he's given
By Him who gives it; let him share
With the needy man who comes and pleads,**
So that he here, temporally, will escape
From poverty, and there fare well.
Who money rightly thus employs
Will find no bar to heaven's joys:
Be loving, fear God, and keep His word††
(Which here, temporally, and there too is heard),
The best of treasures, the highest hoard.

M. R.

Augsburg, at the Shop of Mattheus Rembold, Print Dealer. 1622.

* See James 2:13. For the purpose of his argument, the poet ignores the second part of the verse: "But mercy triumphs over judgment."

† See 1 Cor. 6:13.

‡ See Isa. 35:8.

§ See Eccles. 10:16.

** See the parable of the rich man and Lazarus, Luke 16:19–31, especially verses 22–23.

†† See Mic. 6:8.

Der Lachend vnd wainend Müntz Legat.

Verzaichnus der groben Müntzsorten/ wie die von Año 1609 biß 1623. ingemein gestigen vnd gfallen.

Von dem Auffsteigen vnd Abfahl/ Ist dises ein Memorial/ Darumb der Leser hobgehrt/ Woll in die Spacia vnbschreiben/ Selbst wo Er waist mehr zeichnē ein/ Wie dann drumb leer gelassen sein/

Es hat golten in dem Jar	Monat	Der Reichsthaler. fe: kr	Guldenthaler. fe: kr	Philipsthaler. fe: kr	Die Silbercronen. fe: kr	Silbern Groschen mit 72 fe: kr	Der Ducat oder Zeggin. fe: kr	Goldgulden. fe: kr	Die Spanische Duplonen fe: kr	Creitzducaten. fe: kr	Spanisch einfache cronen fe: kr	Französische einfach cronen fe: kr	Welsch einfach cronen fe: kr	Engellotten. fe: kr	Rosenobel. fe: kr	Schiffnobel fe: kr	Acht Real. fe: kr	Kö. Engl. Spil. fe: kr
1609.	Julio	1:24	1:14	1:30	1:36	1:24	2:15	1:40				2:—						1:30
1610.	Octobri	1:24	1:14	1:30	1:36	1:24	2:18	1:45		2:—								1:30
1611.		1:24	1:14	1:32		1:24	2:20	1:45							4:30			1:32
1612.	Novemb	1:24	1:15	1:32		1:24	2:20	1:45				2:—				4:—		1:32
1613.	Februa	1:24	1:16	1:32		1:24	2:20	1:45					2:—					1:32
	Septemb	1:26	1:16	1:33		1:26	2:20	1:45										1:33
1614.	August	1:28	1:16	1:34		1:30	2:20	1:45			2:10				5:—			1:34
1615.	Martio	1:28	1:16	1:34		1:30	2:20	1:45										1:34
	Novemb	1:30	1:20	1:34		1:34	2:30	1:52										1:40
1616.	Octobri	1:30	1:20	1:40		1:36	2:30	1:52		2:12		2:8						1:40
1617.	Maio	1:30	1:20	1:40		1:37	2:31	1:52										1:40
1618.	Maio	1:32	1:22	1:42		1:30	2:32	2:—		2:12		2:16						1:42
1619.	Octobri	1:48	1:36	1:58		1:54	2:48	2:10		2:28		2:30						1:58
1620.	Februa	2:4	1:50	2:15	2:15	2:8	3:4	2:18										2:15
	Junio	2:8	1:56	2:18	2:20	2:10	3:12	2:20	5:40	2:58	2:50	2:50	2:45	4:40	7:—	6:12		2:18
	Novemb	2:20	2:—	2:30	2:30	2:24	3:30	2:30	6:—	3:4	3:—	3:—		5:—	7:40	6:45	2:10	2:30
1621.	Januari	2:20	2:—	2:30	2:30		3:30	2:30	6:—									2:30
	Februa	2:24	2:6	2:36	2:36		3:36	2:36	6:30									2:36
	Martio	2:30	2:10	2:50	2:50		3:40	2:40	7:—									2:50
	Aprili	2:36	2:15	3:—	3:—		3:45	2:45	7:30									3:—
	Maio	2:48	2:24	3:—	3:8	2:42	4:30	3:—	8:—	4:10								3:—
	Junio	3:6	2:36	3:30	3:30		4:30	3:30	9:—									3:30
	Julio	3:15	2:52	3:32	4:—	3:20	5:—	3:40	10:—	4:40								3:32
	August	4:—	3:30	4:15	4:30		6:30	5:15	12:—									4:15
	Septemb	4:30	4:—	5:20	5:48		8:—	6:12	13:30									5:20
	Octobri	5:—	4:24	5:36	6:—		9:30	7:—	15:—									5:36
	Novemb	5:30	4:45	6:—	6:30		10:30	7:30	16:15									6:—
	Decemb	6:30	5:30	7:—	7:—		12:—	8:—	19:—									7:—
1622.	Januari	7:30	6:30	8:—	8:—		13:30	10:—	22:—									8:—
	Februa	10:—	8:30	11:30	12:—		16:—	12:—	28:—									11:30
	Martio	10:—	8:30	10:30	11:—	10:6	15:—	11:—	29:—	14:20								10:30
NB. Von disem Monat Martio an ists also verbliben biß auff den Ersten Octobris, da es vmb das halb theil abgewürdigt.																		
	Octobri	5:—	4:30	5:30	6:—		8:—	5:45	13:—	7:20	8:—							5:30
	Novemb	6:—	5:30	6:30	7:20		9:30	7:—	16:—		9:—							6:30
Nota Bey nachfolgendem Tax bleibts biß dato.																		
1623.	Junio	1:30	1:20	1:40	1:44	1:34	2:20	1:44	3:—	2:10	2:4	4:2	2:—	3:24	5:4	4:30		1:40
	Julio																	
	Augusti																	
	Septemb																	
	Octob																	
	Novemb																	
	Decemb																	

Apollo ward von seinē Räthen
Hochfleissig auff ein zeit gebettē.
Er wolte doch in alle Landen/
Ein Gsandschafft wegn der Müntz absanden.
Dieweil sie gstigen vber dmassen/
Auch wider tief herunder glassen.
An wem doch sey die schuld hierūn/
In Kauff/ Verkauff/ Verlust vnd Gwin.
Hierauff Apollo rufft zuhand/
Zween die er zu vns Teutschen sandt.
Den lachenden Democritum,
Vnd wainenden Heraclitum.
Als sie nun/ wie man zweyflet nicht/
Jr Gsandschafft hetten recht verricht:
Sie wider zum Apollo kehrten/
Vor deme vnd vor seinen Glerten
Relation ein jeder thet/
Democritus fieng an vnd redt:

DEMOCRITVS.

DEr Müntz vnd Thewrung halber gschicht/
Bey vilen Leuten anderst nicht.
Dann was sie selber verursacht/
Jhn selber schad vnd vnheil gmacht.
Vnd sollen sie darff ich wol sagen/
Jhr eigne Torheit drumb anklagen.
Dann als nun her bey etlich Jaren/
Jhr etlich so begirig warn.
Vnd wünschten daß zu lautter Gold/
Was sie anrüren/ werden solt.
Da haben sich solch Leuth gefunden/
Die auß Metall Gold machen kunden.
Die nachmals den betrug wol büesten/
Vnd auff Chymistisch sterben müesten.
Sie warden nemblich sublimiert,
Auff Alchymistisch cohibiert.
Das Corpus in den Lufft gebracht/
Vnd an dem Galgen fix gemacht.
Als man nun ist dahinden bliben/
Vnd mehr Außgab als Einnam̄ gschriben.
Da kam man von dem transmutiern,
Auff das spitzfindige legiern.
Das Silber lehrnet man addirn,
Vnd subtil künstlich subtrahirn.
Die Sorten ring multipliciern,
Den guten Thaler diuidiern.
Den man so lang vnd vil beschnitten/
Biß man zum Falliment geschritten.
Nach deme nun von Jahr zu jahr/
Die grobe Müntz gestigen war.
Vnd kleine Müntzen Bastartweiß/
Außgschloffen wie die kale Mäuß.
Habens die Kauff: vnd Handelsleut/
Gehalten noch in Heimbligkeit.
Daß an vil Herren Höfen gar/
Secretum Secretorum war.
Da ist mit wenig groben Sorten/
Vil Guet vnd Wahr erhandlet worden.
Vnd da sonst vor verschiner zeit,
Die Wein: die Fuhr: vnd Bawrsleut
Groß Beutelgschwulsten wolgespickt/
Von Marck't getragen wolgeleckt.
Ist bald ein anders worden drauß/
Sie truegen von dem Marck hinauß
Gar wenig stuck von groben Sorten/
Drauß aber seynd vil Gulden worden.
Mit denen ließ man fantasirn/
Jhr vngesaltznes tolles Hirn.
Deß jhn die Stattleut gnueg gelacht/
Auß Bawren einfalt spott gemacht.
Insonderheit gefiel jhn wol/
Daß man vmb ein Ducaten sol
Den besten Emer Wein einkauffen/
Da möcht ein guter Bruder sauffen.
Daß ein Schaf Korn ein Taler galt/
Ein gute Zech ein Batzen alt.
Da war ein gwaltigs jubiliern/
Wie man ein guten Mneth könn führn
Vmb einen Taler vnd nit mehr/
In Summa es gieng alles her
Gar wolfeil/ vnd nichts thewer war/
Dann nur der Taler: den man zwar
Muest lösen vmb der Gulden vil/
Ins zehendt oder zwölffte zil.
Doch konde man herwiderumb/
Deß Fleisch vil Pfundt auch haben drumb.
Vil Ayr/ deß Schmaltz wol 20. pfund/
Bey 20. Maß Wein man haben kund.
Als nun in solcher Gu'ten zeit/
Man mit dem Gelt kond glangen weit.
Wolt jederman die Gelter zaln/
Der mit dem Gelt war da einmaln.
Da kam die löblich Obrigkeit/
Vnd macht hierinn den vnderscheid.
Sie zog dem Geld die Laruen ab/
Der Bawersman entsetzt sich drab.
Vnd weil dann auch sein Edelman/
Wolt gutes Gelt von jhme han/
Thet er die Augen besser auff/
Gab im Verkauf mehr achtung drauff.
Gen Marckt was führen jhm nit gfelt/
Weil er dann hett noch zimblich Gelt/
Dorfft Gült nicht zahlen/ thete feyrn/
Bhielt er sein Traid in seiner Scheyern.
Obwol nun zlest so böse Sorten/
Durch Schwabenland verrathen worden.
Auff welches man in allen sachen/
Wolt guten Tax vnd Ordnung machen.
Wie man darn gute Anschläg gmacht/
Vnd zierliche Motiua bracht.
Gleichsamb als ob der Bawrsman/
Der Cortesia nach thet gan.
Als ob wer [illegible] Verstand zufinden/
Beym gmainen Mann vnd Bawrenkinden.
Warn doch die Bawrn dazumal/
Verwürrt sehr vnd bestürtzet all.
Von wegen der Dreybätzner böß/
So hetts Jahr sonst auch vil anstöß.
Vnd die Digesta warn eitel/
Man hielt vil mehr auff Kästen vnd Beutl.
Pandecta giengen an dem Rädl/
Die waren in der Bawren Städl.
Dann einmal nach dem Codice,
Der Bawrsman fragt Modicè.
Vnd liesse gleichwol die Juristen/
In den Decretis vmbher nisten.
Den Tax hielt er nur für ein spott/
Acht weder Oberkeit noch Gott.
Dieweil nun das Dominium,
War worden sogar Rusticum
Da braucht der Bawer kein Verstand/
Wolt vil grob Sorten auff die Hand.
Vnd weil das schlagen auff die Wahrn/
So hoch im steigen auffgefahrn
Wolt es der Bawr nit geben nach
Hielt jmmerdar starck auff sein sach
Drumb man sich lang nit kund vergleichen/
Man wolt lang nit herunder weichen.
Nun wil ich aber je noch gern/
Die langgewünschte Zeittung hören.
Wie man sich jetzt werd schicken drein/
Weil Taler, herab gstigen seyn.
Vnd sich demuetig han verkert/
In ein so leidenlichen werth.
Nun muß ich je zu disen sachen/
Nach meinem brauch von Hertzen lachen.
Daß in der Welt so jrrig steht/
Die gleichsamb in der Faßnacht geht.

HERACLITVS.

Als nun Heraclitus die Red/
Mit wainen angehöret het.
Wischt er die Zäher von dem Gsicht/
Vnd gantz mitleidig also spricht.

APollo du vil klarer Schein/
Deß allerschönsten Liechtes dein
Hett man fürwar noch nie so sehr/
Als eben jetzt bedörfft bißher.
Daß etlich dise Jar voran/
Jr vnhail möchten schawen an.
Dann ob gleichwol die Teutschen sind/
Deß Adlers Bruet vnd liebe Kind.
Hats doch bey disen Jahren eben/
Gar wenig Generosos geben.
Die jre Augen vnd Gesicht/
An deine stralen hetten gericht.
Vil giengen leider so blind drein/
Es möcht erbarmen einem Stein.
In so vil vnerschätzlich schaden/
Seynd durch jr schmeltzen vil gerathen/
Daß die Nachkommen an beschwerden/
Noch wol zuschmürtzen haben werden.
Es seufftzen wol die arme Leuth/
Nach einer guten Wolfelkeit.
Wem aber ist der Taler bliben/
Vnd in der Truhen abgestigen/
Dem wird es Thewr gnueg noch seyn/
Was er darumb sol kauffen ein.
Wie manches Junckerl das bißher
Auff seine Taler bochet sehr/
Die jhn sehr groß vnd prächtig machten/
Mueß jetzt nach Herrn Diensten trachten.
Ach Witwen vnd die Waisen klein/
Wer ist der sie doch gnueg bewein?
Die durch diß wesen wie vermelt/
Seynd spöttlich kommen vmb jr Gelt.
Wann ich wolt dran gedencken recht/
Vor wainen ich nit reden möcht.
Hör was auß diser Müntz vnruhe/
Für grosses vnhail folgen thue.
Weils Geld hett kein gewisen lauf/
Bracht man gen Marckt nichts zum verkauf.
Das liebe Traid bhielt man zusam̄/
Daher dann grosser Hunger kam.
Vnd weil das Holtz so vil gekost/
Muest mancher leyden grosser Frost
Von wegen mangel guter Speiß/
Kam Kranckheit auff vil manche weiß.
Biß letztlich gar der bitter Todt/
Wegen der jämmerlichen Noth.
Die Vnzucht grassiert in der Welt/
Dieweil man müst verdienen Gelt.
Der Neyd vnd Haß war mannigfalt/
Weil Brüderliche Lieb erkalt.
Auß Geitz vnd Neyd kam Tödtlichs Mordt/
Wie man erfuhr an machen Orth.
Glaub/ Hoffnung/ Lieb/ all gute Sitten/
Die waren elend gnueg beschnitten.
Vnd desto grösser ist der schad/
Weil man jhn erst empfind so spat.
Die Thewrung hat den gmainen Man
Am allermaisten t[illegible] an.
Die Bawrendölpel rissen sich/
Vmb seine Taler embsiglich.
Der Reiche hett noch vil in gwalt/
Daruon er hett sein auffenthalt.
So hett sich auch der Handelsman/
Längst auff die Taller grichtet schon.
Der Bettelman sliß sich der Wort/
Vnd kam desto leichter also fort.
Daher nur maists der mittle Man/
Den Thewrungs schaden müste han.
Diß waren rechte Bawrenjahr.
Vor acht vnd neuntzig Jahren zwar/
Da haben sie es so weit gewagt/
Durch Edleut die spieß gejagt.
Jetzt Jagen sie in grosser Sum̄/
Der grossen Herrn Bildnuß vmb
Die auff den Talern seyn gebräckt/
Daß manchen vbermuet erweckt.
So ist der Bawren Teuffel karg/
Jetzt nunmehr worden also arg/
Vom Taler sie vor theten sagen/
Jetzt aber weil er abgeschlagen/
So wöllen sie durchauß die zahl
Vom Gulden bhalten vberal
Hat also auch das Bawrengsind/
Den Stätten zwagen jren Grind
Vnd jhnen zeigt wie die vom Adl/
So wenig Korn auß jrem Stadl
Vmb ein par Seiden strimpff thuen geben/
Sie merckten gleichfals auch darneben/
Wie wenig Traid der Bawren Stock/
Geb vmb der Gredta Lindisch Rock.
Das Rusticalisch Jahr wars je/
Das Iubilate pfiffen sie.
Cantate sangens auch allda:
Liessens Misericordia
Den hungerigen Märckt vnd Stätten/
Die sie schon außgesäugert hetten.
Man wird zum Müntz herunder springen/
Vocem Iucunditatis singen.
So kombts Exaudi an die Bawrn/
Daß manchem wird Haut noch schaurn.

APollo ließ gefallen jhm/
Jhr beeder angebrachte Stim̄.
Vnd sagt wie er all sach zuhand/
Wöll stellen in ein guten stand.
Nach solchem gieng man auß dem Rath/
Jetzt wart die gantze Welt auff gnad.

PLATE XXIII. The Laughing and Weeping Money-Mission

On the left side, in a throne room a seated Apollo, with a scepter in one hand and an orb in the other, presides over an audience with Democritus and Heraclitus. In attendance are Apollo's advisers: to his right sit Plato's Republic and Paracelsus's Alchemy, to his left, Coinage and Aristotle's Politics. On their advice he has called the audience to determine the causes of the inflation in Germany. On the left, Democritus points to the sphere on the floor, which represents the world, and laughs at the folly of people, whom he sees as having caused their own harm. In contrast, Heraclitus, on the right, laments the harm that the inflation has caused common people. On the right side is a list of coin values from 1609 to June of 1623, above which are six verses:

Of the climbing and the fall
  This chart is a memorial.
Thus, the reader, much esteemed,
  Can fill the empty spaces in
With more notations easily:
  And that's why they must empty be.

Apollo by his Councilors
  Was urgently implored one day
To send abroad, to every land,
  A mission investigating coins,
Since coinage had climbed measurelessly
  And also fallen to the depths,
To see who might deserve the blame
  In buying, selling, loss, and gain.
Herewith Apollo called at once
  Two men, whom he sent to us Germans,
The laughing sage Democritus*
  And Heraclitus, wet with tears.†
Now when they (as one dare not doubt)
  Had carried out their mission well,
To Apollo they again returned;
  Before him and his learned men
Each one delivered his report.
  Democritus began and spoke:

* Democritus (c. 440–371 B.C.) was from Abdera in Thrace, a town proverbial for the stupidity of its inhabitants, although it was also the birthplace not only of Democritus but of the philosophers Anaxarchus and Protagoras. Literary tradition calls Democritus the "laughing philosopher."

† Heraclitus (fl. c. 500 B.C.)—from Ephesus—was called the "weeping philosopher" and was often paired with Democritus.

DEMOCRITVS:

The course of coinage and inflation
  Runs much the same with many a nation,
For what they cause themselves are but
  Harm to themselves and great despair,
And they shall, as I well may say,
  For their own folly bear the blame.
It happened several years ago
  That some of them grew covetous
And wished that everything they touched
  Into pure gold would be transformed.
Just then such people did exist
  Who claimed from metal to make gold
And afterwards paid for their deceit
  And had to die chymistically.
They were, you see, all sublimated
  And alchemistically cohabitated;*
Their corpus flew into the air
  And to the gallows was affixed.
When now men came upon the truth
  And noted greater loss than gain,
They turned away from transmutation

* The writer of the verses employs technical terms of the alchemists (or gold-makers) to describe their own public execution.

To the clever art of adulteration.
Of silver they learned to make addition
And subtly do artful subtraction,
The lesser coin-sorts multiplying,
The solid Thaler coins dividing,
Which they so long and much trimmed down
Until they strode to bankruptcy.
Hereafter now, from year to year,
Large coins had risen high in worth,
And little coins in bastard fashion
Were shut out like calvitic mice,
The merchants and tradespeople too
Still kept them hid in secrecy,
And at the courts of many lords
They were *Secretum Secretorum*.*
Thus, with a few large kinds of coins,
Much wealth and wares have been acquired,
And where, elsewhere, in times gone by,
The vintners, draymen, peasantry
Bore great purse-goiters, stuffed quite full,
Home from the market, spick and span,
A different matter soon occurred:
They carried from the market home
But few coins of the larger sort.
From them, though, many Guldens came,
With which they let their addled brain,
Unseasoned, run to fantasies,
At which the townsfolk laughed aloud,
Mocking the peasants' stupidity.
Especially, they were quite pleased
That they for but a single ducat,
Of the best wine could buy a bucket,
From which a good fellow would gladly guzzle,
That a bushel of grain would cost a Thaler,
And a good carouse an old-time Batzen.
There took place a mighty celebration
At how one could achieve high spirits
For only a Thaler and no more.
In summary: everything proceeded
So cheaply indeed, and nothing was dear
Except the Thaler, which to be sure
For a pile of Guldens must be exchanged,
Up to the count of ten or twelve.
Yet one could, on the other hand,
In return, get many pounds of meat,
Of eggs a lot, twenty pounds of fat,
Twenty quarts, almost, of wine as well.
When now, in such a golden age,
People with money quite far could go,
Everyone wished to pay his debts.
The man with money was present once more.
Then the government, worthy of praise, appeared
And made in these matters a decision:
It stripped from the money the masks away.
The countryman was horrified,
And since, as well, his nobleman
By him in good money would be paid,
He opened his eyes to a better way
And took, in selling, more careful heed.
To bring things to market he'd not condescend;
Since he still had money in some amount,
He would not pay rent, and went on vacation,
Keeping his grain within his barn.
Although at last such rotten coinage
Throughout all Swabia had been discovered,
Hereupon one wished in every matter
To make good values, put things in order,
Coming up with excellent proposals
And issuing elegant *motiva*,*
As if the peasantry would be
Glad to behave with *cortesia*,†
And as if common sense were to be found
'Midst common people and peasants' sons.
Yet the peasants at that very time

* This term refers to the secret of secrets or the secret of making gold, another phrase from the alchemistic vocabulary.

* From the late Latin, meaning "motivation."

† From the Spanish, meaning "civility."

Were much confused and much confounded.
On a bad triple Batzner's account,*
So that also, that year, much objection arose,
And the *Digesta* were in vain.†
More heed was paid to chests and purses,
Pandecta were broken in the wheel,‡
Which were on the peasants' side;
Once then about the *codice*§
The peasant inquired *modice***
Letting, likewise, the jurists search
Around in all the law's *decreta.*
They took the values as a joke,
And heeded not government nor God.
Meanwhile the *dominium*
Had grown indeed quite *rusticum.*
The peasants showed no sense at all,
But wanted big coins in their hand,
And since the inflation of wares' cost
Had climbed so high into the air,
The peasants would not give way, and kept
Strongly insisting on their cause,
So that they long could not agree,
And long weren't willing to back down.
Now I, however, want to hear
The news that long has been desired:
How finally they will agree,
Since Thalers have in value decreased,
And humbly have transformed themselves
Into a worth that's tolerable.
Now I must laugh repeatedly,
(As is my wont) most heartily,

* This line may refer to a specific case of cheating or counterfeiting.

† The Digests are the main part of the *Corpus juris civilis,* fifty excerpts from the Roman jurists, made by order of Emperor Justinian (527–565).

‡ The Pandects are synonymous with the Digests.

§ The mention of the codex, i.e., lawbook, is an allusion to the *Codex Justinianus.*

** This word means "modestly" or, more likely, "slightly" or "fleetingly."

Because the world has grown so crazed,
As if it were entering Shrovetide's days.

HERACLITVS:

When now Heraclitus had heard,
Amidst his weeping this oration,
He dried the tears from off his face,
And, all compassionate, spoke thus:

Apollo, you clear-shining ray,
Of your supremely fairest light
There truly has never been such need
Until now, as there is today,
For some folk in these years just past
Might readily behold their ruin.
Although the Germans are indeed
The eagle's brood and beloved child,*
There have been in these present years
Of *Generolos* precious few,†
Who willingly would turn their sight
And eyes toward your sunbeams' light,
And rather strolled along so blind,
That a stone to pity would be moved.
Into what immeasurable harm
Have they with their alloying come,
That their descendants will someday
Suffer burdens painful to be borne.
Indeed, the poor cry out aloud
To get some blessed price-decrease.
However, he who's kept his Thalers
And stored them in his chests away,
For him too, things grow passing dear,
Whatever he may wish to buy.
How many a squireen who till now
Has boasted loud about his Thalers,
Which made him seem so grand and splendid,

* The eagle was the symbol of the Holy Roman Empire, as it had been of the Romans.

† The Spanish word *Generolos* is actually a misprint for *generosos* (noble, valiant persons) or possibly a contamination with *generales* (generals).

Must now seek service with some master.
Oh, the widows and the orphans small
(What man can weep for them enough?)
Who through this practice as described
Have lost their money shamefully:
If I should ponder this aright,
I could not speak for all my tears.
Hearken to what from this coin-commotion
Would come as a great catastrophe.
Since money no certain value had,
To market naught was brought for sale.
Precious stores of grain were kept untouched,
And so great famine came to pass,
And since wood itself became so dear,
Many had to suffer awful chill.
For lack of proper nourishment
Sickness arose in many a wise,
Till bitter death at last appeared.
Because of this piteous distress,
Whoredom ran wild throughout the world,
For money somehow must be earned.
Envy and hatred were manifold,
Since brotherly love had turned to cold.
From greed and envy cruel murder came,
As people in many a region learned,
Faith, hope, and love, all morals good
Were miserably enough curtailed.
And all the greater was the harm
Because it was found out so late.
Inflation, most openly of all,
Upon the common man did fall,
The peasants squabbled doltishly
About their Thalers busily.
The rich man kept in his control
Still much on which his life depended.
The tradesman too had long since turned
His care toward his stock of Thalers.
The beggar polished up his words,
And all the easier survived.
So it was mostly the average man
Who from inflation suffered harm.

Now those in truth were peasant years
Some eight and ninety years ago,*
When they were bold enough to dare
To run the nobles through with spears,†
And now they chase, in great amount,
The great lords' images about,
Which on the Thalers have been stamped,
Thereby much insolence awaking.
This way the greedy peasant-devil
Has in these days become so evil:
Before, they liked to talk of Thalers,
But since these now have lost their worth,
They want entirely to keep
Their hoard of Guldens everywhere.
In this way, too, the peasant band
Can scrape the mange of city folk,‡
Showing them, like the nobility,
How little wheat from the granary,
Will be paid for a silken stocking pair,
And likewise they must see besides
How little grain the peasant clod
Will give for a coat of violet hue.§

* The German Peasants' War of 1525 took place principally in Franconia, Swabia, and Thuringia, where some one hundred thousand persons perished in the uprising. Three years after the composition of this broadsheet, a similar uprising occurred in Upper Austria (where, in 1526, the peasants had managed to obtain some concessions). The uprising was put down with measures quite as bloody as those employed in Germany the century before.

† On Easter Sunday, 16 April 1525, the peasants of the Odenwald—led by Jäcklin Rohrbach, an innkeeper—besieged and captured Weinsberg (in Württemberg) and the next day brought its commander, Ludwig von Helfenstein, some fifteen knights, and eighty other defenders to a meadow outside the town, where they drove them through a gauntlet of spears. The massacre helped sway opinion against the peasants, all the more because of the grotesque abuse to which Helfenstein's wife, an illegitimate daughter of the late and very popular Emperor Maximilian (1459–1519), was subjected.

‡ *zwagen iren Grind:* to scrape their mange, i.e., to skin or trick.

§ *der Greta Lindisch Rock:* from the French *gris de lin* (grayness of flax); cf. Swedish *gredelin* (lilac, mauve).

The rustic year was ever so:
   They whistled *Jubilate*'s tune,*
And their *Cantate* sang besides,†
   Leaving *Misericordia*‡
To the hungry markets and the towns,
   Which they already had sucked dry.
They will dance downward to the mint,§
   Singing *Vocem jucunditatis.***
Thus, *Exaudi* comes to the peasants all,††
   So that many will feel their skin acrawl.

Apollo let himself be pleased
   By both their voices, thus applied,
And said that he, without delay,
   Would settle things in a proper way.
After which they left the council's place,
      And now the whole world waits for grace.

* *Jubilate* is the third Sunday after Easter, named after the beginning of the introit in its mass, Ps. 66:1: "Jubilate Deo omnis terra" (Make a joyful noise unto God, all ye lands).

† *Cantate* is the fourth Sunday after Easter, named after the beginning of the introit in its mass, Ps. 98:1: "Cantate Domino canticum novum" (Sing unto the Lord a new song).

‡ *Misericordia* is the second Sunday after Easter, named after the beginning of the introit in its mass, Ps. 33:5: "Misericordia Domini plena est terra" (The earth is full of the goodness of the Lord).

§ That is, the mint of hell.

** See Bar. 2:23. The Jews of Babylon send this message to their fellows in Jerusalem, admonishing them to repent their sins; the speaker of the threatened curse (2:21–35) is God himself. The allusion to Baruch shows what confidence the writer of the broadsheet text had in the Bible-versedness of his readers, and it is extremely clever. Interjected into the series of psalmic references (and Sunday nomenclature), it indicates, to the knowledgeable, what the fate of the rejoicing coiners will be. The cruel joke, in the context of the broadsheet, is heightened by the fact that the message of the Jews of Babylon is accompanied by a gift of money (see Bar. 1:10).

†† *Exaudi,* the sixth Sunday after Easter Sunday within the Octave of the Ascension, is named after the beginning of the introit in its mass, Ps. 27:7: "Exaudi, Domine, vocem meam qua clamavi ad te" (Hear, O Lord, when I have cried with my voice).

Verzeichnuß der groben Müntzsorten/wie die von Anno 1582. biß 1623. in gemein gestiegen vnd gefallen.

Von dem Auffsteigen vnd Abfall/ Ist dieses ein Memorial. Darbey auch hie zu mercken ist/ Wo ein Händlein stehet/so wisst: Daß selbiges bedeuten thut/ Ein Obrigkeitlichs Mandat gut. Beym Monat der Versal Buchstab/ Zeiget der Stadt Namen vorab. Vnd weil die erst Edition Abgangen ist/vnd hinwegk schon. Als hab ichs mit rath ehrlicher Leut/ Wider aufflegt/vnd vermehrt weit. Vnd tracht nach den fürnembsten Sortn/ So maist gangbar jetzt dieser Ortn. Woll demnach der Lesr hochgeehrt/ Selbs in die Spacia vnbeschwert Welche leer stehn/mehr zeichnen ein/ Wies dann drumb leer gelassen seyn.

Es hat golten in dem

Jar.	Monat.	Der Reichsthaler	Der Guldenthaler.	Der Philipsthaler.	Die Silbercronen.	Reichstaler mit 72.	8 Ducat oder Zeggin.	Der Goldgulden.	Spannische Duplon.	Der Creutzducaten.	Spannische einfache cron.	Frantzösische einfache cron.	Welsch einfache Cron.	Der Engellott.	8 Gwichtige Rosenobel.	Der Schiffnobel.	Königische kopfstück 5:10
		fl: kr.	fl: kr.	fl: kr.	fl: kr.	fl: kr.	fl: kr.	fl: kr.	fl: kr.	fl: kr.	fl: kr.	fl: kr.	fl: kr.	fl: kr.	fl: kr.	fl: kr.	fl: kr.
1582		1: 8	1:	1: 20	1: 24	1: 12	1: 45	1: 15	3: 20	1: 40	1: 32	1: 36	1: 32	3:	3: 30	2: 38	1: 20
1587		1: 9	1:	1: 20	1: 24	1: 12	1: 50	1: 17	3: 20	1: 40	1: 32	1: 36	1: 32	3:	3: 30		1: 20
1590		1: 10	1:	1: 20	1: 24	1: 12	1: 50	1: 18		1: 40		1: 36					1: 20
1594		1: 11	1: 2	1: 20	1: 24	1: 12	1: 50	1: 19		1: 41		1: 36					1: 20
1596	Septemb. 13(23) F	1: 12	1: 4	1: 20	1: 24	1: 12	1: 50	1: 20			1: 34	1: 36	1: 34	3:	3: 30		1: 20
1597		1: 12	1: 4	1: 20	1: 24	1: 12	1: 56	1: 20		1: 43	1: 34	1: 38	1: 34		4:		1: 20
1598		1: 12	1: 4	1: 20	1: 24	1: 12	2:	1: 20	3: 34	1: 43	1: 34	1: 40					1: 20
1599		1: 12	1: 4	1: 20	1: 24	1: 12	2:	1: 20		1: 43					4:	3:	1: 20
1600		1: 12	1: 4	1: 20	1: 24	1: 12	2:	1: 20				1: 40			4:		1: 20
1601		1: 12	1: 4	1: 22	1: 24	1: 12	2:	1: 22		1: 45							1: 22
1602		1: 12	1: 4	1: 22	1: 24	1: 12	2:	1: 22					1: 34				1: 22
1603		1: 14	1: 4	1: 22	1: 26	1: 14	2:	1: 22	4:			1: 40					1: 22
1604		1: 14	1: 4	1: 22	1: 26	1: 14	2:	1: 22	4:	1: 48					4:		1: 22
1605		1: 15	1: 4	1: 24	1: 30	1: 15	2: 4	1: 30									1: 24
1606		1: 15	1: 4	1: 24	1: 30	1: 15	2: 4	1: 30					1: 34				1: 24
1607		1: 16	1: 8	1: 24	1: 30	1: 16	2: 7	1: 30						3:			1: 24
1608		1: 20	1: 8	1: 30	1: 36	1: 20	2: 10	1: 30									1: 30
1609	Jul. 7. Decemb. 19. A	1: 24	1: 14	1: 30	1: 36	1: 24	2: 15	1: 40				2:					1: 30
1610	Jul. 10. Octob. 23. A	1: 24	1: 14	1: 30	1: 36	1: 24	2: 18	1: 45		2:							1: 30
1611		1: 24	1: 14	1: 32		1: 24	2: 20	1: 45							4: 30		1: 32
1612	Jul. 19. Nov. 8. A	1: 24	1: 15	1: 32		1: 24	2: 20	1: 45				2:					1: 32
1613	Februario.	1: 24	1: 16	1: 32		1: 24	2: 20	1: 45					2:			4:	1: 32
	Septembri.	1: 26	1: 16	1: 33		1: 26	2: 20	1: 45									1: 33
1614	Augusto.	1: 28	1: 16	1: 34		1: 30	2: 20	1: 45			2: 10				5:		1: 34
1615	Martio 21. N	1: 28	1: 16	1: 34		1: 30	2: 20	1: 45									1: 34
	Novemb. 17. A	1: 30	1: 20	1: 40		1: 34	2: 30	1: 52									1: 40
1616	Jul. 2. A. Oct. 12. N	1: 30	1: 20	1: 40		1: 36	2: 30	1: 52		2: 12		2: 8					1: 40
1617	Majo 22. N	1: 30	1: 20	1: 40		1: 37	2: 31	1: 52									1: 40
1618	Majo 15. N	1: 32	1: 22	1: 42		1: 38	2: 32	2:		2: 20		2: 16					1: 42
1619	October 20 N	1: 48	1: 36	1: 58		1: 54	2: 48	2: 10		2: 28		2: 30					1: 58
1620	Februario.	2: 4	1: 50	2: 15	2: 15	2: 8	3: 4	2: 18									2: 15
	Junio 11. A	2: 8	1: 56	2: 18	2: 20	2: 10	3: 12	2: 20	5: 40	2: 58	2: 50	2: 50	2: 45	4: 40	7:	6: 12	2: 18
	Novemb. 24. A	2: 20	2:	2: 30	2: 30	2: 24	3: 30	2: 30	6:	3: 4	3:	3:		5:	7:	6: 45	2: 30
1621	Januario.	2: 20	2:	2: 30	2: 30		3: 30	2: 30	6:								2: 30
	Februario.	2: 24	2: 6	2: 36	2: 36		3: 36	2: 36	6: 30								2: 36
	Martio.	2: 30	2: 10	2: 50	2: 50		3: 40	2: 40	7:								2: 50
	Aprili.	2: 36	2: 15	3:	3:		3: 45	2: 45	7: 30								3:
	Majo 25. A	2: 48	2: 24	3:	3: 8	2: 42	4: 30	3:	8:	4: 10							3:
	Junio	3: 6	2: 36	3: 30	3: 30		4: 30	3: 30	9:								3: 30
	Julio 29 A	3: 15	2: 52	3: 32	4:	3: 20	5:	3: 40	10:	4: 40							3: 32
	Augusto.	4:	3: 30	4: 15	4: 30		6: 30	5: 15	12:								4: 15
	Septembri.	4: 30	4:	5: 20	5: 48		8:	6: 12	13: 30								5: 20
	Octobri.	5:	4: 24	5: 36	6:		9: 30	7:	15:								5: 36
	Novembri.	5: 30	4: 45	6:	6: 30		10: 30	7: 30	16: 15								6:
	Decembri.	6: 30	5: 30	7:	7:		12:	8:	19:								7:
1622	Januario 18. A	7: 30	6: 30	8:	8:		13: 30	10:	22:								8:
	Februario.	10:	8: 30	11: 30	12:		16:	12:	28:								11: 30
	Martio 8. vnd 15.	10:	8: 30	10: 30	11:	10: 6	15:	11:	29:	4: 20							10: 30
NB.	Von diesem Monat Martio an ists also verblieben/biß auff den 8. Octobris/da es vmb das halbe theil abgewürdigt worden.																
	Octobri 1. A	5:	4: 30	5: 30	6:		8:	5: 45	13:	7: 20	8:						5: 30
	Novemb. 22. A	6:	5: 30	6: 30	7: 20		9: 30	7:	16:		9:						6: 30
1623	Junio 27. A	1: 30	1: 20	1: 40	1: 44	1: 34	2: 20	1: 44	3:	2: 10	2: 4	4: 2	2:	3: 24	5: 4	4: 30	1: 40
Nota.	Adj 28. Julij ist durch die drey löbliche im Müntzwesen *Correspondierende* Fränckisch- Bayrisch- vnd Schwäbischen Craiß mehrere beschlossen worden/es/deß Gelts halben bey letzten Absatz/den Reichsthaler zu anderhalben Gulden/rc. für dißmal verbleiben zu lassen.																
	Septembri.																
	Octobri.																
	Novembri.																
	Decembri.																

Gedruckt im Jahr 1623.

PLATE XXIV. Chart of the Large Kinds of Coins, How from the Year 1582 until 1623 They Have Risen and Fallen*

A list of the values of individual coins from 1582 to June of 1623.

Of the climbing and the fall
This chart is a memorial.
Hereby attention's to be paid:
That where a little hand sign's seen,
You'll know what it is meant to mean:
A good mandate of government.
The capital beside the month
Will indicate the city's name,†
And since the first edition
Has run out and is wholly gone,
I have, on honorable advice,
Printed it anew, and much enlarged,
Including the finest kinds of coins
Most current in these several places,
And so the reader, much esteemed,
Can fill the empty spaces in
With more notations easily:
And that's why they must empty be.

NB. From this month of March on it remained the same, until October 8, when it was devalued by half.

Note: July 28, by the three praiseworthy districts of Franconia, Bavaria, and Swabia, corresponding in their coinage, it was severally decided, on the money's account by the latest issue, to let the Reichsthaler remain at one and a half Guldens, etc., for the time being.

Printed in the Year 1623.

* An anonymous broadsheet with a table that includes the coin values through 1623 was issued in 1643.

† The meanings of the capital letters are as follows: F for Frankfurt am Main, A for Augsburg, N for Nuremberg, and R for Regensburg.

Abschrifft eines Schreibens/ so von dem Obristen Hellischen Fürsten/ dem Lucifer Ermahnungs Weise abgegangen ist/ an alle vnd jede Kipperer vnd Wipperer/ Wucherer vnd Schinder/ daß sie alle wollen beständig vnd willig verbleiben in jhrem angefangenen Handwerck der Kipper- vnd Wipperrey/ Wucherey vnd Schacherey/ Schinderey vnd Schaberey Büberey vnd Dieberey wie mans weiter tituliren mag/ auch was jhnen endlich für jhre Mühe/ vnd getrewe Dienste jmmer vnd ewig soll recompensirt werden.

WJe Lucifer von Gottes Vngnaden/ ein König aller Gottlosen/ ein Ertzhertzog der Finsterniß ein Fürst der Welt vnd Vater der Lügen/ ein Haupt aller Rotten vnd Secten/ ein Verkehrer der Warheit/ ein Stiffter alles Vbels vnd Vnglücks/ Beförderer aller Verderbniß vnd Schadens/ ein Ankläger der Sünder/ abgesagter Feind des gantzen Menschlichen Geschlechts vnd ein Wiederwertiger Gottes vnd aller seiner Heiligen/ ꝛc.

Entbieten euch allen/ vnsern Newgebornen/ außerkornen allerliebsten vnd getrewesten Dienern/ Freunden vnd Söhnen/ Juden vnd Judensgenossen/ vnd allen die jhr mit Kippen vnd Wippen/ Wuchern/ Schinden vnd Schaben vmbgeht/ meinen willigen Dienst vnd freundlichen Gruß jederzeit zuvorn/ ꝛc. Freundliche/ liebe/ ja allerliebste/ gehorsame/ gelernige/ abgefeimbte/ durchtriebene/ wolgeübte/ vnverdrossene/ allzeit willige/ embsige/ aber numehr aller Welt bekandte/ benandte/ beschissene/ betrogene/ verlogene/ verstolene/ meineydige/ von ewerm Gott abgefallene/ Gewissenlosse/ Gottsvergessene/ hellische/ henckermässige/ vngehenckte/ verstockte/ halßstarrige/ vnverschampte Schandbuben vnd Mammons Knechte/ Ehrlose/ hellische getrewe vnd wolgerahtene Ertzdiebische Kipperer vnd Wipperer/ Wucherer vnd Schächerer/ Schinder vnd Schaber/ vnd vieler anderer dergleichen guten Tugenden mehr vntergebene/ die jhr all vnsern geneigten Willen vollbringt/ daran jhr vns ein groß Gefallen thut/ dessen jhr dann auch wieder Ewig bey vns in guten bedacht seyn vnd geniessen solt. Wir können nicht vnterlassen euch zuzuschreiben vnd zuvermahnen/ dieweil jhr von diesem ewerm sonst nicht groß löblichen Handwerck der Kipperey so grossen Nutz habt/ dann einmahl habt jhr grosse summen Geldes zusammen gebracht vnd ewer Hauß wol bestelt eusserlichem Schein nach/ vnd in Summa/ jhr seid vnsere beste vnd letzte/ die ärgste vnd klügeste/ Gottesvergessene/ Ertzdiebische Heler vnd Steler/ so jemals haben gefunden werden mögen/ wie jhr denn dessen von allen Cantzeln benandt/ verbrandt vnd außgeruffen werdet/ aber jhr thut mir einen grossen Gefallen dran/ daß jhr das euch nicht jrren lasset vnd daran kehret/ darumb wollen wir auch euch zu Tag vnd zu Nacht fleissig helffen Rath vnd That geben. Nach dem wir nun von vnsern lieben getrewen/ den Edlen vnd Gestrengen Juncker Wolff von Kipperg/ Laux von Wipperheim/ Wuchershausen vnd Schindeberg/ Fuchs von Greiffhart vnd Hebfest/ wie auch dem Wohl Edlen Herrn vnd Bruder von Schacherheim vnd Müntzberg/ als Herrn vnd MittErben vnsers hellischen Reichs mit grossen Frewden vnd Frolocken vernommen/ daß jhr es durch ewere geflissene/ vnverdrossene mir wolgefellige vnd darneben so wolbekandte Dienst/ mit Kippen vnd Wippen/ wuchern vnd schachern/ schinden vnd schaben so weit gebracht habt/ daß wir numehr versichert vnd jhr hievon schwerlich werdet lassen/ darumb dann die Geld steigerung gar nicht fallen wird/ dadurch dann alle Land ruinirt vnd verderbt/ vnd was durch vnerträglichen aber mir wolgefelligen Krieg nicht verheert vnd verderbt/ verwüst/ verbrent vnd zertrent worden/ das wird doch durch ewer

Ertzdiebische kippische Schinderey/ Schacherey vnd Wechßlerey/ vollends verderbt vnd außgesogen/ also gar/ daß sich ausser ewer Zunfftgenossen kein ehrlicher vnd redlicher Mann mehr wol mit den Seinigen ernehren vnd erhalten kan/ bevorab in dem es so hoch kommen/ daß ein jeder mit Reichsthaler in specie wil bezahlet seyn/ welches den Armen vnmüglichen/ darumb dann sie euch auß Vngedult dermassen verfluchen vnd verschweren/ vnd erzürnen damit auch Gott jhren HErrn höchlich/ dadurch dann vnser Hellisch Reich dapffer gemehret wird/ dieweil sich die Menschen an Gott vnd jhrem Nechsten so hoch versündigen vnd vergreiffen/ welches vns aber ein hertzliebende Frewde ist/ sonderlich aber weil solche ewere in Ewigkeit vnvergessene Wucherey vnd Schinderey/ Schacherey vnd Schrapperey/ Dieberey vnd Triegerey in vielen Landen vngescheucht getrieben/ schleunig vnd wol von statten gehet/ auch an etlichen Orten von solchen Gesellen/ die viel mehr für Ehrliche vnd Redliche/ als für solche Land vnd Leut verderbliche Ertzbuben wollen angesehen sein. Vnter ewer Zunfft gehören auch alle die Jenigen so mit Korn/ Victualien vnd andern zu der Menschen Notturfft gehörigen Sachen stattlich wuchern/ schinden vnd schaben/ seynd auch allbereit in ewer Register verzeichnet/ dann es muß jhnen auch belohnet werden. Weil dann nun solche Kipper- vnd Wipperey von obgemelten Leuten/ darzu von lauter Christen/ dafür sie wollen gehalten seyn/ getrieben wird/ so werden sich die vngetauffte Jüden vnd andere vngläubige Völcker/ daran zum höchsten ärgern vnd in jhrem Aberglauben beharrlich fortfahren/ als welche an jhren Brüdern vnd Glaubensgenossen nicht also schinden vnd schaben vnd sagen/ das seynd der Christen Früchte/ wir Juden haben das ehrliche Handwerck gelernet vnd treibens auch/ weil man vns kein anders treiben lest/ alles zu dem Ende/ daß wir vnser Weib vnd Kinder vnd vnser Glaubensgenossen ernehren vnd erhalten/ vnd der Obrigkeit den schuldigen Tribut vnd Zinß geben können. Die Christen aber bringen dadurch jhr eigene Glaubensgenossen vmb das jhrige vnd in höchste Armut/ vnd was sie rauben vnd stelen mit Kippen vnd Wippen das behalten sie allein für sich vnd die jhrige/ dadurch beharren sie in jhrem vnbußfertigem Leben vnd Vnglauben/ vnd fahren vns also mit Leib vnd Seel fein warm zu/ vnd bringen andere mit sich/ welches das aller ärgste/ vns aber das wolgefelligste ist/ so auß Kipperey entspringen thut/ dann dadurch vnser Reich gemehrt vnd erweitert wird. Zu dem/ so habt jhr durch ewere vnverdrossenen Dienst/ die Sach so weit gebracht/ das nicht allein alles gute Geld auß dem Lande kommet vnd auffs höchste steiget/ sondern auch durch ewer Wipper- vnd Kipperey eine solche vnversehene vnerträgliche/ ja vnerhörte Thewrung vnd Steigerung aller Sachen in gantz Deutschland vnd andere Länder eingefallen/ darinnen viel Menschen an Gott verzagen vnd verzweiffeln/ sich selbst oder die jhrige auß Hungersnoth erstechen/ erhencken vnd ertrencken/ darzu dann auch vnsere wohl ansehnliche vnd dapffere Korn Juden reichlich helffen/ vnd das beste thun/ in dem sie den Segen Gottes auffs thewerste verkauffen vnd damit wuchern. Derowegen sie in dieser Diebeszunfft incorporirt vnd billich in vnserm Reich oben angesetzt werden. Was nun in gantz Deutschland für vnaußsprechlichen Jammer vnd Noth auß ewerm Ertzdiebischen Handwerck entstanden/ wird der Außgang geben vnd werdet eine fewerreichliche Belohnung davon empfangen/ dann von vielen Orten die Seelen hauffen weiß von Kipperer vnd Wipperer zu vns kommen werden/ Derhalben O jhr Kipperer vnd Wipper Wucherer vnd Wächßler/ Schinder vnd Schaber/ sehet nur fleissig zu/ daß jhr hierinnen nichts verseumet/ sondern bey ewerm von vns genommenen Beruff verharret: Gott geb man schrey vnd schreib/ klag vnd sag truck vnd predige darwider was man wolle/ so thut jhr doch als wenn es euch nicht angienge/ solches alles sol euch bey vns in der hellischen Flammen/ da wir auch euch eine schöne Müntzstadt bereiten wollen/ wol belohnet werden/ vnd jhr auch ewig bey vns wohnen vnd Dienst haben solt. In summa es ist vnser höchste Bitt an euch/ daß jhr in solchem verzweifflichen Ertzdiebischen wohlerfahrnen Handwerck embsiglich wolt fortfahren/ in Ansehung das solches Vnwesen zu Mehrung vnsers gantzen hellischen Reichs der Finsterniß/ gar dienstlich ist/ dann kein ärgers/ aber vns angenehmers Werck in der Welt nie ist auffkommen/ darumb wollen wir euch auch beystehen mit Hülff/ Rath vnd That/ so viel wir jmmer können/ damit vnser Reich/ darin wir auch ewer Stell vorbehalten vnd euch auff Pölster von Schwebel vnd Bech bereit setzen wollen/ gemehret werde. Derowegen trachtet vnd suchet/ sinnet vnd erdencket allerley newe List vnd Betrug/ Bescheisserey vnd Finantzerey/ Tück vnd Griff/ wie jhr ewern Nechsten nur tapffer könnet betriegen vnd den armen Mann gar verderben/ damit ewer wolhergebrachtes vnd ruhmwürdiges Lob bey vns vnd der Welt noch mehr angenem werde vnd nicht in Abfall komme/ diß alles sol euch allen reichlich vergolten vnd in alle Ewigkeit nimmer vergessen werden/ welches wir auch fest vnd steiff halten wollen/ Weiter auff dißmal wissen wir euch nichts mehr zuschreiben/ dann daß jhr/ wie obgemelt in ewerm diebischen vnd landsverderblichen Vorhaben vns zu dienst beharrlich vorfahret/ so habt jhr dessen bey dem gantzen hellischen Reich ein grosses Lob vnd Ehr/ dann bißher ewers gleichen in der Hell noch nie gewesen/ noch gefunden worden. Fahret derowegen fleissig also fort vnd höret nicht auff/ biß vnser Legat vnd Commissarius zu euch gesand/ kommen werde vnd euch die Hälß abbreche/ auch zu vns in das hellische schwebelbrennende Bad vnd Müntzstadt führet/ welches/ so jhr also beständig verbleibet/ in kurtzer Zeit geschehen vnd zu euch abgefertigt werden soll. Es lassen euch auch freundlich/ fleissig vnd dienstlich grüssen/ Nabal der alt Herr vom Geitzhalß/ Thalersberg vnd Wucherim Judas der Printz vom Geldsack vnd Verräthersburg/ Gehasi von Kippershausen vnd Schacherheim/ Ahitophel vnd Haman/ Cain vnd Pharao vnd noch viel ansehnliche Herrn/ gute Gesellen vnd Hellbrüder/ so auff euch mit grossem Schmertzen warten thun im warmen Schweißbad/ da wir euch zubereiten sieben tausend Schwebelstützel/ dreyhundert Fewerkugeln vnd neun vnd neuntzig Bechkräntz alles zusammen gehackt vnd zu einem Pulver gemacht/ mit mehrerm Zusatz nach der Alchimisten Kunst auß vnser hellischen Zeugkammer gemehret/ damit solches alles für die Kipper fleissig soll behalten vnd jhnen für die grosse Hitz vnserer Müntzwerckstatt/ daß sie nicht ersticken/ biß sie es gewohnen/ eingeben werde/ welches sie dann brauchen sollen vnd werden. Datum im Abgrund der Hellen Mense so viel in specie/ vnser Regierung im hellischen Fewer im fünfftausend/ fünff hundert vnd zwey vnd neuntzigsten Jahr/

E. D. M.

Lucifer der oberste vnd fürnembste Fürst vnd Regent der Hellen.

Gedruckt im Jahr Christi/ M. DC. XXIII.

PLATE XXV. Copy of a Communication, Which by the Supreme Prince of Hell, Lucifer, Has Been Dispatched as a Reminder to Each and Every Clipper and Whipper, Usurer and Skinner, That They Who Will Desire, Constantly and Willingly, to Remain at Their Task, Already Begun, of Clipping and Whipping, Defrauding and Cheating, Rascality and Thievery as It May Further Be Named, and Finally What Their Compensation Shall Be for Their Labor and Faithful Service, Forever and in Eternity.

Amid clouds of smoke, flames, and the smell of sulfur Judas, with moneybags dangling from a chain around his neck and with a letter from Lucifer in his left hand, approaches a table at which a moneychanger is seated. Inscribed in Latin on the table is an exhortation stating that money must be sought more quickly. Lying in front of him on the table are numerous individual coins, while two sacks already filled with coins rest on the corner of the table. A man to his right brings coins to exchange, and at the left another man brings a metal vessel. Behind the moneychanger stands Belial, who is using a bellows to blow air into the moneychanger's left ear. At the far left a man minting money is being devoured in the jaws of hell.

We, Lucifer, by God's Disfavor, a Monarch of All the Godless, an Archduke of the Darkness, a Prince of the World and Father of Lies, a Perverter of Truth, a Chieftain of all Gangs and Sects, an Originator of All Evil and Misfortune, Promoter of Ruin and Harm, an Accuser of Sinners, Declared Foe of the Whole Human Race and an Opponent of God and All His Saints, etc.

Offer you all, our newborn, chosen, dearest, and most faithful servants, friends, and sons, Jews and consorters with Jews, and all you who have to do with clipping and whipping, usury, skinning and shystering, my willing service and friendly greeting at all times in advance, etc. Friendly, dear and indeed dearest, obedient, educable, cunning, crafty, well-practiced, undaunted, forever-willing, industrious, yet now known to the whole world, benamed, beshitted, betrayed, furtive, perjuring, God-forgetting, hellish, hangman-ready, unhanged, hardened, obdurate, obstinate, unabashed rogues and vassals of Mammon, infamous, hellishly loyal, and well-practiced clippers and whippers, usurers and swindlers, skinners and sharpers, and still more of those devoted to other like-good virtues, all of whom carry out our favorable will, by which you do us a great favor, for which you in turn shall remain in our good opinion and have joy of it! We cannot neglect to write to you and to admonish you, since you have had great benefit from this your otherwise not greatly laudable craft of clipping; for first of all you have assembled great sums of money and put your house in fine order, according to outward appearances, and, in short, you are our best and last, the wickedest and cleverest, God-forgotten, arch-thieving fences and filchers who may ever have existed, just as you are named, flamed, and proclaimed from every pulpit; but

you give me a great pleasure thereby, that you do not let yourselves be led astray and turned away, on which account we shall zealously by day and night help you with word and deed. Even as we presently have heard from our faithful followers, the noble and puissant Junker Wolf of Clipperburg, Laux of Whippingheim, Usuryhausen, and Fraudberg, Fuchs of Seizehard and Hold Fast, as also from our very noble lord and brother of Shysterheim and Coinberg, as the lords and coheirs of our hellish empire, with great joy and rejoicing, that you, by your industrious, undaunted service, well pleasing to me, and at the same time well known, by clipping and whipping, usury and larceny, skinning and shystering, have brought matters to such a point that we are now made sure, and you will scarcely leave off from these practices, for the inflation of money will not fall off, by which then all the nations are brought to wrack and ruin, and whatever has not been ravaged and ruined, wasted, burned down and chopped up by the unbearable war, so pleasing to me, that will now, by your arch-thieving, clippingly skinning, charging and changing, be utterly ruined and sucked dry, so that, save for your fellow guildsmen, no honest and honorable man can nourish and preserve his family, especially since it has gone so far that everyone wants to be paid with Reichsthalers in cash, which is impossible for the poor, on which account they, from their impatience, will curse and accuse you, and thereby enrage God, their Lord, extremely, by which then our hellish empire will be handsomely increased, since humankind so grievously sins and attacks God and its fellow men, which however is for us a heartwarming joy, especially since such usury and treachery, such fraud and villainy, such thieving and skullduggery, unforgotten in all eternity, is carried on fearlessly in many lands, swiftly and well, and in some places by such fellows who wish much more to be regarded as honorable and honest folk than as arch-rascals, ruinous to land and folk. In your guild, too, all those are already registered who proudly profiteer, trick and deceive with grain, victuals, and other things necessary for the need of humankind, for they too must be rewarded. Since now such clipping and whipping is carried on by the people mentioned above, in addition by naught but Christians, as they wish to be regarded, in result of which the unbaptized Jews and other unbelieving people grow highly annoyed, and persist stubbornly in their superstitions, as those who do not skin and trick their brothers and fellow believers and say that these things are the fruits of Christians: "We Jews have learned the honorable craft and likewise practice it, since we are permitted to practice no other, all to the end that we may nourish and preserve our wives and children and fellow believers, and can render unto the authorities the tribute and tax we owe them."* The Christians, however, rob their own fellow believers thereby of what they possess and consign them to the most extreme poverty, and what they steal and rob by clipping and whipping is kept by them, for themselves and theirs alone, thus they persist in their unrepentant life and unbelief, and there they come to us with body and soul handsomely warmed, and bring others with them, which is the worst of all, but which gives the greatest pleasure that from clipping issues forth, because thereby our empire is increased and expanded. What is more, through your untiring service you have furthered our cause so much that not only all good money has vanished from the land and has climbed to the highest point, but also that through your clipping and whipping

* This may be a mocking allusion on Lucifer's part, put in the mouth of the Jews, to Jesus's instructions to the Pharisees (see Matt. 22:21). Paul gives a more mundane version of the rule in Romans 13:7.

such an unexpected, unbearable, indeed unprecedented inflation of all things has entered into the whole of Germany and other lands as well, whereby many people lose faith in God, and fall into despair, stabbing, hanging, or drowning themselves or their family from starvation, in which our very respectable and valiant grain-Jews also help, and do their best, in that they sell the blessing of God exceedingly dear, and profiteer thereby. Accordingly they are incorporated into this guild of thieves,* and fairly are vouchsafed high places in the empire. What now, in the whole of Germany, has arisen of unspeakable misery and need from your arch-thieving craft, is the result, and you will receive a fire-rich reward for it, since from many places, in droves, the souls of clippers and whippers will come to us. On which account, oh you clippers and whippers, usurers and money-changers, skinners and shysters, pay careful heed that you neglect nothing in this matter, but rather persist in the calling you have received from us. God grant that, however much men may cry out and write, lament and speak, print and preach against this, as much as ever they will, you act as if it were not your concern; all such will be well rewarded in the flames of hell, where we shall prepare a fair minting place for you, and you shall dwell with us forever, and have service with us. In short, it is our highest plea to you that you will want to continue zealously in such desperate, well-experienced work, in consideration of the fact that such abuse is truly serviceable for the increase of the entire hellish empire of darkness, for no worse (but to us pleasing) endeavor has ever arisen in the world; therefore we intend to support you, too, with aid, advice, and deed, as much as ever we can, so that our empire, in which you have your place reserved, where we shall seat you on cushions of sulfur and pitch, may be increased. Therefore strive and search, ponder and invent all sorts of new stratagems and deceits, double-dealing and finagling, tricks and feints, as to how you can deceive your fellow men as swiftly as you can, and utterly ruin the poor, so that your traditional and laudable praise, with us and in the world, will become still more pleasing and not fall into decline; all of this will be richly repaid you and never be forgotten in all eternity, a pledge we shall keep solidly and firmly. Further, on this occasion we know nothing more to write to you, save that you, as mentioned above, will sedulously continue in your thieving projects, harmful to the whole country, in our service, so that in the entire realm of hell you will have great praise and honor, because until now the likes of you have never been in hell or have been found there. Therefore continue industriously, and do not cease until our legate and commissioner will be sent to you, and will break your necks, and conduct you to us, into the hellish sulfur-burning bath and mint, which, if you remain thus constant, will take place in a brief time and be prepared for you. Friendly, assiduous, and official greetings are sent to you by Nabal,* the ancient lord of Miserdom, Thalersberg, and Usury, Judas, the Prince of Moneybag and Traitorsburg, Gehazi† of Clippershausen and Jobberheim, Ahithophel‡ and Haman,§ Cain and Pharaoh, and many other distinguished gentlemen, good comrades and brothers in hell, who await you with great pain in the warm sweat-bath, where we are

* The comical notion of such a guild is central to Niclas Ulenhart's brilliant transference of Cervantes' *Rinconete y Cortadillo* from Seville to Prague in his *Historia von Isaac Winckelfelder vnd Jobst von der Schneid* (1617).

* See 1 Sam. 25.

† See 2 Kings 5:9–19.

‡ See 2 Sam. 15–19.

§ See Esther 3–8.

readying seven thousand posts of sulfur, three hundred balls of fire, and ninety-nine wreaths of pitch, all minced and made into a powder with several additions in accordance with the alchemists' art, taken from our hellish armory, so that everything will be properly preserved for the clippers, and be administered to them for the great heat of our coin workshop, so that they will not choke before they have grown accustomed to it, and which they then shall and will need. Given this date in the abyss of hell in the month of so-and-so-much in cash, in the five thousandth, five hundredth, and ninety-second year of our reign in the hellish fire.

E. D. W.*
Lucifer, the Supreme and Most
Splendid Prince and Regent
of Hell.

Printed in the Year of Our Lord MDCXXIII.

* These initials are most likely meant satirically as *Eure Dienstfertige Wenigkeit* (Your Humble Littleness).

Kurtzer vnd einfeltiger/ jedoch klarer vnd sattsamer vnterricht vnd beschreibung/ welches doch eigentlich der ehrlichen Gesellschafft/ so man KIPPER vnd WIPPER nennet/ vrsprung vnd ankunfft sey/ durch was mittel sie zugenommen vnd gestiegen/ was für schöne früchte sie gewircket/ vnd schließlichen/ was für ein end vnd belohnung sie einsten zu gewarten haben:

Allen den jenigen die sich dieser Zunfft theilhafftig gemacht/ oder derselbea in etwas zugethan vnd beförderlich seyn/ zur trewhertzigen warnung/ andern aber zur Lehr vnd Trost vorfasset/ vnd in dieser Figur vorgestellet

Durch

DICÆOPHILUM MISOKIPPUM

Christianopolitam.

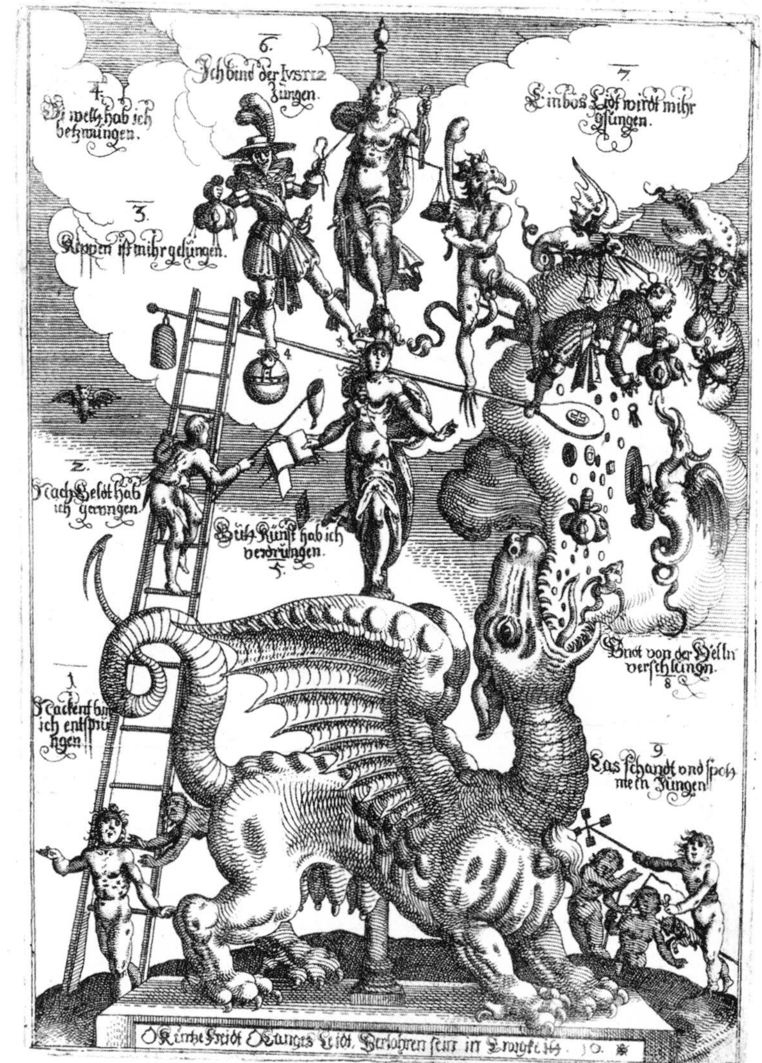

Hier lerne lieber Leser frey/
Was Kippen vor ein Handwerck sey.
Nackend komm ich auff diese Welt/
Ein leere Tasch ohn alles Geldt
Die ist mein Patrimonium,
Doch lest die Kunst nicht kommen vmb/
Durch Kippen schwing ich mich sehr hoch/
Die gantze Welt muß fühln mein Joch.
Pallas vnd jhre liebe Kindt/
Mein Sclaven vnd Leibeigen sindt;
Justitia muß mir wol schweign/
Vnd tantzen wie ich jhr thu geign.
Wo ist der Reichen grosses Gut?
Wo ist der Armen Schweiß vnd Blut?

In meim Sack/ den ich mit gespickt.
In summ mir war alles gelückt.
Vnd dörffte nichts begehren mehr/
Wenn nur das End nicht grausam wer.
Denn lieber Leser wie du siehst
Mein eigen Mutter mich auffrist/
Gantz schön/ dick/ fett/ vnd wolgemest/
In meiner Blüt/ vnd Alter best;
Vnd muß nun in all Ewigkeit
Verzeihen mich der Seligkeit/
Im Leben hatt ich Lust vnd Freud/
Im Tod abr eitel Hertzeleid.
Nun wird Apollo triumphirn
Pallas vnd jhr Heer Jubilirn.

Justitia wird verdammen mich/
Die gantze Welt wird frewen sich.
Mein Kindern laß ich Hohn vnd Spott/
Groß Armut/ Jammer Angst vnd Noth/
Bistu nicht aus der Kipper Gmein
Leser/ so wirstu frölich seyn.
Weil mein Todt ist das Leben dein/
Der Kipper abr die ewig Pein.

Extract des vorhergehenden.

Vom Teuffel bin ich kommen her/
Zum Teuffl ich endlich wider kehr.
Die gantze Welt hab ich verwirrt/
Die Kunst geschwecht Justiz verkehrt.
Dafür die Helle wird mein Lohn
Meinem Nachkommen Spott vnd Hohn.

Gedruckt im Jahr M DC XXIII.

PLATE XXVI. Brief and Simple, Nonetheless Clear and Sufficient Instruction and Description, of What Actually Are the Origin and Arrival of That Honorable Society Which Is Called CLIPPING and WHIPPING, by What Means It Has Increased and Grown, What Fair Fruits It Has Borne, and Finally What Sort of End and Reward It One Day Has to Expect. Composed for All Those Who Have Taken Part in This Guild, or Are Somewhat Inclined and Helpful to It, as a Truehearted Warning, but for Others as Instruction and Consolation, and Represented in This Picture by DICÆOPHILUS MISOKIPPUM,* Citizen of Christianopolis.

The various stages in the life of a money-clipper from birth to damnation are depicted in terms of his ascending a ladder and later plummeting from the sky. At the top of a tall pole Lady Justice, with a sword in one hand and scales in the other, stands atop the goddess Athena, upon whose shoulders rests a beam balance tipping toward her left. In front of this pole stands a monster, who inhales smoke and hellish little demons while at the same time defecating a child. A young money-clipper already standing at the base of the ladder says, "Naked I have been born." On his way up the ladder, the young man, having neglected the gifts of Athena ("Good art I have pushed aside"), is still shabbily dressed and extends a rod with an empty moneybag attached to its end ("I have striven for money"). Once off the ladder, he stands—fashionably attired—with a heavy moneybag in his right hand and boasts, "My clipping has succeeded" and "I've overwhelmed the world." With his left hand tugging on a rope attached to the mouth of Lady Justice, he proudly states, "I bind the tongue of justice." His boasting is, however, hollow, for as he tries in vain to place his left foot on the head of Athena for stability, his right one rests on an orb, an emblem for fickle fortune. To the left of Lady Justice, the scales have tipped against the money-clipper, who now confesses as he plummets toward the earth, "I am sung an evil song" and "I am swallowed by hell." A devil with raised club stands ready to knock him down if he tries to raise himself up. The money-clipper's moneybag and coins fall before him to be devoured by the monster, who will digest them to produce new progeny. The demise of the money-clipper has an impact on his children: "Shame and ridicule for my sons." The inscription on the base upon which the monster stands sums up the money-clipper's life: "O brief joy, O long suffering, I am lost for eternity."

Learn here, dear reader, readily
What sort of handwork clipping is.
Naked I come into this world,
An empty purse, all money lacking,
That is my *Patrimonium*.
But this art does not let me die;

By clipping I swing myself on high.
The whole world now must bear my yoke.
Pallas and her children dear*
Have now my slaves and serfs become;
Before me Justice must fall mute,

* This name means "Justice-Lover Clipper-Hater."

* The poet means Pallas (Athena) as the goddess of wisdom and of the arts and crafts.

And dance to what I fiddle for her.
Where is the great wealth of the rich?
And where the poor man's sweat and blood?
They're in my bag, which I've stuffed full.
In brief: all turned out well for me,
And I could wish for nothing more,
If the end were not so horrible.
For, dear reader, as you see,
My very mother gobbles me,
All fair, fat, greasy, fully fed,
In my life's flowering and prime,
And now for all eternity
I must abandon sanctity.
In life I had joy and merriment,
In death, though, naught but grief of heart.
Apollo now will celebrate,
Pallas and her army jubilate,
Justice will my name condemn,
And all the world know happiness.
To my children I leave scorn and shame,
Great poverty, misery, dread, and need.
If you're not of the clippers' band,
Oh reader, then you may rejoice,
For from my death you life will gain,
Whereas the clipper gets eternal pain.

Extract of the Previous

From the devil hither I have come,*
To the devil I at last return.
I have confused the world entire,
Enfeebled art, made justice lame.
Thus, hell my recompense will be,
And scorn and shame for my progeny.

Printed in the Year MDCXXIII.

* The poet parodies here the opening line of Luther's famous Christmas song, "Von Himmel hoch da komm' ich her" (From Heaven Above to Earth I Come).

Juch Hoscha/ der mit dem Geld ist kommen.

Weil nach mir schreyet alle Weldt/ So bin jch kommen mit dem Geldt. Will geben jedem nach gebier/ Das man nicht weitter schrey nach mir.

Ein Reutters Mann vff der strassen.

Halt still/ das dich botz Marter schendt/
Mein theil will ich an disem Endt.
Kurtzumb haben/ das sage ich dir/
Oder kombst vngezauset nicht von mir.

Der mit dem Geldt.

Thu gemach gut Kerls/ nicht also/
Will Geldt von mir bekommen/ so:
Kom morgen in die Statt hienein/
Will ich dir geben auch das dein.

Der Edelmann.

Deß Gelds ein Theyl ich haben will/
Dann in meim Schloß brauch ich sein vil.

Der mit dem Geld.

Biß gschmeidig im Haußhalten dein/
So wird am Geld kein mangel sein.

Der erste Kauffmann.

Ein Wechsel ich erlegen soll/
Drumb kombst mir mit dem Geld jetzt wol.

Der mit dem Geld.

Fürsichtig richt dein Handel an/
So wirstu Geld zum Wechsel han.

Der ander Kauffmann.

Die Wahr ist jetzt in rechtem Kauff/
Darumb gib mir des Gelds vollauff.

Der mit dem Geld.

Thu dich zu vil nicht vberladen/
So kriegst du Geld ohn deinen schaden.

Der Wirth.

Deß Gelds thu mir ein Summ verehren/
Das ich die Gest kan wol Trackturen.

Der mit dem Geld.

Nicht schind die Gest Tracktir sie recht/
Ein theil deß Gelds gib ich dir schlecht.

Der Handtwercksmann.

Jnn meim Hauß will mir nichts erklecken/
Drumb thu mir etlich Geld fürstrecken.

Der mit dem Geld.

Mach fleissig Arbeyt nichts verschwendt/
So kriegstu Geld biß an dein Endt.

Der Handtwercks Gesell.

Mein Bott gib mir auch Gelds genug/
So hab ich zu dem Wandern fug.

Der mit dem Geld.

Mach nicht drey Feyrtag in der Wochen/
So kombst nicht ohn Geld her gekrochen.

Der Lands Knecht.

Ach Bott wie lang hab ich dein geward/
Es will doch nichts thun auff der gart.

Der mit dem Geld.

Zu einem Herren solst dich fügen/
So kriegst du Gelds ein gut genügen.

Der Bawer.

Die Gült mein Herr will haben schlecht/
Drumb kombst mir mit dem Geld gar recht.

Der mit dem Geld.

Bauw fleissig/ das Wirthshauß du meyd/
Vertrawe Gott/ Geld ist nicht weit.

Der Bott.

Biß willkom/ Bruder mit dem Gelt
Hast mein Theil auch zusammen zelt.

Der mit dem Geld.

Sey fleissig/ Treuw/ verschwigen/ schnell/
Ein theyl deß Gelds ich dir zustell.

Der Taglöhner.

Wenn mich doch auch ein Glück anging/
Das ich ein Theyl deß Gelds empfing.

Der mit dem Geld.

Jn deiner Arbeyt ruff zu Gott/
So gibt er dir auch Geld zur noht.

Die Pancketirer/ als Spieler/ Sauffer/ vnd dergleichen.

Erst wölln wir ligen in dem Luder/
Der bringt deß Gelds ein gantzes Fuder.

Der mit dem Geld.

Wolt jhr nicht besser Garn spinnen/
So wird mein Geld an euch zerrinnen.

Der Bettler.

Jch bin auch einer von den Armen/
Billich solte ich dich Erbarmen.

Der mit dem Geld.

Von Recht solst du der erst sein gewesen/
Dein Geld ist schon besonder gelesen.

Der Narr.

Es ist nun kommen dieser Gast/
Nach dem Mann hat geschrihen fast.
Nun sag mir einer jetzundt her/
Wem ist worden der Beuttel schwer.

Gedruckt zu Straßburg/
Anno 1625.

PLATE XXVII. Hip-Hip-Hurray: The Moneyman Has Come

In the background to the left a highwayman on horse and with a raised pistol approaches a moneychanger transporting a large cargo of coins and is advised to visit the moneychanger the next day. In the foreground the well-dressed moneychanger, with a bag of coins in his left hand, is seated at a table, in front of which is a money chest and several large sacks of coins. He is joyfully greeted by men from various walks of life: to his right a courier, a peasant, a lansquenet, a beggar, and two merchants, and to his left a nobleman, a journeyman, an innkeeper, a day laborer, an artisan, and a gamester. Each asks for money and is in turn given advice on how to be industrious and frugal; only for the beggar has money already been set aside on the table. Overseeing all of this activity is a fool, who wonders whose moneybag will be heaviest. Above the scene are four verses:

Since all the world cries for me,
I've come with sacks of money,
Which I'll distribute to each accordingly.
So there'll be no further cries for me.

A Highwayman:
Stand and deliver, in rapine's name,
To get my share is here my aim.
Do it, I tell you, immediately,
Or you will not get off scot-free.

The Moneyman:
Gently, good fellow, speak not so,
If you want money from me, then
Come tomorrow into town,
And I shall give you yours as well.

The Nobleman:
Of money I will have a share,
For in my castle much I require.

The Moneyman:
If you are clever at keeping house,
There'll be no lack of money at all.

The First Merchant:
I have to pay a debt today;
Thus, you come with money in good time.

The Moneyman:
Be circumspect in your affairs,
And then you'll have money for your debt.

The Second Merchant:
Just now's a good time to buy wares,
So give me money generously.

The Moneyman:
Take not too much on your account,
And then you'll get money without fail.

The Innkeeper:
Honor me, do, with a certain sum,
That I may serve my guests properly.

The Moneyman:
Don't cheat your guests and serve them well,
Then I'll gladly give you of money a share.

The Artisan:
In my house nothing turns out well,
So advance me money in some degree.

The Moneyman:
Ply your craft diligently, do not waste,
And then you'll get money on the spot.

The Artisan's Apprentice:
Dear courier, give me money too,
Enough to set out on my journeys.*

The Moneyman:
Don't take three holidays a week,
And you'll not come creeping moneyless.

The Lansquenet:
Oh courier, how long I've awaited you,
For in my trade there's naught to do.†

The Moneyman:
You should find service with some lord,
And then you'll get money abundantly.

The Peasant:
My master will have my rent right now,
And so your money comes handily.

The Moneyman:
Plow hard and see that you shun the inn,
And trust in God, money's not far off.

The Courier:
You're welcome, brother, with your money,
You have my share, too, counted out.

The Moneyman:
Be busy, loyal, mum, and quick,
And I'll hand you of money a share.

The Day Laborer:
Oh, would that good fortune fell to me,
And of money I too would get a part.

The Moneyman:
In your labor cry out unto the Lord,
Then He'll give you money to meet your need.

The Banqueters, Gamesters, Topers, and the Like:
First off, we want to dissipate:
For that, he'll bring a cartload of money.

The Moneyman:
If you're not willing to mend your ways,
My money will vanish in your hands.

The Beggar:
I too belong to the poor folk's band,
In fairness, I deserve your money.

The Moneyman:
Rightly, you should have been the first,
Your money's already been set aside.

The Fool:
This visitor has now arrived,
The man for whom loudly has been cried.
Now let it by someone here present be told:
Whose purse is filled with the heaviest load?

Printed in Strasbourg, Anno 1625.

* The apprentice, who apparently has completed his training with a master, wants to set out as a journeyman.

† The unemployed mercenary is ubiquitous in German literature of the time and in reality presented a serious social problem.

Repositories

Augsburg, Staats- und Stadtbibliothek Augsburg (Plate IV).
Bamberg, Staatsbibliothek Bamberg (Plate VI).
Brunswick, Herzog Anton Ulrich-Museum (Plate VIII).
Coburg, Kunstsammlungen der Veste Coburg (Plate XXVI).
Erlangen, Universitätsbibliothek Erlangen-Nürnberg (Plate XII).
Gotha, Schloßmuseum Gotha (Plates IX and XXV).
Halle, Stiftung Moritzburg (Plate XXVII).
Hamburg, Staats- und Universitätsbibliothek Hamburg (Plates V, X, and XI).
Nuremberg, Germanisches Nationalmuseum (Plates III, VII, XIV, XXI, XXII, and XXIII).
Ulm, Stadtbibliothek Ulm (Plates XV, XVI, XVII, and XIX).
Wolfegg, Kunstsammlungen der Fürsten zu Waldburg-Wolfegg (Plate XVIII).
Wolfenbüttel, Herzog August Bibliothek (Plates I, II, XIII, and XX).
Zürich, Zentralbibliothek Zürich (Plate XXIV).

Plate Sizes

The first measurement is for the printed area, height before width in millimeters; the second is for the copper plate. Where only one measurement is given, the sheet is either unillustrated or fully etched. A "t" indicates that something is either trimmed or cropped.

Plate I:	305 × 182; 136 × 165
Plate II:	336 × 300; 154 × 282
Plate III:	367 × 252; 133 × 250
Plate IV:	375 × 255; 151 × 203
Plate V:	t378 × t279; 162 × 245
Plate VI:	350 × 242; 127 × 177
Plate VII:	t353 × t245; 127 × 173
Plate VIII:	360 × 255; 292 236
Plate IX:	290 × 167
Plate X:	383 × 255; 180 × 262
Plate XI:	t363 × t249; 173 × 258
Plate XII:	690 × 291; 162 × 295
Plate XIII:	441 × 309; 183 × 314
Plate XIV:	378 × 270; 126 × 244
Plate XV:	333 × 289; 160 × 119
Plate XVI:	248 × 322; 172 × 115
Plate XVII:	298 × 200
Plate XVIII:	331 × 289; 163 × 114
Plate XIX:	355 × 244; 139 × 245
Plate XX:	359 × 277; 160 × 242

Plate XXI:	306 × 345; [left to right:] 139 × 47, 141 × 129, 140 × 90, and 140 × 46
Plate XXII:	344 × 253; 94 × 124
Plate XXIII:	498 × 315; t223 × 288
Plate XXIV:	355 × 255
Plate XXV:	350 × 278; 88 × 124
Plate XXVI:	349 × 256; 196 × 143
Plate XXVII:	324 × 364; 179 × 350

Credits

Plate I	Herzog August Bibliothek IE 183
Plate II	Herzog August Bibliothek IE 184
Plate III	Germanisches Nationalmuseum HB 23592/1278
Plate IV	Staats- und Stadtbibliothek Augsburg Einblattdrucke nach 1500, Nr. 120
Plate V	Staats- und Universitätsbibliothek Hamburg Scrin. C/22, 52
Plate VI	Staatsbibliothek Bamberg VI G 160
Plate VII	Germanisches Nationalmuseum HB 24698/1363
Plate VIII	Herzog Anton Ulrich-Museum Flugblätter

Plate IX	Schloßmuseum Gotha G 88, 4
Plate X	Staats- und Universitätsbibliothek Hamburg Scrin. C/22, 201
Plate XI	Staats- und Universitätsbibliothek Hamburg Scrin. C/22, 80
Plate XII	Universitätsbibliothek Erlangen-Nürnberg A III 53
Plate XIII	Herzog August Bibliothek IE 193
Plate XIV	Germanisches Nationalmuseum HB 23594/1293
Plate XV	Stadtbibliothek Ulm Einblatt 312
Plate XVI	Stadtbibliothek Ulm Einblatt 326
Plate XVII	Stadtbibliothek Ulm Einblatt 317
Plate XVIII	Kunstsammlungen der Fürsten zu Waldburg-Wolfegg Flugblätter 250, 112
Plate XIX	Stadtbibliothek Ulm Einblatt 330
Plate XX	Herzog August Bibliothek IE 194
Plate XXI	Germanisches Nationalmuseum HB 12439/1278
Plate XXII	Germanisches Nationalmuseum HB 19420/1293

Plate XXIII	Germanisches Nationalmuseum HB 2081/1278
Plate XXIV	Zentralbibliothek Zürich EDR 1623, Münzsorten, Ia, 2
Plate XXV	Schloßmuseum Gotha G 19, 9
Plate XXVI	Kunstsammlungen der Veste Coburg XIII, 443, 62
Plate XXVII	Stiftung Moritzburg Kunstmuseum des Landes Sachsen-Anhalt F 34/47